I CAN'T
COOK
BOOK

FIONA HAMILTON-FAIRLEY

I CAN'T COOK BOOK

LONDON   NEW YORK   SYDNEY   TORONTO

To
Tilman, Sebastian and Melinda

I would like to thank: Tilman, Sarah, Chris, Belinda, Anna, Rip and Tessa, Robert and Tracy, and the numerous guinea pigs for their support and encouragement in preparing this book. It is the fact that they said they would never be able to cook, and now they can, that convinced me to write the *I Can't Cook Book*.

This edition published 1993 by BCA by arrangement with
Bloomsbury Publishing Limited
2 Soho Square, London W1V 5DE

CN4083

The moral right of the author has been asserted.

Copyright © Fiona Hamilton-Fairley 1993

A copy of the CIP entry for this book is available from the British Library.

Designed by Elizabeth Pitman
Photoset by Parker Typesetting Service, Leicester
Printed in Britain by Clays Ltd, St Ives plc, Bungay, Suffolk

Contents

1. All-season menu
Taramasalata with pitta bread
Savoury omelette
Fresh green salad or peas
Sweet cherries with sour cream

2. Quick pre-theatre supper
Fresh melon with port
Minute steak with herb butter
Pan-fried onions and potatoes
Garlic and ginger spinach
Cheese platter with fresh fruit

3. Vegetarian menu – spring or summer
Aubergine and ginger dip with pitta bread
Baked cheesy eggs with leeks
White, brown or wild brown rice with
sweetcorn
Fresh fruit salad with cream

4. Fast supper from the store cupboard
Tuna dip with hot toast or melba toast
Pasta carbonara with peas
Grilled peaches

**5. Weekend break menu
(This menu can be made in advance and
frozen for emegencies.)**
Home-made lasagne
Mixed salad with French dressing
Baked sultana and egg custard

6. Chinese stir-fry menu
Spinach and prawn stir-fry
Fried beef in oyster sauce
Boiled rice
Lychee and mango fruit salad

7. Vegetarian winter or spring menu
Stuffed tomatoes with avocado cream
Baked vegetable casserole with Quorn and
cashew nuts
Scallop potatoes
Apricot and banana bake

**8. Summer and winter menu
(Omit the bacon for vegetarians.)**
Seafood salad with Melba toast
Pasta and bacon hot pot
Mangetout or peas
Apple and almond jalousie with cream

9. Sunday roast menu
Sour cream mushrooms with croûtons
Roast beef with roast potatoes, parsnips,
carrots and onions
Fresh broccoli or Brussels sprouts
Yorkshire pudding with gravy
Baked orange and lemon dessert with crème
fraîche or cream

10. Winter menu
Prawn and asparagus vol-au-vents
Lamb bourguignonne
Potatoes au gratin
Fresh red cabbage
Rich orange and lemon syllabub

**11. Vegan menu
(This menu would suit vegetarians who
don't eat dairy products.)**
Artichoke and cucumber salad with croûtons
Stuffed spinach cannelloni baked in tomato
and tofu sauce
Glazed caramelized carrots
Mixed fruit crumble

**12. Summer grill menu
(Suits people who don't eat meat, but eat
fish.)**
Chilled watercress and orange soup
Grilled trout or mackerel stuffed with
mushrooms and tomatoes
New potatoes
Fresh mixed salad
Fruit flan and cream

13. All seasons menu
Cream of mushroom soup with French bread
Grilled lamb or pork chops
Cauliflower and onion cheese
Parsnip and potato cream
Meringue baskets filled with fruit and cream

14. Barbecue menu
Garlic bread
Chicken satay with peanut sauce
Home-made hamburgers
Mixed salad and new potatoes
Fresh strawberry and raspberry cream

15. Curry menu
Poppadoms, onion bhajis or samosas with
yogurt and cucumber sauce
Special chicken curry
Boiled rice
Mango chutney
Mango water ice

16. Mexican taco menu
Baked potato skins with sour cream
Taco shells with spicy Mexican mince,
avocado, lettuce, cheese and sour cream
Baked banana sponge with crème fraîche or
cream

17. Spring dinner party menu
(This menu suits people who do not eat
red meat.)
Smoked mackerel pâté with Melba toast
Chicken breasts in white wine sauce
White or brown rice
Baked courgettes
Baked banana puffs with fresh cream

18. Summer buffet menu
Smoked haddock mousse with brown rolls
and butter
Coronation chicken
Mixed rice salad
Bean salad with yogurt dressing
Tomato and chive salad
Rich chocolate mousse with wafer biscuits
and strawberries
Selection of cheeses
Fresh fruit

19. All seasons menu
(This menu suits young hungry guests.)
Avocado and prawn salad with brown rolls
and butter
Sweet and sour meatloaf
Baked potatoes with sour cream
Fresh broccoli
Apple and pear tumble with fresh cream

20. Cocktail or drinks party menu
Avocado dip or blue cheese dip with crudités
Smoked salmon rolls
Asparagus rolls
Ham and cream cheese rolls
Devils on horseback
Honey-roast cocktail sausages
Chicken nuggets with mayonnaise

21. Hungry winter menu
Chicken liver pâté with Melba toast
Pork fillet Normandy
Fresh green tagliatelle
Brussels sprouts
Lemon cheesecake

22. Summer fish menu
(This menu suits people who don't eat
meat, but who eat fish.)
Stuffed mushrooms with brown rolls
Baked salmon trout with hollandaise sauce or
mayonnaise
New potatoes
Mixed salad with French dressing
Old English trifle with cream

23. Formal dinner party menu
Haddock au gratin with French bread
Stuffed beef olives
Mange-tout or French beans
Potato and parsnip castles
Lemon soufflé with wafer biscuits

Introduction

This book is unique: it is designed to make cooking as simple as possible, and to persuade you that it can be fun rather than a chore.

Aimed at the working person who has little time and perhaps little or no experience of cooking, this book presents a step-by-step approach to creating a successful meal. All the planning is done for you, with lists of equipment and shopping, and a minute-by-minute count-down to the preparation of the meal. In many cases, there is even time planned into the menu for you to have a break. Just think how satisfying it will be to invite friends round to a home-cooked meal rather than serving shop-bought items that they have probably eaten many times before. And think too of all the money you will save.

The 23 menus cover nearly every eventuality, includ-ing informal suppers, vegetarian meals, buffet snacks, dinner parties, barbecues and stir-fries. Simply choose a menu to suit you and your guests, and the rest is plain sailing. If you like, it is possible to mix the menus, taking a starter from, say, Menu 1, a main course from Menu 2, and a dessert from Menu 3. The unique countdown sys-tem allows you to mix and match dishes at will. You also have the option of leaving out a course if time or money are limited: omit the starter, for example, or serve cheese and biscuits instead of dessert. All the recipes serve four people, but it is easy to double the ingredients if you are making dinner for eight, or to halve them if cooking for two.

Unlike most other cookery books, this book does not assume that you already know a lot about cooking. Every step in preparing each menu is clearly explained, as are the basic skills of cooking. There are no difficult cookery terms to confuse you, and there is no need for any unusual utensils. The equipment list given at the begin-ning of each menu allows you to check before starting that you have all the necessary hardware.

The shopping list is set out in three sections, one for each course, so it is easy to omit a section if you are not preparing one of the courses. Quantities are given in metric and imperial measures, but make sure you use one system only, not a mixture of both. Items that you may already have in your store cupboard are marked with an asterisk (*), so you can check first and thus avoid buying them again.

One of the skills emphasized throughout the book is sauce-making – a vital part of many recipes, whether a base sauce for a casserole, a gravy for a roast, or a white sauce for a cauliflower cheese. Sauces are especially important when cooking dishes in the oven, as they prevent meat and vegetables from drying out. They also combine with all the meat juices and thus help to create a deliciously flavoured dish. Conquer the art of sauce-making and many of your cookery problems are over.

It takes time and effort to become a good cook, but this book aims to minimize both and maximise your potential. It will not turn you into a master chef overnight, but it will help you to feel confident in your kitchen and show you that cooking can be a real pleasure.

Fiona Hamilton-Fairley
April 1993

Healthy eating

Over the years an increasing amount of information has become available on diet and health, and the British population is constantly being urged to change its eating habits. Long gone are the days when fine cooking called for lashings of butter and cream. Thanks to the inventiveness of good cooks everywhere, it is now possible to eat a healthy diet without sacrificing taste.

All the menus in this book have been carefully planned. They are well balanced in terms of fat, fibre and protein; they combine interesting and colourful ingredients; they consider the calorie content and cost; and they indicate the time involved.

Given the current health advice, do try to minimize the following items in your cooking:

Animal fats, such as butter and lard, should be avoided. Replace them with sunflower cooking margarine or oil (see Handy Tip 1 on page xvii). When a recipe requires milk, use skimmed or semi-skimmed. Serve cream separately, rather than cooking with it, so that guests can choose whether or not to eat it.

Salt is the most over-used flavouring, and can be harmful to health in large amounts. Use the minimum in your cooking, or even cut it out altogether. Remember that it is always possible to add more salt if necessary, but it cannot be taken out. As we all have different tolerances, invite your guests to add as much salt as they like at the table.

Sugar is another flavouring that is much abused. Try to cut down on the amount you use in desserts, but put a bowl of sugar on the table so that those with a sweet tooth can help themselves to the desired amount. Like salt, more sugar can be added to a dish, but it cannot be taken away, so do not be heavy-handed.

Notes for vegetarians

Given the growing number of people who prefer to eat little or no meat, the following guidelines may be helpful when planning a meal for vegetarian friends.

Lacto vegetarians
These are people who eat no meat, meat products, fish or shellfish. They *do* eat eggs and dairy produce, such as butter and yogurt, but cheese must be rennet-free. Products suitable for vegetarian consumption frequently have a symbol on the packaging.

Vegans
These people eat no meat, meat products, fish, shellfish, eggs or dairy produce. Take care to check your cooking fats and oils if preparing food for vegans, as some are blended and may contain animal fat.

This book contains two menus for lacto vegetarians (pages 17 and 47) and one for vegans (p83), but there are many dishes in other menus which can be adapted for them. Substitute the meat with beans or pulses such as chick peas, lentils or buckwheat, or use a variety of minced nuts and grated root vegetables. Alternatively, use one of the modern meat substitutes which are both nutritious and versatile.

Quorn – a high-protein food made from mushrooms
Tofu (bean curd) – a high-protein food made from soya beans
Textured vegetable protein (TVP) – soya mince or chunks
Tempeh – fermented tofu

These ingredients tend to be rather bland, so make sure you use them in conjunction with a well-seasoned sauce.

There are also many ready-made vegetarian dishes available in health food stores; these include bean burgers, vegebangers and vegetable grills.

If you think that some of your guests might not enjoy a completely vegetarian menu, you could grill a few chops to serve to the die-hard carnivores.

Party planning checklist

1. Make sure you know beforehand whether your guests have any particular food foibles or if they are vegetarians (see px). Nowadays more and more people prefer not to eat much meat, and they are also more conscious of the fat content in their diet. Choose a menu to suit your guests, the time of year (if it is cold outside, you should have at least one hot course), and check what foods are in season. Serving fresh strawberries in winter, for example, may be fiendishly expensive, or even impossible.

2. The menus in this book are designed to cover all occasions and every season. They also cater for different budgets, so plan beforehand how much you want to spend, and don't forget to add in the cost of wine and soft drinks. If you decide to serve courses from different menus, make sure you have the right equipment and that you have enough room in the oven for all the courses.

3. Check that you have enough cutlery and crockery for each course. You can wash up between courses, but this takes time and is an additional worry. To maximize your time with your guests, try to choose a menu that won't involve you in extra washing up. Also ensure that you have enough serving dishes.

4. Remember to check your store cupboard before going to the shops as you may already have some of the basic ingredients and would not want to buy them again. For special occasions, you may want to add pretty napkins, candles and a bunch of flowers to your shopping list. Small touches like these create a good impression and show that you have really made an effort to please.

Equipment

The list below is a detailed and comprehensive equipment list. I have explained as much as possible about all the different types of utensils and dishes. I am very aware that not many people will have all the equipment on the list below, but as you run through this book you might want to stock up on a few extra gadgets which will save you time and energy. This list does look rather long and daunting, so I have marked all the basic essentials with an asterisk.

★ = Basic essential equipment.

1*	Chopping board for savoury things. (See Handy Tip 2, pxvii.)
1*	Chopping board for sweet things. (See Handy Tip 2, pxvii.)
1*	Large chopping knife (all purpose).
1	Medium-sized serrated edged knife for bread and some vegetables.
1*	Small chopping knife (all purpose).
1	Small saucepan with fitted lid.
1*	Medium saucepan with fitted lid.
1	Large saucepan with fitted lid.
1*	Medium-sized frying pan.
1	Grill and grill pan.
1*	Medium-sized ovenproof casserole dish with fitted lid.
1	Large-sized ovenproof casserole dish with fitted lid.
1	Medium-sized ovenproof glass dish with fitted lid for vegetables and desserts.
1*	Large roasting tin (all purpose).
1	Medium roasting tin (all purpose).
1*	Flat baking tray (non-stick makes washing up easier).
1	12-hole bun tin (you will only need this if you are a Yorkshire pudding fan or want to make fairy cakes etc.).
1	20cm (8 inch) plain or fluted loose bottom cake tin. You will need this if you make a lot of cheesecakes and cakes; you can also use a plate or normal cake tin but it won't be as easy to remove it from the tin.
2	Non-stick 20cm (8 inch) cake tin. You will only need these if you don't have a loose bottom cake tin.
6–8	Ramekins. These are individual ovenproof dishes. I use them a great deal both for starters and desserts. They can go straight from the oven or fridge onto the table to be served. They are also very useful for small dips, sauces, mustard and peanuts.

2 (1*)	Wooden spoons (savoury, i.e. onions, vegetables etc. – see Handy Tip 2, pxvii).
2 (1*)	Wooden spoons (sweet, i.e. fruits, chocolate etc. – see Handy Tip 2, pxvii).
1	Soft and bendy spatula (all purpose).
1	Colander for vegetables, fruit and pasta etc.
1*	Medium-sized fine sieve.
1	Small-sized fine sieve.
1*	Swivel-bladed all-purpose potato peeler.
1	Hand-held electric mixer.
OR	
1*	Balloon whisk – this is a metal whisk made from thin metal wires formed into a balloon shape. It is excellent for whisking up eggs, cream and getting lumps out of sauces and gravy. A balloon whisk is essential if you don't have a hand-held electric mixer or a food processor.
1*	All purpose square grater, i.e. a grater with 4 different sized and shaped graters.
1	Rolling pin with solid ends. These are useful for crushing biscuits and nuts. You can also use a clean wine bottle to roll out pastry if you don't have a rolling pin.
1	Kitchen scale. This is essential if you want to be accurate in your measurements. It doesn't have to be expensive or modern. You can use tablespoons to measure quantities but this method is not as accurate.
2*	Tablespoons for cooking. They should be the same size, especially if you are going to use them to measure with.
1	Non-stick spatula for turning food when frying.
1*	Measuring jug, with both metric and imperial measurements.

1*	Lemon squeezer. It should be big enough to hold the juice of at least one whole lemon or orange.
2 (1*)	Plastic or glass mixing bowls. Plastic bowls make less noise when whisking egg whites, cream etc. with an electric hand whisk or a balloon whisk. Glass bowls can also be used for serving if necessary.
1	Double saucepan.
OR	
1	Heatproof mixing bowl. This must be a glass or ceramic bowl which will fit

over one of your saucepans. It can be used to melt chocolate or whisk egg yolks for mousses and soufflés. You will need such a bowl if you don't have a double saucepan.

1*	Tin opener (all purpose).
1*	Corkscrew and bottle opener.
1	Pair of kitchen scissors.
1	Potato masher.
1	Salad shaker or spinner. This is not an essential item, but is useful if you have to dry a lettuce quickly. A wet salad will not mix easily with a French dressing.

I have tried to make all the recipes adaptable to the equipment you will have in your own kitchen. If you are working from the basic essential equipment list always check the menu equipment list before starting to prepare the recipes; this will ensure that you don't get halfway through the menu only to find that you can't complete it because you haven't got a vital piece of equipment. The more you cook and enjoy it the more likely you are to start to collect some useful utensils and machinery. It is a good idea to borrow a piece of equipment from a friend and try it out to see if it helps you before spending money on some expensive gadget which might not suit your style of cooking.

Dishes needed for serving

This is a detailed list and I would not expect you to have all these dishes; use the basic essential serving list which is marked with an asterisk. I have assumed that you have a set of china and cutlery to serve at least 4 people, so the list below is what you will need in the way of extra serving dishes to serve the food in or on once it has been prepared and cooked.

* = Basic essential equipment.

6–8	Ramekins (see equipment list for details).
1*	Large salad bowl (wooden or glass).
1*	Pair of salad servers.
1	Large glass bowl for fruit salads etc.
2 (1*)	Vegetable dishes with lids. The lids will help to keep food hot.
2 (1*)	Pairs of serving spoons for vegetables.
1	Flat oval plate for serving meat, fish, pasta, or even a dessert.
1	Round or oval bread basket (this could also be used for baked potatoes or cheese biscuits).

2	Casserole dishes (see equipment list). Try to buy a nice looking casserole dish which can go straight from the oven to the table.
1	Soup tureen (or a large bowl or a saucepan if you have nothing else).
1	Soup ladle.
1	Flat fish slice for serving fish, meats, cheesecakes and cakes.
1	Cheeseboard.
1	Cheese knife.
1	Butter dish (or you can use an extra ramekin).
1	Butter knife.

Food processors, liquidizers and blenders

There is a great deal talked about food processors, liquidizers and blenders. My own feeling is that you can manage without them if the recipes are simple and give you alternatives, as I do in this book. Once you move on and really enjoy cooking and do a lot more, there is a lot to be said for the speed and accuracy you can get from a good food processor.

I managed with only an electric hand mixer for many years. I didn't feel that I needed anything bigger until I started to cater for a large number of guests and needed to cut down on time and energy. I would suggest that you buy yourself a small electric hand mixer and see how you get on before splashing out on more complicated and costly equipment that might not suit your style of cooking.

Dry ingredients

Plain flour
Self-raising flour
Cornflour (the best thickening agent)
Stock cubes (chicken, beef, vegetable)
Granulated sugar
Caster sugar
Demerara sugar
Dried breadcrumbs
Sultanas
Gelatine or Agar (vegetarian setting agent)
White long-grain rice (easy-cook)
Pasta (white or green)
Salted peanuts or crisps
Flaked almonds
Parmesan cheese
Plain chocolate
Vanilla essence
Cheese biscuits (keep in an airtight tin)
Boudoir or Langues de chat biscuits (to serve
    with a dessert)
Croûtons
Kitchen paper
Cling film
Tin foil

Dry herbs and seasonings

Cooking salt
Black peppercorns (if you have a pepper mill)
Ground black pepper
Ground white pepper (it is only necessary to
    have white pepper if you don't want black
    speckles in a white sauce)
Dried mustard powder
Ground nutmeg
Oregano
Mixed herbs
Bay leaves
Curry powder (hot, medium or mild)
Chilli powder

Packet mixes

*Don't feel embarrassed about using packet mixes –
they will save you time and effort, especially if you
get home late and want to cook something quickly.*

Instant custard powder
Instant hollandaise sauce
Stuffing (sage and onion)
Instant bread sauce
Instant savoury sauce
Instant soups (mushroom, French onion)
Instant potato granules
Vacuum-packed pizza base

Tins and bottles

Worcestershire sauce
Soy sauce
Tabasco sauce
Tomato ketchup
Tomato purée
Lemon juice
Vegetable and/or Sunflower oil
Olive oil
White wine vinegar
Plum tomatoes
Sweetcorn
Tuna fish
Peach halves
Mandarin oranges
Condensed milk
Olives
Thick honey
Chutney (mango or peach)
Orange marmalade
Peanut butter
Carton UHT milk (in case you run out of fresh
    milk)

Fridge stores

Cooking margarine (see Handy Tip 1 on page
    xvii)
Table margarine (sunflower)
Eggs (size 1 or 2)
Mayonnaise
Milk
Cheddar cheese
Mustard (wholegrain, French, English)
Garlic and herb butter

Fresh stores

Onions
Garlic
Ginger (see Handy Tip 11 on page xx)
Potatoes

Most people have a freezer, even if it is only a tiny one at the top of fridge. If this is the case, choose carefully what to keep in it, as space will be precious.

Basic deep-freeze stores

Ice cream
Brown rolls or **sliced brown bread**
1 packet puff pastry
Frozen vegetables (such as peas or spinach)

If you have a separate deep-freeze with lots of space, it's a good idea to stock a few items that can be made in a short time when you get home from work. It is always a good idea to have something you can fall back on when friends arrive unexpectedly and you would like to make them a hot snack or supper dish. Such items include:

Basic pizzas (individual meat and vegetarian ones)
These are cooked from frozen and are made even better by adding extra tomato purée, cheese, salami, onions, herbs, olives or whatever you fancy. Put the pizzas under a hot grill first to crisp them up and then add all the extra toppings. The whole process takes no more than 20 minutes. Serve them with a fresh green salad, or some hot tinned sweetcorn from the store cupboard.

Vol-au-vent cases (medium-sized)
The cases are cooked from frozen and can then be filled with a number of delicious fillings.

Sausages (which can be cooked from frozen)
Chicken nuggets (cooked from frozen)
1 packet of butter or margarine

Leave enough room for some of your own home-cooked food. It is always a good idea when you are making a stew or dessert to make a little extra, especially if you are making it for only one or two people. When freezing freshly cooked food or leftovers, always allow the food to cool to room temperature and label it clearly with the date, contents and number of people it will feed. Food should not be kept longer than 3 months in the deep-freeze.

Handy tips

1. What is the difference between cooking margarine and eating margarine?

Cooking margarine is a margarine that can be cooked at high temperatures without burning. It will burn if you get it too hot, but in general it has a much higher melting point. Some recipes call for both cooking margarine and oil to be added to the pan, this is to increase the heat resistance and to prevent burning. You might have experienced problems with other margarine or even with butter which does burn easily. Have a look in your local supermarket for cooking margarine, (it will always be clearly labelled on the packaging). Use a better quality margarine for eating and serving when entertaining, or use butter. I state what kind of margarine to use in all the menus.

The general rule is: When cooking a dish either in the oven or on top of the hob you should always use a cooking margarine or oil. The exception will be for delicate dishes when you should either use a better margarine or butter. I tend to use a low fat good quality margarine for eating for health reasons.

2. Chopping boards and wooden spoons

I have included 2 chopping boards and 2 wooden spoons in the recipes. My first chopping board and wooden spoon are for savoury items, eg; onions, garlic, leeks, vegetables or any strong smelling savoury fish or meat. My second chopping board and wooden spoon are for sweet things, eg strawberries, peaches, nuts, chocolate etc.

Wooden utensils are prone to absorb strong flavours. If you use the savoury board for strong smelling things, and a sweet board for soft fruits etc. you should never have a problem with tastes getting mixed up.

3. General rule for cooking vegetables

I have stuck to one general rule when cooking vegetables which I think makes a lot of sense and is easy to remember and follow.

Vegetables that grow under the ground, i.e. in the cold damp soil, such as carrots, potatoes, parsnips, turnips, etc. should always be put into cold water and brought slowly up to the boil. They should then be allowed to simmer until cooked, with a lid half on.

Vegetables that grow above the ground, i.e. in warmer conditions, such as broccoli, beans, peas, Brussels sprouts, courgettes etc. should be plunged into boiling water, or boiling water should be poured over the vegetable in the saucepan. The vegetable should be swiftly brought up to the boil, then simmered until cooked.

Always cook vegetables in as little water as possible but with enough to cover them. Don't forget that a large percentage of the goodness is lost in the water while cooking.

Most of us have become very 'salt conscious' these days so only use a pinch of salt in the water when cooking vegetables. Remember to put some salt and pepper on the table to give your guests the option of adding extra seasoning if they wish.

4. How to crush garlic without a garlic press or crusher

This is a very simple method for crushing garlic, I think it saves time and washing up. Once you have mastered it, you will find that it is quick and easy to do.
Peel the garlic clove and place it on a savoury chopping board (see Handy Tip 2, above). Take a round-ended knife and a teaspoon of cooking salt. Place the salt near the edge of the board, take one hand and hold the garlic clove down hard, using your other hand take the round-ended knife, dip the knife into some of the salt and start working away at the garlic. Once you have broken the outer skin of the garlic, add a little more salt and with a sharp up and down movement of the knife work away at the garlic clove. You will find that the garlic starts to break down and become a paste. Keep working at the garlic adding more salt as you need it, until you only have a small piece left. Add a little extra salt and squash the remaining piece of garlic under the weight of the knife. You should be left with a fine paste of garlic which is ready to use. Discard any excess salt. Remember that you have used a large amount of salt with the garlic, so you probably will not need to add any extra salt to the dish you are making.

5. How to get rid of lumps in a sauce or gravy

The main reason why you end up with a lumpy sauce or gravy is if the margarine and flour (the 'roux') is too thick or overheated. It is very important to add a cold liquid to a hot roux or a hot liquid to a cold roux. Usually the lumps appear during the process of adding the liquid to the roux. You should add the liquid to the roux away from the heat, as slowly as possible, stirring all the time. If the mixture starts to 'clump' stop adding the liquid at once. Take a balloon whisk or a strong wooden spoon and beat the sauce or gravy as hard as possible to work the lumps out. Within a few minutes you should be left with a smooth mixture. Once you are sure that the sauce is smooth again, you can continue to add the liquid slowly, stirring all the time. However, if you still have a very lumpy sauce or gravy the best thing to do is to sieve it into another saucepan or bowl, make sure you get as much of the roux through the sieve as possible, add the remaining liquid if you still have any and put the sauce or gravy back on a medium heat and bring it up to the boil. Cook for a further 2–3 minutes to remove the starch. This prevents the sauce or gravy from having a floury taste. If the sauce or gravy is too thin you can always use some cornflour to thicken it up later on (see Handy Tip 6).

6. How to use cornflour

Take a tablespoon and a small bowl. Place 1 level tablespoon of cornflour in a small mixing bowl and add enough water to make a thin paste. Stir well and add the cornflour paste slowly to the sauce or gravy, off the heat. Put the saucepan back over a low heat and slowly bring back up to the boil. Stir constantly. You should find that the sauce thickens on boiling. It is very important that the sauce cooks for several minutes after thickening to cook out the starchy taste found in cornflour. If the sauce is still not thick enough, repeat until you reach the correct consistency.

7. If you cry when you peel onions

If you find that the onions you are chopping are very strong and are irritating your eyes, move the chopping board over to the sink and gently run some cold water. Continue to chop the onion as close to the running water as possible. You should find that this eases the problem.

8. How to separate eggs

The hardest thing in separating an egg is conquering your fear of breaking through the shell and breaking the egg yolk. However, practice makes perfect and as soon as your confidence grows you are sure to have success. This method seems to work for most people and it also builds confidence, which is half the problem.

First wash your hands well. Take 2 bowls, one will be used for the egg yolk the other for the egg white. Make sure both bowls are large enough to hold the egg and any other ingredients, especially if you are going to whisk them. (This saves time and washing-up.) Take an egg and make a crack in the middle of the shell by knocking it hard on the side of the bowl or on the edge of a work surface. When you have a good break in the centre of the shell, slowly prize the egg shell apart. Hold one cupped hand over the egg-white bowl and empty the whole egg into your cupped hand. Allow the egg white to run between your fingers into the bowl underneath. You should find that the egg yolk remains in the centre of your hand. Open your fingers out a few times to ensure that all the egg white has fallen into the bowl. In the end you should be left with a well separated egg. Carefully put the egg yolk into the yolk bowl and repeat the process with any remaining eggs. Practice makes perfect!

9. How to cook and serve eggs

Whether you are hard boiling or soft boiling eggs there are a few general rules which you should follow to get the best results.

- Always check that eggs are not cracked or broken before starting to cook them.
- Always boil the water in the saucepan first before adding the eggs. This means you can be more accurate with the timing as you will know exactly when they start to cook.
- If possible, use an egg hole-puncher to pierce a small hole in the egg shell. This releases the air inside the egg and stops it from exploding during the cooking time. If you do not have an egg-puncher you can make a hole with a clean needle or safety pin. This can be a bit fiddly so be careful not to break the egg. Another method of preventing the egg from bursting is to add a teaspoon of salt or vinegar to the water.
- Plunge all the eggs into the saucepan at the same time, so that they cook evenly, and start the timer at once.
- Cook a hard boiled egg for 8–10 minutes.
- Cook a soft boiled egg for 4–6 minutes. The time will vary depending on the size of the egg.
- Once the eggs are cooked take the saucepan off the heat and run some cold water over the eggs to stop them from cooking and to stop a black ring appearing around the yolk. This makes removing the shell much easier.

• A soft boiled egg must be eaten immediately, whereas a hard boiled egg should be left to sit in cold water until it has cooled down.

• You can distinguish between cooked eggs and raw eggs by spinning them on a work surface. Boiled eggs spin smoothly and evenly, whereas raw eggs tumble around from side to side, as the liquid inside moves about.

• If you have problems peeling a hard boiled egg, run some warm water and peel the egg underneath the tap.

• You always cut an egg lengthways and not around its middle. This is in case the egg yolk has moved down into one half of the egg. If you cut the egg lengthways you will always ensure that both halves of the egg have a yolk.

10. Squeezing oranges and lemons

When you need to squeeze the juice from oranges or lemons, it is a good idea to roll the fruit under the palm of your hand on a flat surface. This will release the flesh inside the fruit and make squeezing more efficient and easy.

11. Fresh root ginger

Fresh root ginger is readily available in the vegetable sections of supermarkets and many good vegetable market stalls. It is something you have probably seen and wondered what it was, and what you would do with it. Once you have started to use root ginger you will find that it makes a change from standard spices. Fresh ginger in a savoury dish is delicious and often gives food an oriental flavour. I have used ginger in several of the menus in this book. Ginger is a knobbly root. It has a thin grey skin and looks a little like an artichoke. Some roots can be very big but in general you can always break a piece off.

To use fresh ginger, first of all peel it with a sharp potato peeler. If this is difficult use a sharp knife. Once the ginger is peeled, grate it into the dish you are making using a fine grater. Most recipes ask you to cook ginger before you eat it as it can be very strong. It is delicious with fresh vegetables, casseroles and in fresh cakes and desserts.

NB: Keep fresh root ginger in a cool dry place (perhaps with your onions and garlic). Remember that the longer you keep root ginger the stronger and more woody in texture it will become. You might have to cut down the amount you use if you have kept it for quite some time.

12. How to ripen an avocado

Remember to buy avocados 3 to 4 days before you need to use them. If you are having a dinner party for 4 guests, buy 3 hard avocados. Make sure that they are not already bruised or their skins broken. It is always best to buy more avocados than you will actually need so that you can choose the ripest ones.

Take the avocados and place them in a brown paper bag (use 2 bags if the avocados are very large). Place the paper bag in a warm place. I always put mine in a kitchen cupboard near the cooker but they could go in an airing cupboard if you have one.

After 2–3 days check the avocados, they should be ripening slowly. You might need to turn them over in the bag. By day 3 or 4 they should be ripe and ready to eat. To determine whether they are ripe, squeeze the top of the avocado. It should be soft to the touch (the top of the avocado is the narrow end where it would have hung from the tree). Always cut an avocado lengthways i.e. from the narrow end downwards, and not around the middle. If the avocado is ripe the stone should fall out easily and you should be able to peel the skin away from the flesh with ease.

Measurements

Grams	Ounces
(Recommended conversion to the nearest unit of 25 grams.)	
25g	1oz
50g	2oz
75g	3oz
100g	4oz (¼lb)
125g	5oz
175g	6oz
200g	7oz
225g	8oz (½lb)
250g (¼Kg)	9oz
275g	10oz
300g	11oz
350g	12oz
375g	13oz
400g	14oz
425g	15oz
450g	16oz (1lb)
475g	17oz
500g (½Kg)	18oz
550g	19oz
575g	20oz (1¼lb)
1000g (1Kg)	2lb 3oz

For the best results you should measure things out accurately with kitchen scales. If you do not have any scales then the general rule is: 25g (1oz) = 1 tablespoon.

If you measure out small amounts with a tablespoon always use the same tablespoon for all the ingredients, this will ensure relative accuracy.

Liquid measurements

Metric measure nearest ml. (litre)	Imperial measure	Imperial measure fl oz
150 ml	¼ pint	5 fl oz
300 ml	½ pint	10 fl oz
450 ml	¾ pint	15 fl oz
600 ml	1 pint	20 fl oz
900 ml	1½ pints	30 fl oz
1000 ml (1 litre)	1¾ pints	35 fl oz

Oven settings

	°C	°F	Gas Mark
Very Cool	110	225	¼
	120	250	½
Cool	140	275	1
	150	300	2
Moderate	160	325	3
	180	350	4
Moderately Hot	190	375	5
	200	400	6
Hot	220	425	7
	230	450	8
Very Hot	240	475	9

Ovens can differ tremendously – from modern fan-assisted ovens to conventional ovens or Agas. I have always had an electric oven and a gas hob, so I have enjoyed the best of both worlds. I believe that gas is easier to work with as it is far easier to control the temperature and keep things simmering, rather than boiling.

Experiment with your oven. You will soon discover how best to control your oven and hob, but don't forget it might take a little time before you feel confident and happy using it.

All-season menu
Easy to prepare and cook
Cost level: inexpensive
Serves: 4

There is no break incorporated in this menu.

| **Starter** | Taramasalata with pitta bread | Preparation time = 5 minutes
Cooking time = None |

| **Main course** | Savoury omelette
Fresh green salad or peas | Preparation time = 30 minutes
Cooking time = 12 minutes |

| **Dessert** | Sweet cherries with sour cream | Preparation time = 12 minutes
Cooking time = None |

This menu is very easy to prepare and cook, and is useful if you come home late after a long day at work and want something light but nutritious to eat. If you are cooking for only two, halve all the amounts.

You should find all the ingredients you need in your own storecupboard or fridge, but if not, the corner shop should stock all the necessary items. Don't forget this is a fast and flexible menu, so you can always leave out the starter or dessert and add extra ingredients to suit your taste. For this menu you will need to buy or make French dressing (see recipe p196).

If any of your guests are vegetarians (see page x), omit the bacon from the omlette.

Equipment Needed – **Menu 1**

Starter

1 small serving bowl
1 knife to cut the pitta bread
1 bread basket or bowl (for serving)

Main course

1 savoury chopping board
1 sharp knife
1 frying pan (non-stick if possible) with
   lid or plate that will fit on top
1 mixing bowl
1 fork or balloon whisk
1 measuring jug
1 wooden spoon
1 cheese grater
1 metal pallet knife (if you are not using a
   non-stick pan)
1 non-stick plastic spatula (frying utensil)
1 colander
1 vegetable peeler
1 salad bowl OR
1 saucepan with lid (for vegetables)

Dessert

1 tin opener
1 measuring jug
1 serving bowl (preferably glass)
1 saucepan
1 sweet wooden spoon
1 small mixing bowl
1 tablespoon
1 knife
1 lemon or orange squeezer
1 small sieve

Shopping list – **Menu 1**

Starter

225g (8oz) pot fresh taramasalata
1 packet (approx. 6–8) pitta breads
★1 jar pitted black or green olives (optional)

Main course

★1 large onion
★25g (1oz) cooking margarine
★8 fresh eggs
★150ml (¼ pint) milk
★8 rashers back bacon
★175g (6oz) mild Cheddar cheese
★4 fresh tomatoes
★salt, pepper and a pinch of dried mustard
★225g (8oz) packet frozen peas OR
   1 iceberg lettuce or 2 round lettuces
   2 raw carrots
   ½ green pepper
   ½ red pepper
★150ml (¼ pint) French dressing

Dessert

*★1 425g (15oz) tin pitted black cherries in
   natural juice*
★1 sachet quick-set gel mix (red)
200g (7oz) carton sour cream OR
200g (7oz) carton crème fraîche
25g (1oz) caster sugar
1 whole orange

★Check store cupboard

Countdown – **Menu 1**

If you want to prepare and cook the whole menu, you will need 60 minutes. As this is such a fast menu I have not allowed for a break. However, if you would prefer a break, the starter, salad and dessert can be made in advance and put into the fridge to chill. If you are a slow cook, add 5–10 minutes to each course to ensure you do not run out of time. Remember, the times are only a guide as each cook will take different lengths of time to complete each task. If you do take a break, when you return you will only have to prepare your omelette and dress your salad, or cook your peas. The omelette must be cooked and eaten immediately, otherwise it will spoil.

Dessert

Preparation time: 12 minutes
Cooking time: None

Assemble all the ingredients and equipment you will need for the dessert. Set your timer for 12 minutes.

12 mins Open the tin of cherries and drain all the juice into a measuring jug. Put the cherries straight into your serving dish (or a glass bowl if you have one).

10 mins Take the quick set gel mix and read the packet instructions. These will differ slightly depending on the brand. Bring the mixture up to the boil and stir well for at least 1 minute.

6 mins Now pour all the jelly over the cherries, making sure they are well covered. Leave to cool slightly, then place the cherries and jelly in the fridge while you make the cream topping.

5 mins Take 200g (7oz) of sour cream or crème fraîche and place in a small mixing bowl. Measure out 25g/1oz (1 tablespoon) of caster sugar and add it to the cream. Take one orange and roll it firmly under your hand on a hard work surface to loosen the flesh inside, cut it in half and squeeze the juice from both halves. Add the juice to the cream and mix well.

1 mins Take the cherries and jelly out of the fridge and gently pour the orange cream all over them. Put the dessert back into the fridge to chill until required.

0 mins Wash up and clear away.

PROBLEMS AND HANDY TIPS

If you have bought cherries with pips by mistake you can either de-pip them by hand (which will take some time), or inform your guests that the dessert has pips in it and supply a pip bowl or plate on the table.

If you have used too much water in the jelly and you can't get it to thicken, either start again with a new packet, or continue with the recipe and leave out the jelly. The dessert will still be delicious with the cherries and cream topping.

If you have lumps in the jelly mix before it has thickened, it would be a good idea to sieve the jelly before cooking it and discard any lumps left in the sieve.

The jelly should set very quickly once you put it into the fridge. If it doesn't, you can still make the cream topping and pour it over the jelly once it has set, just before serving. Don't worry if the cream merges with the jelly and cherries – it will still taste the same.

Starter

Preparation time: 5 minutes
Cooking time: None

This starter can either be served as a dip to your guests while they are standing up, or as a starter sitting down. Set your timer for 5 minutes.

5 mins Take the taramasalata out of the fridge and either place it all in a serving bowl (from which your guests can help themselves), or on to individual plates. Take the pitta bread and cut it into diagonal slices, then place in a bread basket ready to serve.

You can serve the pitta bread warm by using a microwave, placing them under a grill for a minute, or putting them in a toaster on a low setting. Only do this just before serving.

2 mins If you are using olives, either garnish the top of the taramasalata with them, or serve them separately.

0 mins Wash up and clear away.

You can cut the olives into halves or quarters to garnish the top of the taramasalata. Serve the remaining olives in a bowl.

Salad

(If you are using frozen peas instead of salad, ignore these instructions.)

Reset your timer for 10 minutes.

10 mins Take the iceberg lettuce and cut into thin shreds using a sharp knife. Place the lettuce in a colander ready to be washed. If you are using round lettuces, discard the outside leaves, then tear the remaining leaves up and place them in a colander. Wash the lettuce or lettuces well. Drain and pat dry on kitchen paper.

Don't make the lettuce shreds too big, otherwise they can be awkward to eat.

5 mins Take 2 carrots and peel them, then use a sharp knife to cut the carrots into thin slices (try to make them as thin as possible). Place the sliced carrot straight into your salad bowl. Take the 2 halves of pepper, remove the seeds and stalk from both, then wash them under cold running water. Using a sharp knife, chop the peppers up into thin slices. Add the peppers to the carrots in the salad bowl and cover with a clean tea towel, or if you have enough room put the salad bowl into the fridge until required. Leave the lettuce to drain and dry until required.

Make sure you get rid of all the tiny seeds in the peppers. This is best done by placing the peppers under cold running water before cutting them up.

0 mins Wash up and clear away.

Relax

If you want to have a break, now would be a good moment, as the dessert is complete and the starter all laid out. The salad is prepared and only needs to be put together and dressed before serving. When you return, you will only need to make the omelette and serve it.

If you are using frozen peas rather than a salad, you can cook them at the same time as the omelette.

Your break can be as long as you like, depending on when you are expecting your guests.

Welcome back

Feeling better after your break?

Main course

Preparation time: 20 minutes
Cooking time: 12 minutes

Assemble all the ingredients and equipment needed for the omelette. Set your timer for 20 minutes.

20 mins Take one large onion and chop it as finely as possible. Measure out 25g/1oz (1 tablespoon) of cooking margarine. Place the margarine in a frying pan and put it over a medium heat. When the margarine begins to bubble and foam, add the onion and cook. Meanwhile, break all 8 eggs into a mixing bowl, and using either a fork or a balloon whisk beat the eggs well. Add 150ml (¼ pint) of cold milk. Whisk up again. Season with a very small amount of salt. Add some ground black or white pepper and a good pinch of dried mustard.

14 mins Stir the onions and if they are cooking too fast, turn the heat down. Take 8 bacon rashers and remove any rind. Cut the bacon into small, bite-sized pieces and add them to the pan with the onion to cook.

10 mins While the onion and bacon are cooking, measure out 175g (6oz) of Cheddar cheese and using a medium grater, grate the cheese straight into the bowl with the egg and milk mixture. Stir well.

6 mins Don't forget to stir the onion and bacon occasionally. If you feel that it is cooking too fast, don't panic, just turn it off or right down until you are ready to continue.

5 mins Before finally putting the whole omelette together and eating your starter, quickly wash up and clear away, putting things back into the fridge, etc. Once you have started cooking the omelette there will be little time, as it

PROBLEMS AND HANDY TIPS

Make sure that no shell falls in when you break the eggs into the bowl. If you are nervous about this happening, use a small bowl and break each egg into it before adding it to the large mixing bowl with all the other eggs.

Don't use too much salt if you are using bacon, as the bacon is already salty. Don't forget you can always add more salt, but you can't take it away once it has been added.

Grating your cheese straight into your egg bowl saves washing up, but if you prefer, you can always grate it on to a separate plate and then add it to the eggs.

must be served piping hot straight from the frying pan.

4 mins Turn off the onion and bacon and leave them to stand until you are ready to add the egg mixture.

3 mins Take out the dinner plates ready for serving. If you are going to warm your pitta bread, do so now.

1 min If you are using frozen peas instead of a salad, fill the kettle with water and put it on to boil. Take the peas out of the deep freeze and put them into a saucepan, ready to cook. If you have made a salad, mix the lettuce in with the peppers and carrot. Measure about 150ml (¼ pint) of French dressing, pour all over the salad and toss well.

0 min Set the salad aside until required. Wash up and clear away.

The pitta bread only needs to be warmed through and not overheated as it then tends to dry out. Freshen it up by using a microwave for a minute or two, a grill or a toaster.

Don't forget to shake the French dressing really well before you pour it over the salad, otherwise you will end up with an unpleasant, very oily dressing.

Now that everything is ready, you can serve the taramasalata and pitta bread. Once the starter is finished you can cook your omelette and vegetables (if you are using them instead of a salad).

Last-minute tasks

If you have only a small frying pan and don't feel that you will be able to get all the omelette into it, you will have to make 2 omelettes. Pre-heat the oven to 160°C/325°F/Gas mark 3 to keep the first omelette hot while you make the second one. Set your timer for 12 minutes. This is approximately the time it will take you to cook the omelette.

12 mins Pour the boiling water over the peas and put over a medium heat to cook. If you have made a salad, put it on the table.

10 mins Before cooking the omelette, quickly wash the tomatoes under cold running water. Take a sharp knife and cut them into thin slices. Set aside until required.

8 mins If you are cooking 2 omelettes, remove half the amount of onion and bacon from the frying pan and set aside for the second omelette. Heat the frying pan up again with the bacon and onion, and when the cooking margarine begins to foam and look hot, whisk up the egg and cheese mixture again and pour it in. Allow the egg at the bottom of the frying pan to start to set, then take a non-stick plastic spatula (or pallet knife if the pan isn't non-stick) and start to pull the egg mixture into the centre of the frying pan. This allows the runny egg mixture to fill up the edges again so that the omelette cooks

If you prefer your tomatoes skinned, pour enough boiling water over them just to cover, leave for 10–15 seconds, then remove them from the boiling water and plunge into cold water. You should find that the skin comes off easily. If not, repeat.

If you feel that you have put too much egg mixture in your frying pan, take a bowl and pour off some of the excess. You can always add it once the omelette has cooked further. Or if you are making a second omelette you can use it then.

evenly. (The omelette will cook much faster on the sides than in the middle.)

5 mins Taste the peas, if you are using them, to see if they are cooked. If they are, turn the heat off and drain away the water through a colander. Put the peas back into the saucepan to keep warm and put the lid on.

3 mins By now the omelette should be almost ready. Take the tomato slices and place them neatly all round the sides of the omelette, slowly working your way inwards towards the centre of the pan. If you are using a non-stick frying pan and feel brave, try this method for turning the omelette over: take a plate big enough to cover the whole frying pan, turn off the heat and, using some oven gloves, cover the frying pan with the plate. Hold the handle of the pan tightly with your other hand and turn upside down. Do this either over a clean work surface or over the sink. You should be left with the whole omelette on the plate. The omelette now needs to cook and brown on the other side, so take your plate and slide the whole omelette back into the frying pan. Return the omelette to the heat and cook rapidly over a high heat to brown.

1 min Put the omelette into the oven to keep warm if you have to make a second omelette.

0 mins To serve, either turn the omelette out again on to the plate, or if you feel one excitement is enough, use your spatula to serve out the portions. Don't forget to serve the peas either straight on to the plates, or put them on the table for your guests to help themselves. Eat immediately while everything is piping hot. Wash up and clear away.

When the main course is finished, serve the dessert.

Make sure the peas do not overcook. Vegetables are always best served undercooked rather than overcooked. Don't forget that they will continue to cook even while they are waiting to be served.

If you can't manage to turn the omelette with the plate method, try using one or two spatulas. First cut the omelette in half and then push one or both spatulas underneath either end of each half and flip it over very quickly. Don't worry too much if the omelette falls apart; you can always patch it up later.

The omelette does look and taste better if both sides have been well browned.

The dessert is best served in small bowls rather than on plates.

MENU

2

Quick pre-theatre supper
Easy to prepare and cook
Cost level: good value
Serves: 4 people

There is no break incorporated in this menu.

Starter   Fresh melon with port

Preparation time = 10 minutes
Cooking time = None

Main course   Minute steak with herb butter
Pan-fried onions and potatoes
Garlic and ginger spinach

Preparation time = 65 minutes
Cooking time = 45–50 minutes

Dessert   Cheese platter with fresh fruit

Preparation time = 10 minutes
Cooking time = None

This menu is quick and easy to prepare. The melon and port make a deliciously light starter. The steak is complemented by the garlic and ginger spinach and the pan-fried onions and potatoes.

The cheese and fruit round off the meal nicely. You could do the shopping for this menu a few days in advance to give the melon and cheese time to ripen and mature. This menu is always useful for a quick dinner for friends before the theatre or cinema, or for a special occasion when you want to splash out a little.

Equipment needed – **Menu 2**

Starter

1 sweet chopping board
1 sharp knife
1 teaspoon or dessertspoon
1 tablespoon

Main course

1 potato peeler or food processor with fine
   slicing blade
1 sharp knife
1 savoury chopping board
1 large mixing bowl
1 frying pan with lid or plate that will fit
   on top
1 cheese grater
1 small bowl
1 savoury wooden spoon
1 garlic crusher (or see handy Tip 4,
   pxviii)
1 medium-sized saucepan
1 large saucepan
1 colander
1 grill and grill pan

Dessert

1 cheese board or large plate
1 cheese knife
1 butter dish
1 fruit bowl
1 basket or plate for the cheese biscuits

Shopping list – **Menu 2**

Starter

*2 honeydew or cantaloupe melons (ripe – soft
   and pleasant-smelling)*
★4 tablespoons port
★4 teaspoons demerara sugar

Main course

450g (1lb) potatoes or 6 large old potatoes
★2 small onions
★25g (1oz) cooking margarine
★100g (4oz) Cheddar cheese
*★salt, fresh ground pepper, nutmeg, pinch
   mustard powder*
*900g (2lb) fresh spinach or packets frozen leaf
   spinach*
★1 clove garlic
2.5cm (1 inch) piece fresh root ginger
★25g (1oz) cooking margarine
100g (4oz) sour cream
4 sirloin or fillet steaks (175g/6oz per person)
100g (4oz) herb butter

Dessert

225g (8oz) Brie
225g (8oz) Cheddar
225g (8oz) Stilton
black and/or white grapes
apples, pears
★225g (8oz) butter
★cheese biscuits

★Check store cupboard

Countdown – **Menu 2**

If you want to prepare and cook the whole menu, you will need 85 minutes. If you are a slow cook, add 5–10 minutes to each course to ensure that you do not run out of time. The times are only a guide as each cook will take different lengths of time to complete each task. The starter should be made first and allowed to chill while you prepare the rest of the menu. Put the cheese out early as this will allow it to breathe and so taste better. There is no break in this menu, but you could quite easily have a rest before making the main course.

Starter

Preparation time: 10 minutes
Cooking time: None

Assemble all the ingredients and equipment you will need for the starter. Set your timer for 10 minutes.

10 mins Take the 2 melons and cut them in half around the middle, not from top to bottom. Remove all the seeds, using a teaspoon or dessertspoon. Set the melons on a plate or in bowls.

4 mins Take the port and add 1 tablespoon of it to each half of the melon. Sprinkle 1 teaspoon of demerara sugar all over each melon half.

1 min Place the melons in the fridge to chill until required.

0 mins Wash up and clear away.

PROBLEMS AND HANDY TIPS

If the melon halves will not sit evenly take a sharp knife and carefully cut a thin slice off the bottom of each. Make it a very fine sliver or the port will run out.

The port should not sit in the melon longer than 1–2 hours.

Dessert

Preparation time: 10 minutes
Cooking time: None

Set your timer for 10 minutes

10 mins Take all the cheese out of the fridge, unwrap it and place on a cheeseboard, ready to serve. Wash the grapes well and arrange a few bunches around the cheeseboard for decoration.

6 mins Place the cheese biscuits on a plate or in a basket ready to serve. Take the butter out of the fridge to soften

PROBLEMS AND HANDY TIPS

If you don't have a cheeseboard, use a large plate or serving dish.

and place it on the table in a serving or butter dish.

2 mins Arrange the rest of the fruit in a bowl or on a plate, place on the table or sideboard.

0 mins Wash up and clear away.

Relax

You could take a short break here before preparing your main course. The length of the break will depend on when you are expecting your guests and when you have to leave for the theatre or cinema.

Main course

PROBLEMS AND HANDY TIPS

Preparation time: 65 minutes
Cooking time: 45–50 minutes

Assemble all the ingredients and equipment you will be using for the main course. Set your timer for 25 minutes. This is how long you will need to prepare the onions and potatoes.

25 mins Take the potatoes and peel them. Place the potatoes on a chopping board and slice them as evenly and thinly as possible. (If you have a food processor, use the fine slicing blade.) Place the sliced potatoes in a large mixing bowl, add some hot tap water leave to stand.

If all the potato slices are roughly the same size, they will cook more evenly. The hot water helps to remove the excess starch which is found in the potatoes, and it also stops them from sticking together when they cook.

14 mins Take 2 small onions and peel and slice them as thinly as possible. (Again if you have a food processor, use the fine slicing blade.) Take out your frying pan and add 25g/1oz (1 tablespoon) of cooking margarine to the pan. Turn the heat on to medium and allow the fat to melt. Add the sliced onions and allow them to cook.

9 mins While the onion is cooking take 100g (4oz) Cheddar cheese and grate it on to a plate or into a bowl. Set aside.

Make sure the onion doesn't burn. If it is cooking too fast, turn the heat down or off.

6 mins Stir the onions and turn them over once they are lightly browned. Turn off the heat. Remove the onions from the frying pan, leaving as much fat behind as possible. Place the onions in a small bowl to cool.

4 mins It is now time to put the whole potato dish together. Take the sliced potatoes and drain all the water from the bowl. Arrange half the potato slices on the bottom of the frying pan, overlapping slightly. Once you have covered the bottom of the pan, take half the onions and sprinkle them over the potato slices. Now season

It doesn't matter if the order of the layers changes. Try to end up with potatoes as the top layer. They will go a lovely brown colour and look more appetizing when served.

with a pinch of salt, nutmeg, mustard powder and some fresh ground pepper. Use half the grated cheese and sprinkle it over the top of the onions and potatoes. Repeat with another layer of potato, onions, seasoning and cheese. Reserve a few extra slices of potato to finish off the top. Season well.

Season well as the potatoes will soak up the seasoning.

1 min Place the frying pan on a low heat to allow the potatoes and onions to cook. If you have a lid, place it on the frying pan; if not, use a plate or baking sheet to cover it. The potatoes need approx. 20–25 minutes on each side.

Place on a very low heat, otherwise the potatoes will burn.

0 mins Wash up and clear away.

Spinach

Set your timer for 20 minutes.

20 mins While the potatoes are cooking, prepare the spinach. If you are using fresh spinach, you must wash it very well under cold running water and remove the long stalks. This is easily done by using either a sharp knife or your fingers; cut or pull the stalk away.

Spinach always has a lot of sand and grit in it, as it grows so close to the ground. Always wash it very well.

15 mins Leave the spinach to drain in a colander.

14 mins Fill the kettle with water and put on to boil.

13 mins Take one garlic clove, peel it and crush it into a medium-sized saucepan.

See page xviii, Handy Tip 4, for an easy way to crush garlic if you don't have a garlic crusher.

10 mins Take the fresh root ginger and using a sharp vegetable peeler or knife, remove the skin. If the peeler won't get into all the nooks and crannies, use the knife. Grate the ginger into the saucepan with the garlic (use a fine grater).

Make sure you use a fine grater and use all the juice and ginger that gets stuck on the reverse side of the grater.

5 mins Take the washed spinach and place it in the large saucepan. Pour in the boiling water, using no more than 300ml (½ pint), as the spinach will cook right down and all the goodness will otherwise be lost in the water. Half cover the saucepan with a lid and place it on a medium to high heat. Cook for approx. 8 minutes. If you are using frozen spinach, follow the instructions on the packet. It should say something like: place the frozen spinach in a saucepan and add boiling water (do not use too much water – only enough to cover). Bring to the boil and cook for 3–4 minutes. Drain well.

Use as little water as possible; this makes your spinach taste much richer.

1 mins Check the potatoes and turn them over to cook on the other side. To do this, first turn off the heat, then take a plate which is either the same size or bigger than the frying pan. Put the plate on top of the potatoes (remove the lid or baking tray first). Hold one hand firmly on the plate and the other on the frying pan handle.

Be careful not to burn yourself on the frying pan when you are turning over the potatoes.

Make sure you hold the plate tightly, as once the potato lands on the plate it can become quite heavy.

Quickly turn the whole pan upside down. You should end up with the whole potato cake on the plate. Now put the frying pan back on the hob and slowly and carefully slide the whole potato cake back into the frying pan. The potato cake should remain whole. Put the frying pan back over a low heat and continue to cook for a further 20–25 minutes. Replace the lid.

0 mins Wash up and clear away.

If the potato falls apart don't worry too much. Still cook it again on the opposite side. When you serve the potato, no one will notice if it has fallen apart once it is on the plate.

Last-minute tasks

Set your timer for 20 minutes, which is when you should be ready to serve your starter. Your potatoes can continue to cook while you eat the melon and port.

20 mins Check the spinach and stir it well.

18 mins Take 25g/1oz (1 tablespoon) of margarine and put it into the saucepan with the garlic and ginger. Put the heat on low and allow the margarine to melt and mix with the garlic and ginger. Stir well. Do not allow the garlic and ginger to burn; turn off the heat once they look slightly brown.

Don't allow the garlic and ginger to burn as this will impair the flavour of the dish.

16 mins Drain the spinach through a colander and squeeze out the excess water.

13 mins Add the spinach to the garlic and ginger in the pan. Stir well and put back over a low heat. When the spinach has heated through, add 100g (4oz) of sour cream. Stir well and replace the lid. Cook for a further 2 minutes, then turn the heat off.

Try to remove as much water as possible from the spinach by pressing a tablespoon onto it while it is in the colander.

10 mins Now everything is ready. The only thing left to cook is the steak. The potatoes will happily cook on until required. The spinach can be heated up again before serving. The length of time the steak will take to cook depends on what type of steak you have bought, how thick it is and how your guests like it cooked.

Make sure the spinach is well heated through before adding the sour cream and leaving it to stand.

Leave the spinach in the saucepan with the lid on to keep warm.

8 mins Ask your guests how they like their steak cooked – rare, medium or well done. The steak can be cooking while you eat the melon. Preheat the grill while you prepare the steaks. Put the steaks on the grill pan and season lightly with some fresh ground pepper and a pinch of salt. If some of the guests prefer the steak well done and others rare, start the well-done ones ahead of the rare ones. Add the others a few minutes later. Thin cut sirloin steak needs approx. 2 minutes each side for rare to medium, 5 minutes each side for well done.

Preheating the grill helps to cook the steaks more effectively.

Remember, the steaks will continue to cook for a few seconds after removing them from the heat. It is harder to cook rare steak than medium or well done.

You can half cook the steaks and turn the grill right down while you eat the starter. Turn the grill up again while you are finishing off the vegetables.

6 mins Eat the melon and port while the steaks are cooking. If the steak is cooking too fast or you are worried, turn the heat off and continue to cook it once you have eaten the melon. It takes only a few minutes, and you need to finish off and serve the potatoes and spinach anyway.

0 mins Check the potatoes, which should now be cooked and ready. The test is to take a sharp knife and push it into the potatoes all the way to the bottom. (Be careful if it is a non-stick pan, as you don't want to scratch the non-stick surface.) If the knife goes through the potatoes with ease, they are ready. Turn the potatoes out on to a heated plate if you can, as they look more attractive served this way. Wash up and clear away.

If the potatoes fall apart while you are turning them out, don't worry. You can patch them up without anybody noticing.

Place the steaks under the grill if you haven't cooked them yet, or if you stopped halfway through the cooking time. Finish them off while you serve the rest of the main course.

Reheat the spinach quickly over a medium heat, stir well and serve either in a heated serving dish or from the pan.

Toss the spinach around quickly over a high heat to reheat it.

Serve the steaks with a knob of herb butter on each one.

You can present the meal in serving dishes for people to help themselves or serve it on plates, which saves on washing up.

Finally, don't forget the cheese, biscuits and fruit for dessert.

Vegetarian menu – spring or summer
Easy to prepare and cook
Cost level: inexpensive
Serves: 4

A 30-minute break is incorporated in this menu.

Starter   Aubergine and ginger dip with   Preparation time = 35 minutes
pitta bread   Cooking time = 40–50 minutes

Main course   Baked cheesy eggs with leeks   Preparation time = 65 minutes
White, brown or wild rice with   Cooking time = 15–20 minutes
sweetcorn

Dessert   Fresh fruit salad with cream   Preparation time = 25 minutes
Cooking time = None

This menu is suitable for vegetarians.

The starter can be made in advance and is a delicious dip served with pitta bread. The main course can be finished off in the oven or under the grill, and is easy to prepare on the day. The fruit salad can also be made in advance, but don't add the bananas until just before serving or they will discolour.

If time is short, or if you prefer to make only a two-course meal, one of the courses could easily be left out.

Equipment needed – **Menu 3**

Starter

1 savoury chopping board
1 sharp knife
1 or 2 plates
1 potato peeler
1 cheese grater
1 garlic crusher (or see Handy Tip 4, pxviii)
1 small saucepan
1 mixing bowl
1 savoury wooden spoon or a fork
1 colander
1 baking tray
1 lemon squeezer
1 tablespoon

Main course

2 saucepans with lids (1 egg saucepan, if you have one)
1 egg-puncher or pin
1 sharp knife
1 savoury chopping board
1 colander
1 tablespoon
1 savoury wooden spoon
1 ovenproof dish (no lid required)
1 cheese grater

Dessert

1 tin opener
1 fruit salad bowl
1 sweet chopping board or a plate
1 sharp knife
1 potato peeler
1 tablespoon

Shopping list – **Menu 3**

Starter

3 medium aubergines
★salt, pepper and nutmeg
1cm (½ inch) piece fresh root ginger
★1 clove garlic
★12g (½oz) cooking margarine
225g (8oz) cream cheese
1 lemon
2 tablespoons natural yogurt
1 packet (approx. 6–8) pitta breads
1 tin (200g/7oz) olives (optional)

Main course

★6 eggs, (free range, if possible)
4 medium leeks
★50g (2oz) cooking margarine
★50g (2oz) plain flour
★300ml (½ pint) milk
salt, pepper
★1 teaspoon dried mustard powder
225g (8oz) easy-cook rice (white, brown or wild)
★½ teaspoon margarine
225g (8oz) mild vegetarian Cheddar cheese
★50g (8oz) wholemeal breadcrumbs
1 tin (275g/10oz) Sweetcorn

Dessert

Choose fruits which are in season
★425g (15oz) tin mandarin segments or 1 tin peaches in syrup
2 bananas
1 pear
1 red apple
225g (8oz) grapes (preferably seedless)
1 kiwi fruit (if available)
★1–2 tablespoons caster sugar
300ml (½ pint) single cream or 1 small tub/ vanilla ice cream
1 tablespoon liqueur (optional)

★Check store cupboard

Countdown – **Menu 3**

If you want to prepare the whole menu, you will need 165 minutes. This includes a 30-minutes break. If you are a slow cook, add 5–10 minutes to each course to ensure you do not run out of time. Remember, the times given are only a guide as each cook will take different lengths of time to complete each task. You can leave out any course if time is short. Both the starter and dessert can be made in advance. The main course is best made on the day so that it remains as fresh as possible.

Starter

PROBLEMS AND HANDY TIPS

Preparation time: 35 minutes
Cooking time: 40–50 minutes

Assemble all the ingredients and equipment you will need for the starter. Preheat the oven to 190°C/375°F/Gas mark 5. Set your timer for 35 minutes.

35 mins Take the 3 aubergines and cut them into slices, starting at the stalk end. Discard the stalk and cut the aubergine slices into 1cm (½ inch) pieces. Place each piece on a flat plate or board and sprinkle lightly with enough salt to make a thin layer (you might need two plates). (The salt helps to degorge, or draw out, the bitter flavour which is sometimes present in aubergines.) Leave the aubergines to soak up the salt for at least 10 minutes before turning them over. The salting process then needs to be repeated on the other side.

You will find that the aubergines start to lose liquid once the salt has started to work. This is meant to happen, and is the process of removing bitterness from the aubergines.

27 mins While you are waiting for the aubergines to degorge, peel the root ginger with a sharp vegetable peeler. Grate the ginger through a fine grater over a plate or bowl.

23 mins Next, take the clove of garlic, peel it and crush it, either through a garlic crusher or with the round-ended knife and salt method (see Handy Tip 4). Place the garlic and ginger in a small saucepan ready to cook.

If the root ginger is very 'knotty' you might need to use a sharp knife to peel it with. If you have kept the root ginger for some time be careful as it becomes stronger the longer you keep it. If this is the case, use only a very small 5mm (¼ inch) piece.

20 mins Turn the aubergines over and sprinkle more salt over them. Leave them to soak up the salt for a further 10 minutes.

17 mins While the aubergines finish degorging, take 12g (½oz) cooking margarine and add it to the garlic and ginger in the saucepan. Put over a medium heat and cook until the garlic and ginger go slightly brown.

The garlic and ginger need to be cooked to remove some of the strong flavour found in them.

14 mins Take a bowl, or if you have one, a food processor (use the sharp chopping blade) and place 225g (8oz) of cream cheese in it. Add the cooked garlic and ginger and mix well, either with a wooden spoon, fork or in the processor. Mix until well blended.

10 mins Take the aubergines and put them into a colander. Wash them thoroughly under cold running water to remove all the salt. Pat dry on kitchen paper. Take a flat baking tray and place all the aubergines on the tray either way up. Place the tray into the preheated oven and cook for approx. 40–50 minutes.

8 mins Take 1 lemon and cut it in half lengthways. Squeeze one half of the lemon, and cut the other half into 4 wedges for serving with the dip. Set these aside until required.

When making the lemon wedges, make sure you cut the lemon lengthways (i.e. not around its middle).

4 mins Season the cream cheese mixture lightly with salt, pepper, nutmeg and ½ teaspoon of the freshly squeezed lemon juice. You can adjust the seasoning when you add the aubergines. (Keep the extra lemon juice safely as you might need it later on.)

2 mins This is as far as you can go with the dip until the aubergines are cooked.

0 mins Wash up and clear away.

Season lightly; don't forget that once the dip has stood for a while you will need to adjust the seasoning. If the taste of ginger is overpowering you have used a very strong piece. Try adding 3 tablespoons chopped plum tomatoes and 1 tablespoon tomato purée to lessen the flavour.

Dessert

PROBLEMS AND HANDY TIPS

Preparation time: 25 minutes
Cooking time: None

The dessert can be made the day before and kept in the fridge until required. Do not add the bananas until the last minute as they will discolour.

Preparation time for the fruit salad will depend on the types of fruit being used.

Assemble all the ingredients and equipment you need for the dessert. Set your timer for 25 minutes.

25 mins Open the tin of mandarins or peaches and pour both the fruit and juice into the fruit salad bowl (this should be big enough to hold all the fruit).

The juice in the tinned fruit will be used for the fruit salad.

17 mins Take all the fruit that needs to be washed, i.e. the apples, pears and grapes and wash them well. Leave the grapes to soak. Cut the apple and pear in half and then into quarters, remove and discard the core in each quarter and cut the fruit into small, bite-size pieces. Add the chopped fruit to the juice and fruit already in the bowl, stir well and cover the fruit with cling film or a plate to stop from discolouring.

Try to cut all the fruit into roughly the same size pieces; it then looks much nicer and is easier to eat.

Make sure all the apple and pear are well covered so that they don't discolour.

10 mins Take the grapes and dry them well. If they are very small and seedless, you can leave them whole. If they are large, they will need to be cut in half, and if they have pips, these will need to be removed. Be warned, if you have to deseed all the grapes, this can take some time, so be patient. Add all the grapes to the rest of the fruit in the bowl. Stir well and cover again.

4 mins Take the kiwi fruit, peel it using a sharp peeler or knife, and cut it into thin slices. These can either be left whole or cut in half, whichever you prefer. Mix all the fruit well and check for sweetness. You might need to add 1–2 tablespoons of caster sugar if the fruit is very tart.

0 mins Mix well and cover the fruit again. Place in the fridge to chill until required. Wash up and clear away.

Kiwi fruit can sometimes have a hard core running right through its middle. If this is the case, cut the kiwi fruit in half lengthways and use a sharp knife to remove the core. Then slice the fruit up thinly.

Watch points

The bananas should be added at the very end just before serving, otherwise they go black and soggy.

For extra richness you could add 1 tablespoon of a liqueur, such as Grand Marnier or Kirsch, just before serving.

Do not keep the fruit salad for longer than 2 days, otherwise it starts to ferment and go soft.

The kiwi fruit can be left at the top of the fruit salad for decoration as it is both pretty and colourful.

Complete the starter

Set your timer for 10 minutes.

10 mins The aubergines are cooked when they have shrunk and the skin is darker and is shrivelled-looking. Take a sharp knife and pierce the flesh, it should be soft and the knife should go through easily. If they are cooked, remove them from the oven. Turn the oven off and place the aubergine somewhere to cool.

8 mins Once the aubergine is cool enough to handle, remove and discard the black skin. (If you are using a food processor, you can use the black skin if you prefer.) Place the aubergine flesh in the bowl or food processor containing the cream cheese mixture. Mix until all the ingredients are well blended. Stir in 2 tablespoons of natural yogurt. Check the seasoning and adjust if necessary. Add extra lemon juice, which you squeezed earlier, if required. Once you are happy with the taste of the dip, place it in a small serving bowl and chill until required. The aubergine dip can be garnished with olives and lemon wedges if you like.

0 mins Wash up and clear away.

If you have a food processor, you should find this procedure faster and that you get a finer blend than by hand, but both methods are excellent.

Main course

Preparation time: 40 minutes
Cooking time: 20 minutes

Assemble all the ingredients and equipment needed for the main course. Set your timer for 40 minutes.

40 mins Take an egg saucepan and fill it with cold water, bring it to the boil with the lid on. Pierce the pointed end of the eggs with an egg-puncher or pin to allow air to be released when the eggs are plunged into the water. This prevents them from cracking open. Take care when piercing the eggs as they can easily break. While waiting for the water to boil, take the leeks, cut a small amount off the root end and a small amount from the dark green end. Discard any very dark green or dirty-looking leaves.

32 mins Cut the leeks into thin slices and wash well under cold running water. Leave to drain in a colander.

27 mins The water for the eggs should now be boiling. Using a metal spoon, lower the eggs carefully into the boiling water. Check your timer, as the eggs will need approx. 10–12 minutes.

25 mins While the eggs are cooking, measure out 50g/2oz (2 tablespoons) of cooking margarine and place in a medium-sized saucepan. Place over a medium heat and allow the margarine to melt. Now add the sliced leeks to the pan and cook for 5 minutes. Lower the heat, place the lid half on the pan and allow to cook slowly for a further 5 minutes.

17 mins Now the eggs should be ready. Take the saucepan off the heat and place it in the sink. Pour some cold water on to the eggs and leave them to stand in it while you return to your leeks.

12 mins Turn the heat off from under the leeks and measure out 50g/2oz (2 tablespoons) of plain flour. Add to the leeks and mix well. Turn the heat back on to low and cook the flour for 1–2 minutes, stirring continuously with a wooden spoon.

10 mins Turn the heat off from under the flour and leek mixture and measure out 300ml (½ pint) of milk. Slowly add the milk to the leek and flour mixture, stirring continuously to prevent any lumps forming. Once all the milk has been added and the mixture is smooth, put over a low heat and bring the leek sauce slowly to the boil, stirring continuously.

5 mins While waiting for the sauce to come to the boil,

Eggs leave a stain on certain stainless steel saucepans, so it is best to keep a special pan specifically for them if possible.

It is true that if you put a pinprick in an egg, it releases any excess air and stops the egg from bursting open. Alternatively, you can add either a teaspoon of salt or vinegar to the water.

Wash the leeks very well as they often have a lot of sand and grit in them.

The eggs need to sit in cold water once they are cooked so that they stop cooking.

The secret of making a smooth sauce is to add the flour and milk off the heat and to stir constantly so that no lumps form. If at any time you find some lumps, stop adding the milk and beat the mixture well until the lumps disappear. Then you can continue to add the milk as normal. Season well and taste before setting aside.

season with ground black or white pepper, a small pinch of salt and a teaspoon of dried mustard powder. Stir the sauce well and once it is boiling allow it to simmer for 2 minutes, stirring continuously. If you think the sauce is too thick, add a little extra milk to thin it down. Don't forget, the sauce should be quite thick as it must bind the eggs together.

1 min Turn the heat off from under the sauce and place a lid over it to keep it warm. Take the eggs out of the water and set aside until after your break.

0 min Wash up and clear away.

Relax

Have a 30-minute break. When you return you will only need to assemble the egg dish, put it in the oven, and cook the rice. The starter and dessert are complete except for a few last-minute touches.

You do not have to have a break – continue if you prefer.

Welcome back

Feeling better after your break?

Last-minute tasks

Set your timer for 25 minutes. This is how long you have until you serve your starter. Preheat the oven to 190°C/375°F/Gas mark 5.

25 mins Fill the kettle with water and put it on to boil.

24 mins Measure out the rice, you will need 50g (2oz) per person (total amount 225g (8oz)). Place the rice in a medium-sized saucepan and add a teaspoon of margarine.

22 mins Peel the shells off the hard-boiled eggs. (This is easier under running water.) Once all the eggs are peeled, cut them in half lengthways so that each half has exactly half a yolk.

Always cut an egg lengthways (not around the middle) in case the egg yolk has moved to one end of the egg.

The eggs should peel easily if you use some warm water to assist you.

17 mins Pour the boiling water over the rice (check packet instructions for the amount) and stir well until all the margarine melts (this prevents the rice from sticking together). Put over a medium heat to cook slowly.

15 mins Take the pitta bread and place it on a baking tray. Put it on the bottom shelf of the preheated oven to warm through before serving the starter.

13 mins Now is the time to decide whether you are going to add the sweetcorn to the eggs or serve it separately (by warming it up in a saucepan). Open the tin of corn and drain off the liquid.

11 mins Arrange the eggs in an ovenproof dish with the yolks facing upwards. If you are going to use the sweetcorn, sprinkle it in the dish evenly. Reheat the sauce, uncovered, over a very low heat, slowly warm it through, stirring occasionally.

Spread the eggs out in the dish so that they have enough room for some leek sauce all around them. Cover the eggs well, otherwise they will dry out while cooking.

6 mins While waiting for the sauce to heat through, take 225g (8oz) of Cheddar cheese and grate it through a medium-sized grater over a plate or bowl.

2 mins Pour the leek sauce all over the eggs in the ovenproof dish. Make sure you cover the eggs well. Take the grated cheese and sprinkle it all over the top of the sauce. Finally, take 50g/2oz (2 tablespoons) of breadcrumbs and scatter them evenly over the cheese. Put the whole dish in the top of the preheated oven to cook for 15–20 minutes.

The breadcrumbs soak up any excess fat from the cheese and give it a crunchy finish.

0 mins Check the rice. If it is boiling too fast, turn it down to low while eating the starter. Wash up and clear away.

Remember, if you are using brown rice or wild rice, it will take much longer to cook than normal white rice.

Watch points

Obviously, once the meal has started it is impossible to give specific times, so the following checklist should be used only as a guide.

If have not used the sweetcorn yet, you can heat it up in a saucepan or microwave just before serving.

Put the main course plates in to warm if you have the facility on your cooker.

Take the pitta bread out of the oven and serve it either whole or cut into slices in a basket or on a plate.

Serve the aubergine dip with some olives, if you have any, and don't forget the lemon wedges you made earlier.

Before sitting down to eat the starter, check on the rice. If it is ready or nearly ready, turn the heat off, but leave the rice in the water to keep warm. If you drain the water away now the rice will become sticky. If it needs to cook further, leave it on while you eat the starter.

The egg dish won't spoil if you are running behind time and it has to sit in the oven a little longer.

When ready, drain the rice through a colander. Check the egg dish, which should be golden brown and bubbling.

Serve the eggs on top of the rice.

When the main course has been eaten, cut the bananas up into diagonal slices and place them in the bowl with the rest of the fruit salad. Stir well. Add 1 tablespoon of liqueur now if you are going to do so.

Don't forget to serve the cream or ice cream with the fruit salad.

Fast supper from the store cupboard
Easy to prepare and cook
Cost level: inexpensive
Serves: 4

There is no break incorporated in this menu.

Starter Tuna dip with hot toast or melba toast

Preparation time = 8 minutes
Cooking time = None

Main course Pasta carbonara with peas

Preparation time = 20 minutes
Cooking time = 20 minutes

Dessert Grilled peaches

Preparation time = 10 minutes
Cooking time = 5 minutes

This menu will be useful when you find that your fridge is bare and you have had little or no time for shopping.

You should find all the ingredients you need in your store cupboard, but a corner shop can always assist with a few minor items, if necessary.

This menu can also be adapted to suit any ingredients you already have, and to your own taste. If you would prefer not to use bacon or ham, you could substitute 225g (8oz) of fresh mushrooms. Don't forget, you can always leave out a course if you don't have the ingredients or the time.

Equipment needed – **Menu 4**

Starter

1 tin opener
1 mixing bowl or serving bowl
1 fork
1 savoury wooden spoon
1 tablespoon

Main course

1 medium saucepan, with fitting lid
1 savoury chopping board
1 sharp knife
1 large saucepan, with fitting lid
1 colander
1 garlic crusher (or see Handy Tip 4, page
    xviii)
1 savoury wooden spoon
1 cheese grater
1 plate
1 tin opener

Dessert

1 tin opener
1 glass ovenproof dish
1 tablespoon
1 teaspoon
1 grill

Shopping list – **Menu 4**

Starter

200g (7oz) tin tuna fish in oil or brine
salt and pepper
1 tablespoon lemon juice
2 tablespoons mayonnaise
100g (4oz) butter or margarine
4 slices fresh bread or melba toast

Main course

225g (8oz) tagliatelle, dried white or green
38g (1½oz) cooking margarine
salt, pepper and nutmeg
2 small onions
1 clove garlic
4–6 rashers bacon or any ham or gammon you
    may have
100g (4oz) Cheddar cheese
450g (16oz) tin peeled plum tomatoes
200g (7oz) evaporated milk tin OR
300ml (½ pint) single cream
450g (16oz) frozen peas
225g (8oz) mushrooms (optional)

Dessert

200g (7oz) tin peach halves in syrup
4 tablespoons evaporated milk (left over from
    main course) OR *4 tablespoons single cream*
12g (1oz) demerara sugar

Countdown – **Menu 4**

If you want to prepare the whole menu, you will need 65 minutes. There is no break in this menu as it is so fast. If you are a slow cook, add 5–10 minutes to each course to ensure that you do not run out of time. Remember that the times given are only a guide as each cook will take different lengths of time to complete each task.

Starter

Preparation time: 8 minutes
Cooking time: None

Assemble all the ingredients and equipment you will need for the starter. Set your timer for 8 minutes.

8 mins Open the tin of tuna fish and drain off the oil or brine. Place the tuna in a mixing bowl and mash with either a fork or wooden spoon until it becomes flaky.

8 mins Season well with ground black pepper and add 1 tablespoon of lemon juice and 2 tablespoons of mayonnaise. Mix well, check the seasoning and place in a serving bowl.

1 min Put the dip into the fridge and chill until required. The 100g (4oz) of butter or margarine will be used when you serve the tuna dip in case your guests want it on their toast.

0 mins Wash up and clear away.

PROBLEMS AND HANDY TIPS

If the tuna is hard to mash, add the mayonnaise, which should make it easier.

You can make and serve the tuna dip in the same bowl.

Main course

Preparation time: 20 minutes
Cooking time: 5 minutes

The use of single cream rather than evaporated milk makes the pasta dish richer, but really delicious. If you prefer not to use bacon or ham, add 225g (8oz) of fresh button mushrooms instead.

Assemble all the ingredients and equipment you will need for the main course. Set your timer for 20 minutes. You will need 5 minutes to cook the carbonara after you have eaten the starter.

20 mins Fill the kettle and put it on to boil.

19 mins Empty the tagliatelle into a medium-to-large

PROBLEMS AND HANDY TIPS

sized saucepan and add 12g/½oz (½ tablespoon) cooking margarine. Once the water in the kettle has boiled, pour it all over the pasta (just enough to cover), add a pinch of salt and put the pan over a low heat to cook.

17 mins While the pasta is cooking, take the 2 small onions, cut them in half, discard the skin and chop as finely as possible. Place the chopped onion in a large saucepan (which will be big enough to hold all the cooked ingredients).

10 min Check the pasta, which should be cooked by now. If ready, turn off the heat and drain the pasta through a colander. Run some hot water through it to get rid of any excess starch and to stop the pasta cooking further. Leave the pasta in warm water in the saucepan while you cook the onions.

8 mins Add 25g/1oz (1 tablespoon) of margarine to the onions in the saucepan and put over a low heat to cook. Crush the clove of garlic, add it to the onions and continue to cook for a further 2 minutes. Make sure the garlic is stirred well.

4 mins While the onions and garlic are cooking, take the bacon or ham and chop it into small, thin slices, then add to the onions and garlic. Stir well and continue to cook for a further 2–3 minutes on a low heat.

0 mins Turn off the heat under the onion, garlic and bacon mixture, and put a lid on the saucepan. Leave to stand. Wash up and clear away.

Dessert

Preparation time: 10 minutes
Cooking time: 5 minutes

Assemble all the ingredients and equipment you will need for the dessert. Set your timer for 10 minutes.

10 mins Open the tin of peaches, drain the juice into a jug, then place each peach half round-side down (i.e. the hollowed-out bit looking up at you) in an ovenproof dish. Pour the syrup all around the peaches but not in the hollows.

7 mins Open the tin of evaporated milk and spoon a small amount into each peach hollow – just enough to fill them. Set the remaining evaporated milk aside if you are also using it in the carbonara; otherwise, use any extra to pour around the peaches. (If you are using single cream instead of evaporated milk, prepare the peaches as above,

The margarine is added to the pasta to stop it from sticking together.

The pasta is cooked when still slightly firm in the middle; test by tasting a little. The pasta will sit quite happily in the warm water while you do other things

To use the round-ended knife method for crushing garlic, see page xviii, Handy Tip 4.

If you are using mushrooms instead of bacon or ham, wash and slice them now and cook with the onion and garlic.

PROBLEMS AND HANDY TIPS

You can also serve each peach half in individual ramekins or bowls, but first make sure that the bowls are ovenproof.

but serve the remaining cream separately, just before serving.)

5 mins Sprinkle about ½ a teaspoon of demerara sugar into each peach half. You can either grill the peaches now and serve them cold, or set them aside and grill them a few minutes before needed. They will need approx. 5 minutes to cook once the grill has heated up.

0 mins Wash up and clear away.

You can use less sugar if you prefer, as this can be rather a sweet dessert.

Last-minute tasks

Either finish off the main course now and keep it hot while you eat the starter, or eat the starter first and then cook the carbonara.

Set your timer for 5 minutes.

5 mins Make some toast and cut into triangles, or put out some melba toast, to eat with the tuna dip. Put out the butter or margarine in case any of your guests would like it.

0 mins Take the dip out of the fridge and serve it with the toast.

You can eat the starter standing up as a dip, or sit down and serve it more like a pâté.

Reset your timer for 20 minutes. This is the time you will need to cook the carbonara.

20 mins Drain the tagliatelle, which has been sitting in warm water, through a colander. Leave to drain thoroughly.

19 mins Fill the kettle and put it on to boil. Place the frozen peas in a small saucepan, add a teaspoon of sugar and a pinch of salt.

The teaspoon of sugar brings out the flavour of the peas.

15 mins Remove the lid and put the saucepan containing the onion, garlic and bacon back over a medium heat. Continue to cook.

13 mins Take the 100g (4oz) Cheddar cheese and grate through a medium grater. Set aside.

9 mins Pour the boiling water over the peas and cook over a medium heat.

8 mins Open the tin of plum tomatoes and add the contents to the onion and bacon mixture. Stir very well to break down the tomatoes.

3 mins Once the tomatoes, bacon and onions look well cooked, add the drained pasta to the saucepan and stir well. Season well with fresh ground pepper, salt and a pinch of nutmeg. Replace the lid so that the whole mixture can heat through.

You can break the tomatoes up with a spoon or fork, which will make them easier to mix into the onion and bacon mixture. Don't use too much salt in the carbonara as the bacon or ham will be salty anyway. Let your guests make their own decision on how much salt to add.

2 mins Once the pasta is hot, add the grated cheese, then half the tin of evaporated milk. Allow the mixture to heat right through. (If you are using single cream, add it now and allow the mixture to heat through.) The cheese must have melted before serving.

If you have used mushrooms, you can add a little more salt at this point.

0 mins Drain the peas through a colander and place them in a serving dish or on the individual plates. Serve the carbonara piping hot with the peas or a green salad. Wash up and clear away.

The peas are cooked after approx. 5 minutes, when they go crinkly and bright green.

Watch points

If you have not already cooked the peaches, heat the grill up now. Once you have eaten the main course, and the grill is hot, place the peaches under it. Allow the sugar to bubble and turn a rich golden brown as it caramelises before serving the peaches. If you have already browned them, they may be served cold or reheated under the grill; they will need approx. 5 minutes to warm through.

Be careful not to burn the peaches and sugar. This can happen very easily, so watch them closely.

Serve the peaches. If you are using fresh cream, remember to serve it now.

Weekend break menu
Easy to prepare and cook
Cost level: inexpensive
Serves: 4

Two 30-minute breaks are incorporated in this menu.

| **Main course** | Home-made lasagne
Mixed salad with French dressing | Preparation time = 40 minutes
Cooking time = 60 minutes |

| **Dessert** | Baked sultana and egg custard | Preparation time = 10 minutes
Cooking time = 45–60 minutes |

This menu is for an easy weekend meal. The lasagne can be made in advance, either the day before or even frozen a few weeks ahead of time. The egg custard is quick to prepare and will cook quite happily in the bottom of the oven while the lasagne is cooking or heating through.

The salad is made on the day and should be served with a French dressing, either home-made or bought. Both the lasagne and egg custard can sit in a warm oven without spoiling, which is useful if you are running late or your guests are delayed.

Don't forget you will need a French dressing for the salad. If you want to make your own, turn to page 196, otherwise you can buy a bottle of ready-made dressing.

Equipment needed – **Menu 5**

Main course

1 savoury chopping board
1 sharp knife
1 medium saucepan with lid
1 savoury wooden spoon
1 tin opener
1 tablespoon
1 teaspoon
1 small saucepan with lid
1 measuring jug
1 cheese grater
1 ovenproof dish (preferably glass)
1 spatula (optional)
1 salad bowl

Dessert

1 mixing bowl
1 fork
1 measuring jug
1 teaspoon
1 tablespoon
1 ovenproof dish (preferably glass)
1 roasting tin

Shopping list – **Menu 5**

Main course

2 medium onions
★75g (3oz) cooking margarine
★450g (16oz) tin peeled plum tomatoes
★2 level tablespoons tomato purée
450g (1lb) minced beef
★salt and ground black pepper
★2 teaspoons dried oregano
★dried mustard powder
★1 tablespoon Worcestershire sauce
★25g (1oz) packet white sauce mix OR
  600ml (½ pint) milk
★50g (2oz) plain flour
★450ml (¾ pint) milk
225g (8oz) Cheddar cheese
150g (5oz) quick-cooking lasagne sheets
1 iceberg lettuce
4 tomatoes
1 cucumber
1 bunch radishes (optional)
150ml (¼ pint) French dressing

Dessert

★ 3 large eggs
600ml (1 pint) milk
★ ½ teaspoon vanilla essence
★ 25g (1oz) margarine
25g (1oz) caster sugar
★ 50g (2oz) sultanas
★ 1 pinch grated nutmeg

★Check store cupboard

Countdown – **Menu 12**

If you want to prepare and cook the whole menu you will need 125 minutes. This includes two 30-minute breaks while you wait for the food to cook. If you are a slow cook, add 5–10 minutes to each course to ensure that you do not run out of time. Remember that the times given are only a guide, as each cook will take different lengths of time to complete each task. The lasagne can be made in advance, either the day before and kept refrigerated, or several days before and frozen. Make sure it is de-frosted for at least 12 hours before reheating. The egg custard should be made fresh on the day and placed in the bottom of the oven while the lasagne is cooking or heating up. Serve a salad or some vegetables with the main course.

Main course

PROBLEMS AND HANDY TIPS

Meat sauce for the lasagne

Preparation time: 15 minutes.
Cooking time: 30 minutes.

Assemble all the ingredients and equipment you need for the meat sauce. Set your timer for 15 minutes.

15 mins Take two onions and peel and chop them as finely as possible.

10 mins Place the chopped onion in a medium-sized saucepan. Add 25g/1oz (1 tablespoon) cooking margarine and place over a medium heat. Cook until the onions are soft and transparent. Stir occasionally.

Do not allow the onion to brown too much.

8 mins While waiting for onions to cook open the tin of plum tomatoes. Once the onion has softened, add 2 table-spoons of tomato purée and cook for a further 1–2 minutes, stirring continuously.

6 mins Take 450g (1lb) of raw minced beef and add it to the onion mixture. Stir well and leave on a medium heat to cook. Stir occasionally.

Make sure the meat doesn't burn on the bottom of the saucepan; keep stirring to prevent this from happening.

5 mins While the meat is cooking, season with a good pinch of salt, ground black pepper to taste, 2 teaspoons of dried oregano, 1 teaspoon dried mustard powder and 1 tablespoon of Worcestershire sauce. Once the meat has browned, add the tin of tomatoes. Stir well, partially cover and simmer over low heat for approximately 25–30 minutes.

0 mins Wash up and clear away.

To break the tomatoes up as you put them in the saucepan, squeeze them between your fingers. Remove the small stalk if you want to. The tomatoes will break down as they cook.

Relax

Have a 30–minute break while the meat is cooking. When you return you will make the white sauce and put the lasagne together.

Welcome back

Feeling better after your break?

White sauce

Preparation time: 15 minutes
Cooking time: 5 minutes

Assemble the ingredients and equipment you need for the sauce. Set your timer for 15 minutes.

15 mins If using a packet sauce, follow the instructions on the packet. If not, take 50g (2oz) of margarine, put it into a small saucepan and melt over a low heat. Take the saucepan off the heat and add 50g/2oz (2 tablespoons) plain flour or enough to make a thick paste. Cook over a medium heat for 2 minutes, stirring constantly, to remove the starchy flavour.

Do not allow the flour and margarine to discolour or go brown, as this is going to be a white sauce. Always add a cold liquid to a hot roux (the flour and margarine mixture), as this prevents a lumpy sauce.

7 mins Remove from the heat and allow to cool.

6 mins Measure out 450ml (¾ pint) of milk and add slowly to the flour mixture, stirring all the time. Once all the milk has been added, put the saucepan back over a low heat and allow it to thicken and come slowly to the boil. Stir continuously.

4 mins Once the sauce starts to thicken, turn the heat down and allow to simmer for a further 2–3 minutes. If the sauce is too thick, add a little extra milk. Don't forget that the sauce needs to be quite thick, as it is for coating not for pouring. Season the sauce well with a pinch of salt, some white or black pepper and a good pinch of dried mustard powder.

The dried mustard powder enhances the flavour of the cheese.

1 mins Turn the heat off and leave to cool. Take 225g (8oz) of cheese and grate it through a medium grater on to a plate or into a bowl.

0 mins Set the sauce aside with the lid on. Wash up and clear away.

Putting the lasagne together

Preparation time: 10 minutes
Cooking time: 60 minutes

If you haven't already set the oven, do so now to 200°C/ 400°F/Gas mark 6. Set your timer for 10 minutes.

10 mins Take an ovenproof dish and put a layer of meat sauce in the bottom. Cover with a layer of lasagne (approximately 2 sheets); you may need to break up the sheets to fit them neatly in the dish. Cover with a small amount of white sauce, then a small amount of grated cheese. Continue layering the meat, lasagne, white sauce and cheese, finishing with a layer of cheese. (Use a wooden spoon or spatula to spread out layers.)

Do not use too much white sauce or cheese in the layers, keep enough back for the top of the lasagne.

2 mins Place the lasagne in the oven and bake at 200°C/ 400°F/Gas mark 6 for 60 minutes. Alternatively, place in the fridge and cook within 24 hours, or freeze and use within 3 months.

0 mins Wash up and clear away.

You should allow the lasagne to cool before you place it in the fridge or freezer.

Dessert

PROBLEMS AND HANDY TIPS

Preparation time: 10 minutes
Cooking time: 45–60 minutes

Preheat the oven 160°C/325°F/Gas mark 3 if it is not already set for the lasagne. If you are using the same oven for them both, the custard will sit happily at the bottom of the oven, even though the temperature is higher. Assemble all the ingredients and equipment you need for the dessert. Set your timer for 10 minutes.

10 mins Break 3 eggs into a mixing bowl and beat well with fork. Measure out 600ml (1 pint) of milk and add it to the eggs. Add ½ teaspoon of vanilla essence and mix well.

If you can see any coloured specks in the eggs when you break them, they have been fertilized. You can remove the specks with a spoon or fork or by sieving the eggs into a bowl.

5 mins Take an ovenproof dish and grease it well with 25g/1oz (1 tablespoon) of margarine, using either a piece of greaseproof paper or your fingers. Stir 25g/1oz (1 table-spoon) of sugar into the egg and milk mixture, than pour into the greased dish.

4 mins Add 50g/2oz (2 tablespoons) sultanas, then sprinkle a pinch of nutmeg over the top of the custard. Take a large roasting tin, half fill it with cold water and place the custard dish in the centre. Place near the bottom of the preheated oven if it is to cook with the lasagne, or in the middle if it is to cook alone on a low heat.

The tin of water in which the custard dish cooks is called a bain marie. It stops the custard from getting too hot and curdling.

1 min Cook for 45–60 minutes. Once cooked the dessert will sit quite happily in the bottom of the oven without spoiling. The custard can also be served cold.

0 mins Wash up and clear away.

Relax

Have a second break while the lasagne and egg custard cook. Take your timer with you and set it for 30 minutes.

Welcome back

Feeling better after your break? You now have only the last-minute tasks to perform, and then it will be time to serve the lasagne.

Last-minute tasks

Set your timer for 15 minutes. This is how long you will need before serving the lasagne.

Salad

15 mins Take the iceberg lettuce and, using a sharp knife, cut it into bite-sized pieces. Wash the lettuce and any other ingredients you are going to use in the salad.

You can also shred lettuce, i.e. break it up with your fingers, rather than cutting it with a knife.

10 mins Place all the washed and chopped ingredients in a salad bowl and mix well. Shake the French dressing and pour some all over the salad. Toss well, adding extra dressing if the salad still looks dry. Place the salad on the table ready to serve.

If you would like to make your own French dressing, see page 196. The dressing is best made in advance. Don't forget to shake or mix the dressing very well before adding it to the salad.

5 mins Check the lasagne, which should be almost ready to serve. If the cheese is golden brown on top, the lasagne is bubbling away and it has been in the oven for at least 60 minutes, it is ready to serve. The test is to put a knife into the centre of the dish; if it goes through the pasta with ease, the lasagne is ready.

3 mins Check the egg custard; if it is beginning to brown, place it lower in the oven if possible. If you are removing the lasagne to serve, the oven can be turned down to 160°C/325°F/Gas mark 3. The dessert will sit happily in the oven until you are ready to serve it.

The lasagne can be left in the oven to keep warm if your guests are late. It will not spoil, so don't worry.

0 mins Wash up and clear away. Serve the lasagne with the dressed salad. Serve the egg custard as it is, no extras are needed.

Chinese stir-fry menu
Easy to prepare and cook
Cost level: good value
Serves: 4

A 30-minute break is incorporated in this menu.

Starter   Spinach and prawn stir-fry

Preparation time = 30 minutes
Cooking time = 10–15 minutes

Main course   Fried beef in oyster sauce
Boiled rice

Preparation time = 30 minutes
Cooking time = 10 minutes

Dessert   Lychee and mango fruit salad

Preparation time = 10 minutes
Cooking time = None

This stir-fry menu is easy to prepare and cook, but it is time-consuming as each vegetable has to be cut into very thin strips before being cooked. The actual cooking time is very short and should be done at the last minute, just before serving.

All the chopping up of the ingredients for both the starter and the main course can be done in advance, and set aside in small bowls until required. This gives you the opportunity to have a break from the kitchen before returning and putting the whole menu together. The dessert can be made in advance and kept in the fridge.

If you have a food processor with a thin slicing blade, all the vegetables for the starter and main course can be put through it. This will save a great deal of time. However, the menu can still be made quite easily by chopping everything by hand.

Remember, this is a menu which can be cooked in front of your guests. It can be served straight from the wok on to their plates.

If you don't have a wok, a deep frying pan can be used instead. Make sure you have enough room in it as there are a number of ingredients to be cooked. If you don't have a lid for your wok or frying pan, you can always make one out of tin foil.

Equipment needed – **Menu 6**

Starter

1 medium-to-large saucepan
1 potato peeler
1 fine grater
1 wok or frying pan (with a lid, if
   possible)
1 colander
1 large chopping knife
1 savoury wooden spoon
1 savoury chopping board
1 teaspoon
1 tin opener
1 fine sieve
1 tablespoon

Main course

1 sharp knife
1 savoury chopping board
1 food processor with a thin slicer blade
   (optional)
5 small bowls to hold the chopped meat
   and vegetables
1 garlic crusher (or see Handy Tip 4, page
   xviii)
1 tin opener
1 medium-sized saucepan for the rice
1 small mixing bowl
1 tablespoon
1 wok or frying pan (with a lid, if
   possible)
1 stirring utensil for the wok or frying pan
1 fine sieve or colander

Dessert

1 tin opener
1 fine, medium-sized sieve
1 small bowl
1 sharp knife
1 sweet chopping board or plate
1 lemon squeezer

Shopping list – **Menu 6**

Starter

225g (8oz) frozen prawns, defrosted
675g (1½lbs) fresh or frozen spinach
*2.5cm (1 inch) piece fresh root ginger
2 spring onions
*1 teaspoon pure sesame seed oil
50g (2oz) tin sliced bamboo shoots
*1 tablespoon soy sauce
*salt, pepper

Main course

450g (1lb) lean beef (top rump or side)
100g (4oz) button mushrooms
½ green pepper
½ red pepper
½ yellow pepper
2 spring onions
2 cloves garlic
100g (4oz) fresh bean sprouts
50g (2oz) tin sliced bamboo shoots
*1 tablespoon cornflour
*4 tablespoons water
*2 tablespoons dry sherry
*2 tablespoons oyster sauce
*1 tablespoon soy sauce
*1 teaspoon pure seasame seed oil
*salt and pepper
225g (8oz) easy-cook rice or spiced Chinese
   rice

Dessert

*425g (16oz) tin lychees
*425g (16oz) tin mangos
1 lemon
1 small tub water ice or light ice cream (any
   flavour)

*Check store cupboard

Countdown – **Menu 6**

If you want to prepare and cook the whole menu, you will need 130 minutes, which includes a 30-minute break. You will need 70 minutes for all the preparation. Then when you return from your break you will need 15 minutes to finish off the starter and 15 minutes to cook the beef. The joy of Chinese wok cooking is that the actual cooking time is very short; the preparation time, however, can be lengthy. Remember that the times given are only a guide as each cook will take different lengths of time to complete each task. I would suggest that you prepare as much as possible in advance so that you have only the actual cooking to perform when your guests arrive. The dessert can be made in advance and left in the fridge to chill.

Starter

PROBLEMS AND HANDY TIPS

Preparation time: 30 minutes
Cooking time: 8 minutes

Set your timer for 30 minutes. This is the preparation time; you will stir-fry the starter a few minutes before serving it.

Assemble all the ingredients and equipment you need for the starter. Defrost your prawns now by leaving them out at room temperature. They will be ready when you need to use them.

30 mins If you are using fresh spinach, wash it well under cold running water to remove any grit, sand or soil. You will need to remove the tough stalks, best done with a sharp knife or your fingers. Pull away the stalk as close to the leaf as possible and discard. If you are using frozen spinach, place it straight in a saucepan.

It is not necessary to remove the stalks if the spinach is very young and soft.

20 mins Fill the kettle and put it on to boil.

18 mins Place the fresh, washed spinach in a saucepan and pour some boiling water over it. Try to use as little water as possible, just enough to cover the spinach, as it will cook down dramatically.

You should not need to use more than 300ml (½ pint) of boiling water to cook the spinach.

15 mins While you are waiting for the spinach to cook, take the piece of root ginger (2.5cm/1 inch) and peel it with either a potato peeler or a sharp knife. Grate the ginger on a fine grater straight into the wok or frying pan.

Do not use any of the long, hairy parts of the ginger; use only the fine parts.

10 mins Turn off the heat under the spinach and drain through a colander. Press out the excess water using a wooden spoon. Leave it to drain.

8 mins Take 2 spring onions, chop the root off the bottom and discard any old skin. Chop the spring onions finely and add them to the ginger in the wok or frying pan.

5 mins Add 1 teaspoon of sesame seed oil to the wok, turn the heat on to high and cook the ginger and spring onions very quickly, stirring constantly – 2 minutes should be enough. Turn the heat off. Take the ginger and onions out of the wok, place them in a bowl and cover to keep in the flavour.

2 mins Open the tin of bamboo shoots and discard the liquid. Add the shoots to the spinach in the colander.

0 mins Wash up and clear away.

Spinach always holds a lot of excess water, so it is a good idea to press it well and leave it to drain.

If you haven't used your wok for a long time, give it a thorough wash before using it.

Make sure you get the oil very hot in the wok as it is important to cook everything very fast.

The prawns for the starter must be de-frosted before being used. You can speed the process up by running them under cold water and then leaving them to continue thawing.

Dessert

Preparation time: 10 minutes
Cooking time: None

The dessert can be made in advance, put into the fridge to chill and then used when required.

Assemble all the ingredients and equipment you need for the dessert. Set your timer for 10 minutes.

10 mins Open the tins of lychees and mangoes and drain the fruit through a sieve, collecting the juice in a bowl underneath. If the fruit chunks are very large, take a sharp knife and cut them into bite-sized pieces. Place the fruit in a serving bowl.

5 mins Taste the fruit juice; if it is too sweet, take a lemon and roll it under the palm of your hand on a work surface to loosen the flesh inside. Cut the lemon in two and squeeze the juice from one half. Add the lemon juice to the fruit juice and taste again. It might be necessary to use the second lemon half as well.

Rolling the lemon on a hard surface releases the flesh, making it easier to squeeze. You also get more juice from the lemon.

2 mins Pour the fruit juice over the fruit in the serving bowl and put it in the fridge to chill until required. The fruit salad can be served with a water ice or light ice cream.

0 mins Wash up and clear away.

Main course

Preparation time: 30 minutes
Cooking time: 10 minutes

Set your timer for 30 minutes. This is how long it will take to prepare all the vegetables and meat for cooking. The actual cooking time is very short, and should really be done at the last minute – even in front of your guests.

If you have a food processor, you can save a lot of time by using it to chop up all the vegetables.

30 mins Assemble all the ingredients and equipment needed for the main course.

You will have to use a lot of small bowls, but it is a good idea to keep the ingredients separate as the cooking times vary.

25 mins Take the meat and, using a very sharp knife, cut it into very thin slices approx. 3.5cm (1½ inches) long. Place the meat in a bowl, cover and place in the fridge.

Don't worry if the meat takes a long time to cut up; this is quite normal.

20 mins Take the mushrooms and wash them well, discarding the stalks, slice very thinly, place in a bowl and set aside.

16 mins Take the halves of green, red and yellow peppers and remove the stalk and seeds from each. If you find it difficult to remove the seeds, run the peppers under cold water to flush them out. Slice the peppers very thinly; this is best done by first cutting them in half across the middle and then slicing it evenly from top to bottom. Place the slices in a bowl and set aside until required.

10 mins Take 2 spring onions, discard the root and tough outer skin, then chop them as finely as possible. Place in a bowl.

6 mins Peel 2 cloves of garlic, crush them, and add to the bowl containing the spring onions.

See page xviii, Handy Tip 4 for an easy way to crush garlic if you don't have a garlic crusher.

2 mins Measure out 100g (4oz) of fresh bean sprouts. Put them into a bowl until required. Open the tin of bamboo shoots and drain well.

0 mins Wash up and clear away.

Now all the ingredients are prepared, all that is left to do is the last-minute cooking. If you would like a break, now is the time, as once you have started the stir-fry, you can't stop. If you are having a break, make sure you cover all the bowls containing the chopped ingredients. I would suggest covering them with a tea towel, unless you are going to be a very long time, in which case they should be put in the fridge to keep cool.

Relax

Have a break for 30 minutes, or more if you like.

Welcome back

Feeling better after your break?

Last-minute tasks

Set your timer for 15 minutes. This is how long you have before you serve the starter.

15 mins Fill the kettle and put it on to boil.

14 mins Take the defrosted prawns, place them in a sieve and run them under cold water to clean them. Leave them to drain.

12 mins Take the rice and put it into a medium-sized saucepan. If you are using easy-cook rice, measure out 50g (2oz) per person, 225g (8oz) in total. Pour the boiling water over the rice and put it on a low to medium heat to cook. If you have bought spiced Chinese rice, check the packet for cooking instructions, as each variety is different.

The rice will take anything from 10–20 minutes to cook. All brands vary, so check the packet for instructions.

8 mins Place the wok over a high heat and allow the ginger and spring onions to get hot again. Then add all the prawns and stir well. Add 1 tablespoon of soy sauce and stir again. Turn the heat down to very low and cover the pan with a lid.

Make sure the wok is very hot before you add the prawns. It is important that they cook very rapidly and do not become tough and rubbery.

5 mins Check the rice and give it a good stir to stop it from sticking together.

4 mins Turn the heat up under the wok, add all the spinach and bamboo shoots and stir well. Season with a very small amount of salt and pepper. You might need to add more soy sauce if the mixture looks dry.

Make sure you stir the mixture in the wok constantly.

2 mins Get out your bowls ready to serve the starter. Check the rice and if you think it might overcook while you are eating the starter, turn it off. You can continue to cook it while you are cooking the stir-fry.

0 mins Serve the starter, making sure everyone has a good mixture of prawns and spinach. Wash up and clear away.

Finishing the main course

Reset your timer for 15 minutes.

Remember, this should be fun, and your guests should be sitting at the table awaiting the wonders of your wok. If you have the facility to warm your plates, put them in now.

15 mins Check the rice and turn it off; you will drain it just before serving. Uncover all the bowls of ingredients. Take a small mixing bowl, measure out 2 tablespoons of cornflour and 2 tablespoons of water, and mix well to form a thin, milky liquid. Then add 2 tablespoons of dry sherry, 2 tablespoons of oyster sauce and 1 tablespoon of soy sauce. Mix well and set aside until required.

10 mins Put the wok or frying pan over a medium heat. Add 1 teaspoon of sesame seed oil followed by the onions and garlic.

8 mins Fry briskly, tossing and stirring all the time. Turn the rice back on to a medium heat, if it needs to cook for a few more minutes.

6 mins Add all the peppers to the wok and stir well.

5 mins Add the sliced mushrooms and continue to cook rapidly.

Make sure you don't forget any of the ingredients. Check that you have collected all the bowls so that you do not leave any out.

4 mins Now add all the meat to the wok and stir well. Make sure the heat remains very high, as the beef needs to cook quickly.

2 mins Once the beef looks cooked (i.e. brown not red), add the cornflour and sherry mixture. Stir very well.

1 min Add the bamboo shoots and the bean sprouts and stir well. Season with a small amount of pepper if you like. Cook rapidly.

0 mins Turn the heat off and cover the stir-fry while you quickly drain the rice through a sieve or colander. Wash up and clear away.

Make sure you drain the rice well. Leave it in the colander while you get everything ready to serve.

Watch points

Serve the rice and beef stir-fry at once.

If you would like more liquid in the sauce, add a tablespoon of water. Keep adding water a tablespoon at a time until you reach the desired consistency.

When you are ready, serve the fruit salad. Offer your guests some water ice or ice cream to go with it.

MENU

Vegetarian winter or spring menu

Moderately difficult to prepare and cook
Cost level: good value
Serves: 4

A 30-minute break is incorporated in this menu.

Starter Stuffed tomatoes with avocado cream

Preparation time = 35 minutes
Cooking time = None

Main course Baked vegetable casserole with Quorn and cashew nuts
Scallop potatoes

Preparation time = 40 minutes
Cooking time = 30–40 minutes

Dessert Apricot and banana bake

Preparation time = 10 minutes
Cooking time = 40 minutes

This menu would suit vegetarians. It is straightforward to prepare, as well as being nutritious and delicious.

The starter is served cold and the combination of tomato and avocado is light and refreshing. The vegetable casserole is cooked in the oven along with the potatoes, so the cook has a chance for a well-deserved break. The dessert is cooked in the oven while the starter is being eaten.

The starter can be made in advance, either the night before or on the day. The vegetable casserole and dessert are best made fresh and cooked straight away.

The potatoes will be cooking in the oven during the break, but the vegetable casserole should not be put in the oven until after your break, to prevent it overcooking.

Equipment needed – **Menu 7**

Starter

1 sharp knife
1 heatproof bowl
1 tablespoon
1 plate
1 savoury chopping board
1 food processor or 1 mixing bowl
1 teaspoon
1 fork
1 savoury wooden spoon

Main course

1 heatproof bowl
1 potato peeler
1 sharp knife
1 colander
1 savoury chopping board
1 medium ovenproof casserole dish with lid
1 garlic crusher (or see page xviii, Handy Tip 4)
1 fine grater
1 tablespoon
1 measuring jug
1 savoury wooden spoon
1 frying pan
1 small baking tray

Dessert

1 ovenproof dish, preferably glass
1 sharp knife
1 lemon squeezer

Shopping list – **Menu 7**

Starter

4 large tomatoes
★1 small onion
1 ripe avocado (see Handy Tip 12, pxx)
200g (7oz) packet soft cream cheese
★salt and pepper
★2 teaspoons lemon juice
★4 pieces brown bread for toasting
100g (4oz) butter

Main course

★8 small onions or shallots
4 large carrots
2.5cm (1 inch) piece fresh root ginger
4 courgettes
1 small cauliflower
★2 cloves garlic
75g (3oz) vegetarian margarine
★38g (1½oz) plain flour
★1 vegetable stock cube or 600ml (1 pint) fresh stock
★pinch dried mustard powder
★salt and freshly ground pepper
★1 tablespoon Worcestershire sauce
★8 small/4 medium to large potatoes
pinch nutmeg
100g (4oz) mangetout
225g (8oz) mushrooms
250g (9oz) packet cubed Quorn
100g (4oz) cashew nuts
225g (8oz) crème fraîche or natural yogurt (optional)

Dessert

250g (9oz) dried apricots
2 bananas
2 oranges
★pinch of coriander
★pinch of mixed spice

★Check store cupboard

Countdown – **Menu 7**

If you want to prepare and cook the whole menu, you need 130 minutes, which includes a 30-minute break. If you are a slow cook, add 5–10 minutes to each course to ensure that you don't run out of time. Remember that the times given are only a guide as each cook will take different lengths of time to complete each task. All the courses are quite flexible and can sit in a warm oven for some time without spoiling, if for any reason you are running late.

The starter can be made in advance and left in the fridge overnight.

Starter

Preparation time: 35 minutes
Cooking time: None

PROBLEMS AND HANDY TIPS

Assemble all the ingredients and equipment needed to make the starter. Set your timer for 35 minutes. (Remember, using a food processor will save a lot of time.)

35 mins Fill the kettle with water and put it on to boil. Take 4 medium-sized tomatoes and use a sharp knife to make a small cut in the skin near the stalk.

Do not use unripe (green-looking) tomatoes, as they can be very difficult to skin and will not be as tasty as ripe tomatoes. If the tomatoes are ready, you should notice that the skin is coming away where you made the small cut.

33 mins Place the tomatoes in a heatproof bowl and pour over enough boiling water to cover them. Leave to stand for approx. 30 seconds, or until skin begins to come away. Lift the tomatoes out of the boiling water with a tablespoon and plunge them into cold water.

28 mins Peel all the tomatoes. This is best done with your fingers or a sharp knife. The skin should come away very easily. If not, put the tomatoes back into boiling water for another 30 seconds. Place the skinned tomatoes on a plate until required.

Avoid plunging the tomatoes into boiling water more than twice, or they will start to cook and go 'furry'.

23 mins Take one small onion and peel it, then chop it as finely as possible. Place the chopped onion in a mixing bowl. (If you use a food processor, keep the onion in the processor bowl.)

Run some cold water while you peel and chop the onion as this helps prevent your eyes watering.

18 mins Take the avocado and cut it in half lengthways. Remove the stone and discard any black or bruised pieces of flesh. Using a teaspoon, scoop out all the remaining flesh and place it in the food processor or mixing bowl with the onion.

The avocado needs to be quite soft for the best results. A hard avocado will make mashing very difficult. If you have two avocados to choose from, choose the softer of the two. Squeeze the top gently to see which one is riper.

16 mins Process the avocado or mash it with a fork to

make a purée with the onion. Then add 200g (7oz) of soft cream cheese and continue to process the mixture or stir with a wooden spoon. Season well with ground black pepper, a good pinch of salt and 2 teaspoons of lemon juice. Stir again, check the seasoning and adjust if necessary. Set the avocado cream aside.

11 mins Return to the tomatoes. Take a tomato in one hand and using a sharp knife, make an incision right round the stalk end. Carefully lever off this 'lid' and discard it. Then use either a teaspoon or your fingers to scoop out the seeds. You will find that there is a core inside the tomato, which keeps the seeds in place. Try to break this with your fingers or a small knife; this can be quite fiddly.

6 mins If some pips remain in the tomatoes, flush them out under cold running water. Drain the tomatoes and pat dry with kitchen paper.

4 mins If the tomatoes do not stand level, cut a thin slice off the bottom of each one. This will ensure that they do not topple over. The slivers removed can be used as 'hats' on top of the avocado cream.

2 mins Now, using a teaspoon, fill the tomatoes with the avocado cream. Push the mixture down into the tomatoes and fill them to the top. A careful shake ensures that the filling goes right to the bottom and that the tomatoes are completely filled. Place the filled tomatoes in the fridge.

0 mins Wash up and clear away.

Make sure you only cut a thin sliver off the bottom of the tomatoes and that you don't cut into the hollow. If you do, the avocado cream will leak out of the bottom.

The small 'hats' for the tomatoes make them look more attractive.

If you have some avocado cream left, you can serve it in a bowl with the tomatoes, or keep it in the fridge for a few days.

Main course

PROBLEMS AND HANDY TIPS

Preparation time: 40 minutes
Cooking time: 30–40 minutes

Preheat the oven to 180°C/350°F/Gas mark 4 if you are going to cook the casserole straight away; otherwise, preheat it while you are having your break. Assemble all the ingredients and equipment needed for the main course. Set your timer for 40 minutes.

40 mins Fill the kettle and put it on to boil. Place the 8 small onions in a heatproof bowl, cover with boiling water and leave them to soak for 5 minutes.

38 mins Meanwhile, peel the 4 carrots and piece of fresh root ginger with a potato peeler or sharp knife.

34 mins Drain the onions and pour some cold water over them. Using a sharp knife, peel off the outer skin, leaving the small root intact. (This keeps the onion

Soaking the onions in boiling water makes them easier to peel.

If the ginger is very difficult to peel, use a sharp knife instead of a potato peeler.

Plunging the onions into cold water makes it easier to handle them and peel them.

together while it is cooking.) Place the peeled onions in an ovenproof casserole dish and cover with a lid or some tin foil.

29 mins Take the courgettes and wash them under cold running water. Cut the top and tail off each and discard. Cut the courgettes into thin, diagonal slices approx. 5mm (¼ inch) thick. Place the slices in a colander, sprinkle liberally with salt and leave for at least 5 minutes. (This process, called 'degorging', removes the strong, bitter flavour often found in courgettes.)

25 mins Take the 4 carrots and slice them diagonally into 5mm (¼ inch) circles.

23 mins Wash the cauliflower under cold running water and cut it into small, even-sized sprigs.

Make sure all the cauliflower sprigs are roughly the same size so that they cook evenly.

20 mins Peel 2 cloves of garlic and crush them with a garlic crusher or the round-ended knife method (see Handy Tip 4, pxviii). Add to the casserole dish with the onions. Add 38g/1½oz (1½ tablespoons) of vegetarian margarine and place on the hob over a low heat to cook the onion and garlic.

15 mins Meanwhile, take the peeled ginger and, using a fine grater, grate it straight into the casserole dish and cook for approx. 1 minute.

12 mins Turn the heat off, measure out 38g/1½oz (1½ tablespoons) of plain flour, add it to the casserole dish and mix well. Turn the heat back on and allow the flour and onion mixture to cook for 2 minutes.

Do not allow the garlic and ginger to burn; watch closely as this can happen quite quickly. Turn the heat off as soon as they start to brown.

9 mins Turn off the heat and allow the mixture to cool slightly. Crumble 1 vegetable stock cube into the mixture and slowly add 600ml (1 pint) of cold water, stirring all the time. Alternatively, add 600ml (1 pint) of fresh stock. Once all the liquid has been added to the flour and margarine, put the sauce over a low heat and slowly bring to the boil, stirring continuously. Season with a pinch of mustard powder, ground black or white pepper, a small pinch of salt and a tablespoon of Worcestershire sauce. Taste to check the seasoning.

Make sure you add the liquid very slowly so that no lumps form in the sauce. If you find it is going lumpy, stop adding the liquid and beat the mixture as hard as possible until you have a smooth consistency again. Then continue to add the rest of the liquid slowly.

4 mins Once the sauce has come to the boil and thickened, allow it to simmer for a further 5 minutes to remove the starchy taste.

3 mins Now wash all the salt off the courgettes and leave them to drain. You will add the courgettes and cauliflower to the casserole once you have had your break.

Make sure you wash the salt off the courgettes extremely well. This is best done by running them under cold water for several minutes.

1min Turn the sauce off and add all the sliced carrots. Cover with a lid or foil. You will prepare the mangetout and mushrooms when you return from your break.

0 min Wash up and clear away.

Scallop potatoes

Preheat the oven to 180°C/350°F/Gas mark 4.

Set your timer for 10 minutes.

10 mins Peel the potatoes. If they are medium/large, cut them in half. Place them in a medium-sized saucepan and cover with cold water. Add a pinch of salt and put the potatoes on to boil.

5 mins Once boiling, allow to boil for 2 minutes.

3 mins Drain the potatoes and run them under cold water to make them easier to handle. Place the potatoes on a chopping board. Using a sharp knife, cut thin slices down diagonally into the potato, but not all the way through. Grease the baking tray with 12g (½oz) of margarine to prevent the potatoes from sticking. Arrange the potatoes on it and season with a little salt, black pepper and a pinch of nutmeg.

0 mins Put the potatoes into the preheated oven, as near to the top as possible, and leave to cook. Wash up and clear away.

The potatoes should par-boil, which means that they cook for only a few minutes to start them off. Try not to cut right through to the bottom of the potato or it will fall apart while cooking.

Season the potatoes well before putting them into the oven.

Relax

Take a 30-minute break, keeping your timer with you so that you know how much time has elapsed. When you return, you will only need to put the vegetable casserole and the dessert together.

Welcome back

Feeling better after your break?

Last-minute tasks

Set your timer for 5 minutes. This is the time you need to warm up the casserole on the hob before putting it in the oven.

5 mins Put the sauce in the casserole dish on to a low heat on the hob to warm through slowly. Stir in the cauliflower sprigs, then cover the casserole and place in the oven underneath the scallop potatoes, which should be beginning to brown.

The sauce needs to be reheated well before it is placed in the oven.

The rest of the vegetables and the Quorn will be added to the casserole later, 15 minutes before serving, otherwise they would overcook. You may also want to add a little extra water or stock at that time if the casserole looks too dry.

Dessert

Preparation time: 10 minutes
Cooking time: 40 minutes

Preheat the oven to 180°C/350°F/Gas mark 4, if not already set for the potatoes and casserole. Assemble all the ingredients and equipment you need for the dessert. Set your timer for 10 minutes.

10 mins Take an ovenproof dish, preferably glass, and place the 250g (9oz) of apricots in the bottom.

5 mins Peel 2 bananas and slice them on top of the apricots. Take 2 oranges, cut them both in half, squeeze the juice from them and pour it all over the bananas and apricots. Add a pinch of coriander and mixed spice. Set aside until required to cook.

A glass dish is attractive, as you can see all the ingredients bubbling away while they cook.

Make sure the bananas are covered with the orange juice as this will prevent them discolouring.

Set your timer for 15 minutes. This is how long you have before you serve the starter.

15 mins Take the casserole out of the oven, add the courgettes, stir well and put it back in the oven.

10 mins Finish preparing the rest of the vegetables. Top and tail the mangetout. Wash the mushrooms well under cold running water, cut them into quarters and leave them to drain in a colander.

The mangetout need have only a very small amount of top and tail removed.

Make sure the mushrooms are washed well and that they are cooked properly before adding them to the casserole.

5 mins Take the casserole out of the oven and add all the Quorn and mangetout. Put the casserole back in the oven to continue cooking. Check the potatoes, which should be opening out like flowers and browning well. If they haven't opened up very much, take a sharp knife and ease them apart a little. Put them back in the oven to continue cooking.

3 mins Melt 25g/1oz (1 tablespoon) of vegetarian margarine in a frying pan, add the mushrooms and cook quickly, turning all the time. When they are beginning to brown, turn the heat off. Take the casserole out of the oven, add the mushrooms and stir well. Measure out 100g (4oz) of cashew nuts, add them to the casserole and return it to the oven for 15 minutes.

0 mins If you are going to serve toast with the starter, make it now and serve at once. Wash up and clear away.

Watchpoints

Put the dessert in the bottom of the oven now if you have the space. If not, put it in when you take out the main course. It might be a good idea to cover the dessert with tin foil to stop it drying out.

Take the starter out of the fridge and serve with the hot toast and butter.

When you have eaten the starter, add the crème fraîche or yogurt to the casserole and serve at once.

If you haven't put the dessert in the oven, do so now when you take out the main course.

The dessert is cooked once the bananas are soft. If it is very easy to push a knife into the bananas they are cooked.

Set your timer for 40 minutes. This is the time the dessert will need to cook. Turn the oven down after 40 minutes and allow the dessert to sit in a warm oven until you are ready to serve.

Summer or winter menu
Moderately difficult to prepare and cook
Cost level: good value
Serves: 4

A 30-minute break is incorporated in this menu.

| **Starter** | Seafood salad with Melba toast | Preparation time = 15 minutes
Cooking time = None |

| **Main course** | Pasta and bacon hot pot
Mangetout or peas | Preparation time = 35 minutes
Cooking time = 60 minutes |

| **Dessert** | Apple and almond jalousie with cream | Preparation time = 35 minutes
Cooking time = 35 minutes |

This menu would suit anyone who prefers not to eat meat, but enjoys seafood. Omit the bacon in the main course if this is the case. This menu has a wonderful mixture of flavours. The Seafood Salad is best made on the day to keep it fresh. The main course and dessert can be made in advance and reheated when required.

The Apple and Almond Jalousie is a delicious dessert similar to an apple strudel, but made with puff pastry. Beginners may find it challenging, but the finished creation looks and tastes wonderful.

Nothing will spoil in this menu if it has to wait, and there are very few last-minute tasks, as so much is cooked in the oven.

If you are using frozen puff pastry, you must take it out of the deepfreeze at least 90 minutes before you are going to use it, and leave it at room temperature to defrost.

Equipment needed – **Menu 8**

Starter

1 fine sieve
1 tin opener
1 mixing bowl
1 savoury wooden spoon
1 savoury chopping board
1 sharp knife
1 lemon squeezer
1 tablespoon
1 garlic crusher (or see Handy Tip 4, pxviii)
1 colander

Main course

1 savoury chopping board
1 sharp knife
1 small saucepan or frying pan
1 savoury wooden spoon
1 colander
1 large mixing bowl
1 measuring jug
1 fork or balloon whisk
1 cheese grater
1 ovenproof glass dish or casserole
1 garlic crusher (or see Handy Tip 4, pxviii)
1 medium saucepan for the mangetout or peas

Dessert

1 mixing bowl
1 teaspoon
1 sweet wooden spoon
1 sweet chopping board
1 sharp knife
1 lemon squeezer
1 potato peeler
1 tablespoon
1 rolling pin (or clean wine bottle)
1 32.5×25cm (13×10 inch) baking tray (nonstick if possible)
1 small bowl
1 fork
1 pastry brush

Shopping list – **Menu 8**

Starter

225g (8oz) fresh or frozen cooked prawns
175g (6oz) tin crabmeat
200g (7oz) tin red salmon (skinless and boneless)
100g (4oz) tin smoked mussels (cooked and shelled)
1 lemon
★3 tablespoons olive oil
★1 tablespoon white wine vinegar
★1 clove garlic
2 tablespoons fromage frais
1 round lettuce
1 bunch parsley
1 packet Melba toast
100g (4oz) butter

Main course

★1 large onion
★50g (2oz) margarine
★225g (8oz) dried pasta, such as penne (hollow tubes)
100g (4oz) back bacon
225g (8oz) mushrooms (optional)
★3 eggs
★450ml (¾ pint) milk
★salt and ground black pepper
★pinch nutmeg
★teaspoon mustard powder
★150g (6oz) mild Cheddar cheese
225g (8oz) mangetout or frozen peas

Dessert

★100g (4oz) demerara sugar
★100g (4oz) ready-washed sultanas
★1 teaspoon cinnamon
50g (2oz) ground almonds
1 lemon
2 cooking apples
225g (8oz) packet puff pastry (frozen or fresh)
★1 tablespoon plain flour
★1 egg
25g (1oz) flaked almonds

★Check store cupboard

Countdown – **Menu 8**

If you want to prepare and cook the whole menu, you will need 140 minutes, which includes a 30-minute break. If you are a slow cook, add 5–10 minutes to each course to ensure that you do not run out of time. Remember that the times given are only a guide, as each cook will take different lengths of time to complete each task. The starter must be prepared as late as possible. The main course and dessert can both be made in advance and cooked or heated up later on.

Remember, if you are using frozen prawns and frozen puff pastry, you must defrost them approx. 90 minutes before you need to use them.

Dessert

PROBLEMS AND HANDY TIPS

Preparation time: 35 minutes
Cooking time: 35 minutes

Preheat the oven to 220°C/425°F/Gas mark 7. Assemble all the ingredients and equipment needed for the dessert. Set your timer for 35 minutes.

35 mins Measure out 100g (4oz) demerara sugar and 100g (4oz) sultanas. Place them in a mixing bowl. Add 1 teaspoon of cinnamon and 50g (2oz) of ground almonds and mix together.

27 mins Take 1 lemon, cut it in half, squeeze both halves and add the juice to the ingredients in the mixing bowl.

If you roll the lemon on a flat surface under the palm of your hand, you will find that this releases the flesh and makes squeezing the lemon easier. You will also get more juice from the lemon.

24 mins Take 2 cooking apples, peel them and cut them into quarters. Remove the core and slice each quarter into 3 or 4 even-sized pieces; the number will depend on how large the apples are. Add the slices to the mixing bowl and stir well. (The lemon juice will prevent the apple from discolouring while you prepare the pastry.)

Try to make all the apple slices approx. the same size so that they cook evenly.

19 mins Clear a space on the work surface and sprinkle 1 tablespoon of plain flour over it. Roll out the puff pastry as thinly as possible, aiming for a rectangular shape approx. 32.5×25cm (13×10 inches). The size of the pastry is very important. If you do not roll it out big enough, there will not be enough to enfold the apple mixture and to plait along the top.

Use a clean wine or milk bottle to roll the pastry if you don't have a rolling pin. Try to make the pastry as thin as possible and as close as you can to the size given.

15 mins Place the thin rectangle of pastry on the baking tray. (Don't worry if falls over the edges of it at this stage.) Take the apple mixture and spread it along the centre of the rectangle, making sure the apple and sultanas are evenly distributed. Use all the mixture if possible. (If you have some mixture left over, cook it separately in a dish in the oven.)

12 mins Break an egg into a small bowl, beat it with a fork and brush on to all the exposed parts of the pastry using a pastry brush or clean fingers. Take a sharp knife and starting 2.5cm (1 inch) in from one end of the pastry, make diagonal cuts. Start from the apple and cut outwards to the edge, making a herring-bone pattern. Stop 2.5cm (1 inch) from the bottom end. Repeat using exactly the same method on the opposite side.

The diagonal cuts should be approx. 2–3cm (1–1½ inches) apart, so that once they are overlapped you will be able to see the apple mixture inside.

6 mins Now it is time to lattice the pastry over the apple. This is rather like making a plait, but you use only two pieces of pastry. Start at one end of the pastry and work your way down, folding the strips from left then right over the apple mixture so that they meet in the middle each time. The egg should help to stick the pastry strips together. When you reach the end of the pastry, fold it in towards the centre and seal it so that none of the juices can escape during cooking. (You should be left with an attractive latticework that allows you to see the apple filling in the centre.)

If you are totally confused about how to cut the pastry and wrap it up, forget the instructions given. Simply wrap the pastry up the best way you can. Seal it with the egg, as explained, to stop the filling from bursting out.

The egg should help to seal the pastry together; if not, you have probably used too much egg. Brush the excess off and try again to seal the pastry.

2 mins Brush the rest of the beaten egg all over the top of the pastry to give a glazed finish. Bake in the preheated oven for 35 minutes, or until the pastry looks golden brown and the apple is soft when you put a sharp knife into it.

0 mins Wash up and clear away.

When the Apple Jalousie has been cooking for 20 minutes, measure out 25g/1oz (1 tablespoon) of flaked almonds and scatter them over the top of the pastry. Return the jalousie to the oven and continue cooking for a further 15 minutes. Turn the oven down to 200°C/400°F/Gas mark 6 if the pastry is already golden brown.

Watch the flaked almonds as they are oily and can burn easily.

Starter

PROBLEMS AND HANDY TIPS

Preparation time: 15 minutes
Cooking time: None

Assemble all the ingredients and equipment you need for the starter. Set your timer for 15 minutes.

15 mins Take the prawns, and put them in a fine sieve and run them under cold water to get rid of the salt, etc. Set aside to drain.

10 mins Open the tins of crabmeat, red salmon and smoked mussels. Drain them, place in a bowl and mix together well.

7 mins Take 1 lemon and cut it in half lengthways. Make 4 lemon wedges out of the first half and set aside to serve with the salad. Squeeze the second half and pour the lemon juice into a bowl. Add 3 tablespoons of olive oil and 1 tablespoon of white wine vinegar and mix well.

3 mins Peel and crush 1 clove of garlic in a garlic crusher (or see page xviii, Handy Tip 4). Place the crushed garlic in the bowl with the lemon juice, oil and vinegar. Add 2 tablespoons of fromage frais and mix well.

1 min Add the prawns to the rest of the seafood. Mix the lemon dressing again and pour it all over the seafood. Stir well. Cover the seafood with some clingfilm and place in the fridge until required.

0 mins Wash up and clear away.

You will serve the seafood salad on a bed of lettuce with chopped parsley for garnish, prepared just before serving.

Don't forget, you must use defrosted prawns. If you have forgotten, defrost them at room temperature now and add them just before serving. Remember to rinse them under cold water first.

Put the lemon wedges in the fridge to keep fresh until you need them.

Make sure you mix the dressing very well before dressing the salad. The oil always floats to the top very quickly.

The prawns can be mixed in with the rest of the seafood after you come back from your break.

Main course

PROBLEMS AND HANDY TIPS

Preparation time: 35 minutes
Cooking time: 60 minutes

Preheat the oven to 200°C/400°F/Gas mark 6. Assemble all the ingredients and equipment you need for the main course. Set your timer for 35 minutes.

35 mins Fill the kettle with water and put it on to boil. Take 1 large onion and chop it as finely as possible. Place the chopped onion in a small saucepan or frying pan and set aside.

28 mins Once the kettle has boiled, pour the boiling water into a large saucepan and add 12g/½oz (½ tablespoon) of margarine. Pour 200g (8oz) of pasta into the saucepan and turn the heat to medium. Stir well so that the margarine coats the pasta and prevents it sticking. Add a pinch of salt and cook for approx. 6 minutes.

26 mins Add 12g/½oz (½ tablespoon) of margarine to the chopped onion that you set aside and put it on to a medium heat to cook.

You use margarine to prevent the pasta from sticking together. The pasta should only cook for a few minutes, just to start it off. It will continue to cook in the oven.

25 mins Meanwhile, weigh out 100g (4oz) of back bacon and chop it up into bite-size pieces (approx. 2.5cm/1 inch) square. Set aside.

If you are making the dish without the bacon, ignore this point and continue with the recipe.

20 mins Check the pasta, as it must not overcook. Don't cook it for longer than 6 minutes once it has come to the boil. Drain the pasta through a colander and place it in a bowl or in the saucepan with some warm water. This will stop it cooking further and also prevent it from sticking together.

18 mins Once the onion is lightly browned, add the bacon and cook until it starts to curl. If you are using mushrooms, wash them well and cut them into thin slices or quarter them. Add them to the onion and bacon in the saucepan. Once the mixture has cooked for at least 5 minutes, turn the heat off and set aside.

13 mins Break 3 eggs into a large mixing bowl and add 450ml (¾ pint) of milk. Beat with a fork or balloon whisk, and season with a very small amount of salt as the bacon is already salty. (You can be more generous with the salt if you are not using the bacon.) Season with a pinch of nutmeg, some ground black pepper and a small teaspoon of mustard powder.

10 mins Take 150g (6oz) of Cheddar cheese and grate it on a medium-sized grater. Add half to the egg mixture and keep half to use on the top.

Don't forget to keep at least half the cheese back for the top of the dish.

7 mins Use the remaining 12g/½oz (½ tablespoon) of margarine to grease the ovenproof dish so that the pasta doesn't stick. (You can use your fingers or a piece of greaseproof paper to do the greasing.)

Make sure the ovenproof dish is big enough to hold all the pasta and the egg mixture.

5 mins It is now time to put the whole dish together. Drain the pasta which has been sitting in the warm water, and leave in the colander. Take the onion, bacon and mushroom mixture and add it to the egg and milk mixture, stir well. Pour the pasta into the ovenproof dish, then stir in the egg and onion mixture until well combined. Finally, sprinkle the remaining grated cheese on top of the pasta and cook in the preheated oven for 60 minutes.

If the pasta is still very hot it is a good idea to mix it with the egg mixture before putting it in the ovenproof dish. This prevents the margarine on the side of the dish from melting.

0 mins Wash up and clear away. Take the butter out of the fridge to soften (this will be served with the starter).

Relax

Have a break for 30 minutes while the pasta hot pot is cooking. When you return you will only have to prepare the garnish for the seafood salad and finish off the last-minute tasks.

Welcome back

Feeling better after your break?

Last-minute tasks

Set your timer for 25 minutes. This is how long you have before you serve the starter. The main course can sit in a warm oven without spoiling if you find that you are running behind time.

25 mins Take the round lettuce and discard the outside leaves. Pull the young leaves off and wash them well under cold running water. Shake the leaves well and pat dry on kitchen paper to remove any excess water. Place 1 or 2 leaves on the starter plates.

20 mins Take the fresh parsley and wash it under cold running water to refresh it; shake well and pat dry on kitchen paper. Using either a sharp knife or a pair of scissors, chop or snip the parsley.

15 mins Take the seafood salad out of the fridge and place on the lettuce leaves on each starter plate. Sprinkle a little parsley over each serving. Take the lemon wedges out of the fridge and place one wedge on each plate. The starter can be put on the table ready to serve, along with the Melba toast.

11 mins Take the mangetout or peas, depending on which you are using. Top and tail the mangetout and place them in a medium saucepan. If you are using frozen peas, put them in a small saucepan, add a pinch of salt and a teaspoon of sugar. You will cook them a few minutes before serving the main course.

6 mins Before eating the starter check the hot pot in the oven to see how it is cooking. It is ready once the egg mixture has set and the cheese top has become golden brown and crusty. To test whether it is cooked, stick a sharp knife into the centre of the dish; if it goes through the pasta with no problem and comes out clean, it is ready. Another way to tell if the egg is set is to pick the dish up and tip it slightly to see if any liquid is left. If you think it is ready, turn the oven down to 150°C/300°F/Gas mark 2.

2 mins If you have the facility to warm your main course plates and a serving dish for the vegetable, put them in to warm now. Fill the kettle with water and put it on to boil.

0 mins Serve the seafood salad and Melba toast. Wash up and clear away.

You can add the prawns now to the seafood bowl and stir well to coat them with the dressing.

It is a good idea to soak the lettuce in cold water to refresh it.

Make sure all the seafood is well covered with the dressing, use any extra dressing at the bottom of the bowl to cover the ingredients.

Mangetout need only a very small amount taken off their top and tail. This can be done either with a sharp knife or your fingers.

The teaspoon of sugar in the peas gives them a sweet and more delicate taste.

If you are in doubt whether the hot pot is cooked, leave it in for a little longer; it won't spoil and it is important that the egg and milk mixture is well set.

Watch points

Once the meal has started, it is not possible to give specific times, so the following instructions should be used only as a guide.

After you have cleared away the starter plates, pour the boiling water over the vegetable and leave to cook while you get the main course ready to serve. The mangetout and the peas will need only 4–5 minutes.

Do not overcook the mangetout or peas as they are better served crunchy.

Once you have eaten the starter, take the hot pot and the serving plates out of the oven. Place the Apple Jalousie in the oven to warm through while you are eating the main course.

The hot pot should be served in the dish it is cooked in.

Drain the vegetables, put them in a serving dish and place them on the table ready to serve.

Serve the main course.

The dessert is served warm to hot. Don't forget to serve some cream with it, or some vanilla ice cream, if you prefer.

The Apple Jalousie can get very hot, so warn your guests before serving it. Fruit can reach very high temperatures and burn the mouth badly.

Sunday roast menu
Moderately difficult to prepare and cook
Cost level: good value
Serves: 4

A 30-minute break is incorporated in this menu.

Starter   Sour cream mushrooms with croûtons

Preparation time = 25 minutes
Cooking time = 8 minutes

Main course   Roast Beef with roast potatoes, parsnips, carrots and onions
Fresh broccoli or Brussels sprouts
Yorkshire puddings with gravy

Preparation time = 30 minutes
Cooking time = 80–105 minutes

Dessert   Baked orange and lemon dessert with crème fraîche or cream

Preparation time = 40 minutes
Cooking time = 40–45 minutes

This is a traditional Sunday roast beef menu, but it also includes guidelines for other roasts, such as pork, lamb, chicken, turkey and duck, plus the traditional accompaniments. The target when cooking a roast meal is to have everything ready at the same time: the meat, potatoes, parsnips, green vegetables and gravy. The starter is cold, and should ideally be made in advance, to minimize your workload on the day.

The dessert cooks in the oven, is very straightforward and won't spoil if it has to sit there keeping warm for some time. As a roast is very filling, you could omit the starter or dessert, or serve cheese and fresh fruit as a quick alternative.

If you decide not to have the starter or dessert, it would be a good idea to increase the amount of meat you buy, in case you have very hungry guests. About 100g (4oz) extra per person should be sufficient.

Equipment needed – **Menu 9**

Starter

1 savoury chopping board
1 sharp knife
1 colander
1 garlic crusher (or see Handy Tip 4,
  pxviii)
1 small – medium saucepan with a lid
1 tablespoon
1 savoury wooden spoon

Main course

2 roasting tins
1 tablespoon
1 potato peeler
1 savoury chopping board
1 sharp knife
1 medium saucepan
1 colander
1 fine sieve
1 savoury wooden spoon
1 measuring jug
1 small saucepan
1 small bowl
1 bun tin (8–12 spaces)

Dessert

1 large mixing bowl
1 sweet wooden spoon or hand-held
  electric mixer
1 fine grater
1 sharp knife
1 medium mixing bowl
1 small bowl
1 lemon squeezer
1 ovenproof glass dish
1 balloon whisk or hand-held electric mixer
1 fine sieve
1 roasting tin
1 flexible plastic spatula

Shopping list **Menu 9**

Starter

450g (1lb) button mushrooms
★1 clove garlic
★25g (1oz) cooking margarine
★1 tablespoon lemon juice
★black pepper
pinch nutmeg
100g (4oz) sour cream or crème fraîche
1 packet croûtons

Main course

★50g (2oz) lard, cooking margarine or
  vegetable oil, or a combination
4 large old potatoes
2 large or 4 small parsnips
4 large or 8 small carrots
2 medium onions
100–150g (4–6oz) beef, off the bone, per
  person or 150–300g (6–12oz) beef, on the
  bone, per person (choose topside, top rump,
  silverside, rib or sirloin)
900g (2lb) broccoli or Brussels sprouts
1 packet Yorkshire pudding mix OR
  ★50g (2oz) plain flour
  ★pinch salt
  ★1 egg
  ★150ml (¼pt) milk
  ★12g (½oz) cooking margarine
2 tablespoons fat from the roast
★2 tablespoons plain flour
300ml (½pt) fresh stock or 1 beef stock cube
1 glass red wine (optional)
★salt, pepper and mustard powder
1 small jar horseradish sauce
1 small jar English mustard

Dessert

★100g (4oz) margarine or butter
100g (4oz) caster sugar
1 lemon
1 orange
3 eggs
75g (3oz) self-raising flour
★150ml (¼ pint) milk
300ml (½ pint) crème fraîche or cream to serve

★Check store cupboard

Countdown – **Menu 9**

If you want to prepare and cook the whole menu, you will need 160 minutes, which includes a 30-minute break. If you are a slow cook, add 5–10 minutes to each course to ensure that you do not run out of time. Remember that the times given are only a guide, as each cook will take different lengths of time to complete each task. Both the starter and dessert can be made in advance. Don't feel you have to make a starter with a full roast menu; a main course and dessert would be ample.

Starter

Preparation time: 25 minutes
Cooking time: 8 minutes

PROBLEMS AND HANDY TIPS

Set your timer for 25 minutes. The sour cream mushrooms are best made in advance, either the day or evening before. Assemble all the ingredients and equipment you need for the starter.

25 mins Wash the mushrooms in cold water and pat dry on kitchen paper. Cut the stalks down until they are in line with the main body of the mushroom, set aside. Peel and crush 1 clove of garlic and place it in a small saucepan with a lid.

If the mushrooms are very large, cut them in to halves or even quarters.

See Handy Tip 4 for an easy method to crush garlic without a garlic crusher.

15 mins Measure out 25g/1oz (1 tablespoon) cooking margarine and add to the saucepan. Cook over a medium heat until the garlic turns slightly brown. Turn the heat to low and add the washed mushrooms. Leave to cook on a low-to-medium heat for 3–4 minutes, then add a tablespoon of lemon juice, some black pepper and nutmeg. Put the lid on and cook for a further 5 minutes.

6 mins When you notice a dark juice running out of the mushrooms and they have cooked for at least 5 minutes, they are ready. Turn the heat off and place them in a serving dish. Leave to cool.

Try not to overcook the mushrooms as they are always nicer slightly firm rather than soft.

4 mins When the mushrooms are cool, take 100g (4oz) of sour cream or crème fraîche and spoon it over them. If the mixture is cold enough to put in the fridge, chill until required. Serve the mushrooms as they are, or sprinkle croûtons on top of the sour cream or créme fraîche just before serving.

Make sure the mushrooms are not too hot before adding the sour cream or crème fraîche as this might make it curdle or go very thin.

0 mins Wash up and clear away.

Dessert

Preparation time: 40 minutes
Cooking time: 40–45 minutes

Preheat the oven to 180°C/350°F/Gas mark 4. The dessert can either be cooked immediately and heated up while the main course is being eaten, or served cold. Be careful not to let it sit around without cooking, otherwise it might curdle. A hand–held electric mixer will save you a lot of time with the beating processes. Assemble all the ingredients and equipment you need for the dessert. Set your timer for 40 minutes.

The dessert is best made and cooked straight away. You can always heat it up again quickly in the oven before serving.

40 mins Measure out 75g (3oz) of margarine or butter and place in a large mixing bowl. Add 100g (4oz) caster sugar and beat well using a wooden spoon or hand–held electric mixer. The mixture should become soft and much lighter in colour.

The margarine and sugar need to be well beaten so that the dessert will be light and fluffy.

30 mins Wash the lemon and orange well under cold running water. Dry them, then roll them both under the palm of your hand on a work surface. This helps to release the flesh inside and makes it easier to extract the juice. Grate the zest of both the lemon and orange using a fine grater. Make sure you scratch only the surface of the fruit, otherwise you will end up with the white pith which is bitter and should not be used.

Zest is the outside skin of a citrus fruit (the coloured part). The pith is the white fibrous tissue found directly under the zest. It is bitter and should not be used.

25 mins Scrape the zest off the grater using a knife.

22 mins Mix the zest with the margarine and sugar, and set aside. Take 3 eggs and carefully separate them into bowls. The bowl for the whites needs to be bigger than the bowl for the yolks (see Handy Tip 8, pxix for an easy way to separate eggs.)

17 mins Add the egg yolks to the sugar mixture and beat well to prevent the mixture curdling. Set aside.

14 mins Cut the lemon and orange in half; squeeze both halves of the lemon but only one half of the orange. The remaining orange half should be cut into slices for decoration of the top before serving. Prepare the slices now; put them on a plate, cover with clingfilm and place in the fridge, ready for when you require them.

10 mins Take the bowl with the egg whites and use a balloon whisk or hand–held electric mixer to beat them until they are stiff and hold their shape (i.e. they can stand up in peaks on their own).

Make sure the balloon whisk or electric beaters are clean and dry before whisking the egg whites, otherwise they will not fluff up properly.

5 mins Take the ovenproof dish and use the remaining margarine to grease it all over. (This can be done with

Make sure you grease the dish well as this makes it easier to turn out the dessert.

your fingers or with a piece of greaseproof paper.) Place the greased dish in a roasting tin and set aside.

3 mins Measure out 75g (3oz) of self-raising flour and sieve it into the bowl containing the egg mixture. Slowly add all the lemon and orange juice and mix carefully with a wooden spoon until all the ingredients are incorporated. Scrape the wooden spoon with a plastic spatula. Gently fold in the stiff egg whites, using turning *not* beating movements. You might find that the whole mixture curdles now because the citrus fruit reacts with the eggs. Don't worry – the mixture will come back together once it starts to cook. Continue folding gently until you can no longer see any egg white; it is very important that it is completely incorporated. Add 150ml (¼pt) milk and stir well. Pour the mixture into the prepared dish which is sitting in the roasting tin, then pour cold water in the tin until it comes halfway up the glass dish. Place in the preheated oven and cook for approx. 40–45 minutes.

It is important *not to beat* the mixture at this stage in order to keep it light and airy.

0 mins Wash up and clear away.

Main course

PROBLEMS AND HANDY TIPS

Preparation time: 30 minutes
Cooking time: 60–80 minutes

Preheat the oven to 220°C/425°F/Gas mark 7. Assemble all the ingredients and equipment needed for the roast meal. Set your timer for 30 minutes.

30 mins Take one of the roasting tins and add a tablespoon of lard, cooking margarine or vegetable oil. If you are cooking 'all the trimmings' – roast potatoes, parsnips, carrots and onions – you will need a second roasting tin. Both tins will need fat in them and should go into the oven to heat through.

25 mins While the fat is melting in the oven, take the potatoes and peel them. Place them on a chopping board and cut them in half or in quarters if they are very big.

20 mins Place the potatoes in a saucepan with enough cold water to cover them, add a pinch of salt and put them on to boil slowly.

18 mins Now peel the parsnips and carrots. Cut them in half lengthways, or in quarters if they are very large and thick. They should all be roughly the same size. Set the parsnips and carrots aside.

When making roast potatoes, it is always a good idea to par-boil potatoes first, this gives them a good start and makes them crisper at the end. Parsnips and carrots do not need to be par-boiled before cooking.

13 mins Check the potatoes, as they should be almost boiling. Once they have come to the boil and boiled for a couple of minutes, turn the heat off and drain them through a colander. Carefully remove a roasting tin from the oven and add the potatoes, parsnips and carrots. Take care as the fat can spit and burn you. Put back into the oven to cook the vegetables.

8 mins Peel and halve 2 onions; if they are very large, cut them into quarters.

4 mins Check the weight of the beef – the packaging should tell you how heavy it is. Make a note of the weight. Take the second roasting tin out of the oven and place the beef in the centre. Add the onions around it. Season the meat with a little salt and pepper and put back in the hot oven to cook. (See below for roasting times.)

0 mins Wash up and clear away.

Roasting times

Rare: allow 20 minutes per 450g (1lb), plus 15 minutes extra at the end of the cooking time.

Medium: allow 25 minutes per 450g (1lb), plus 20 minutes extra at the end of the cooking time.

Well done: allow 30 minutes per 450g (1lb) plus 30 minutes extra at the end of the cooking time.

Use this time chart regardless of whether the meat is on the bone, off the bone or rolled.

Watch points

Remember that every oven is different, so temperatures will vary. You need to know your own and find out whether it is hotter or cooler than the marked temperatures. Don't forget: even after you remove the meat from the oven, it will continue to cook.

Gas ovens differ greatly from electric and fan-assisted ovens, so you might have to experiment a few times until you get the cooking time for your roast just right.

Check the dessert to see whether it is cooked. If you are short of space in the oven, you can always place it on the bottom, where it will sit quite happily cooking very slowly. When the dessert is cooked, it should be light brown on top and a sharp knife pushed into the centre should come out clean. The dessert can wait in a warm or cool oven, but leave it standing in the roasting tin with the water.

The dessert should be slightly runny at the bottom even when it is cooked.

Baste the meat, vegetables and potatoes by spooning the hot fat over them.

Relax

Have a well-deserved break for 30 minutes. When you return you will only have to finish off some last-minute tasks.

Welcome back

Feeling better after your break?

Baste the meat, vegetables and potatoes again.

Yorkshire puddings

Set your timer for 15 minutes.

The batter can be made in advance or straight away. If you make it in advance, keep it in the fridge until required. Don't forget to stir it well before using.

If you are using a packet mix, follow the instructions on the packet. If you are making the Yorkshire puddings yourself:

15 mins Assemble all the ingredients and equipment you need.

10 mins Measure out 50g (2oz) of plain flour and sift it into a mixing bowl. Make a well in the centre of the flour, add a pinch of salt and break 1 egg into the well. Mix carefully. Once the mixture thickens, slowly add 150ml (¼pt) of milk to the mixture. The mixture should be smooth, runny and lump-free. The batter can either be used immediately or put into the fridge to chill until required.

Make sure you do not get any lumps in the batter. Stir the mixture slowly, allowing the flour to fall down into the bowl.

Last-minute tasks

Set your timer for 20 minutes. This is how long you have before you sit down and eat the starter.

20 mins Fill the kettle with water and put it on to boil.

18 mins Take the green vegetable and prepare it. Trim the broccoli stalks or remove the damaged outer leaves from the sprouts.

Gravy

I have found that the old-fashioned method of making gravy in the roasting tin is not always practical. I prefer to make my gravy in a saucepan before the meat is completely cooked, so there is less chance of something overcooking or going cold.

12 mins Take the roasting tin with the beef in it and carefully drain off all the fat and juices from the meat into a bowl. Leave to stand for a moment to allow the fat to come to the top. Remove 2 tablespoons of fat and place in a small saucepan.

10 mins Put the saucepan over a low heat and allow the fat to come to the boil. Turn the heat off and mix in 2 tablespoons of plain flour. If the mixture is very thin, add a little extra flour. Put the flour and fat back over the heat and cook for 2 minutes. Remove from the heat.

Add 300ml (½ pint) of fresh stock, or crumble 1 beef stock cube into the fat and flour, and add 300ml (1 pint) cold water, stirring continuously to ensure no lumps appear. Add 1 glass of red wine if available. When all the liquid has been incorporated, put the saucepan over a low heat, allow it to come to the boil and simmer for a few minutes. Set aside until required. You will add any extra goodness from the meat to the gravy at the end of the cooking time. Season the gravy with salt, pepper and a little mustard powder.

It is important to take as much of the fat off the top of the sediment as possible to prevent you having greasy gravy.

Add the liquid very slowly so that you do not get any lumps; stop adding the liquid if it becomes lumpy. Beat the sauce hard until it becomes smooth again, then you can continue to add the liquid.

Watch points

Before sitting down to eat the starter, put the Yorkshire puddings in to cook.

Grease a bun tin with cooking margarine or meat dripping. Mix up the batter and pour into the bun tin, making a minimum of 8 puddings (2 each). Place in the oven for approximately 20–25 minutes. You must be ready to eat these promptly as Yorkshire puddings spoil if overcooked or left to stand. They should be well risen and golden brown. The timing will depend very much on how hot your oven is.

Baste the meat, vegetables and potatoes with the hot fat. If you are worried that the beef might overcook, take it out of the oven while you cook the Yorkshire puddings.

Yorkshire puddings rise up to double their size when they are cooked, so it is important to be ready to serve them as soon as they are risen. They will sink quickly once you take them out of the oven.

'Resting' the meat also make it easier to carve.) Cover with foil and a tea-towel to keep it hot.

Pour some boiling water over the vegetables before you sit down and eat the starter. This way they will be ready in time to serve with the main course.

Make sure that the vegetables do not overcook. If you are afraid this might happen, turn them off while you eat the starter and continue to cook them while you are putting the main course together.

Serve the starter

Check the vegetables and see whether they are cooked or not. Check the Yorkshire puddings, meat and potatoes.

Before serving the main course, reheat the gravy, removing excess fat before adding any juices left in the roasting tin. Place the gravy in a gravy boat. Serve the main course, not forgetting all the extras, including the horseradish and mustard.

If you would like to serve the dessert turned out, loosen the sides with a sharp knife, cover with a plate and turn the whole dish over swiftly. Shake hard and the dessert should drop out. The bottom is now on top, and should be slightly runny.

If you feel that it might be too difficult to turn out the dessert, serve it in the bowl as it is.

Decorate with the reserved orange slices, or anything else you might have in store. The extra decorations could also help disguise any disasters.

Serve with crème fraîche or cream, if liked.

Roasting other meats

Lamb
Cuts: Leg, shoulder, fillet end, best end of neck, stuffed, boned breast.
Serving: 250–400g (8–12oz) per person, on the bone.
Temperature: 220°C/425°F/Gas mark 7.
Timing: *Rare to medium* – 25 minutes per 450g (1lb), plus 25 minutes extra at the end of the cooking time.
Well done – 30 minutes per 450g (1lb), plus 30 minutes extra at the end of the cooking time.
Accompaniments: Roast potatoes, parsnips, carrots, onions, green vegetables, gravy, mint sauce, redcurrant jelly.

Pork

Cuts: Leg, loin, fillet end, knuckle end.
Serving: 250–400g (8–12oz) per person, on the bone. 100–175g (4–6oz) per person, off the bone.
Temperature: 200°C/400°F/Gas mark 6.
Timing: 30–35 minutes per 450g (1lb), plus 35 minutes extra at the end of the cooking time.
Note: Pork must always be served well cooked, never rare.
Accompaniments: Roast potatoes, parsnips, carrots, onions, green vegetables, sage and onion stuffing, apple sauce, cranberry sauce, gravy.

Chicken

Cuts: Whole birds or pieces.
Serving: A medium chicken weighing 1.25–1.5kg (3–3½lb) will feed 4–6 people.
Temperature: 200°C/400°F/Gas mark 6.
Timing: 80–90 minutes for a medium-sized chicken.
Accompaniments: Roast potatoes, parsnips, carrots, onions, green vegetables, bacon rolls, cocktail sausages, pork sausage stuffing, bread sauce, gravy.

Turkey

Cuts: Whole birds or pieces.
Serving: 250–400g (8–12oz) per person.
Temperature: 180°C/350°F/Gas mark 4.
Timing: *Small bird*, 2–5½kg (6–12lb), 25 minutes per 450g (1lb).
Medium bird, 5½–7¼kg (12–16lb), 20 minutes per 450g (1lb).
Large bird, 7¼–11¼kg (16–25lb), 15–18 minutes per 450g (1lb).
Accompaniments: Roast potatoes, parsnips, carrots, onions, Brussels sprouts or any green vegetable, chestnut stuffing, pork sausage stuffing, bacon rolls, cocktail sausages, bread sauce, cranberry sauce, gravy.

Duck

Cuts: Whole birds.
Serving: 500–600g (16–20oz) per person.
Temperature: 180°C/350°F/Gas mark 4.
Timing: 25 minutes per 450g (1lb).
Accompaniments: Roast potatoes, parsnips, carrots, onions, green vegetables, sage and onion stuffing, orange and parsley stuffing, apple sauce, gravy.

Winter menu
Moderately difficult to prepare and cook
Cost level: good value
Serves: 4

A 30-minute break is incorporated in this menu.

Starter   Prawn and asparagus vol-au-vents

Preparation time = 30 minutes
Cooking time = 25 minutes

Main course   Lamb bourguignonne
Potatoes au gratin
Fresh red cabbage

Preparation time = 50 minutes
Cooking time = 90 minutes

Dessert   Rich orange and lemon syllabub

Preparation time = 15 minutes
Cooking time = None

This is a rich and filling winter menu. The starter is made with light puff pastry and contains a delicious combination of the prawn and asparagus.

The lamb is cooked in the oven. There is quite a lot of preparation for this dish as all the vegetables and meat cook in the bourguignonne. The potatoes au gratin (which means potatoes cooked in stock and cheese) are always popular and go extremely well with the lamb. They also cook in the oven.

The syllabub rounds off the meal with a strong, clear flavour of orange and lemon. This dessert is very rich, so make only small portions for each guest if you are serving it in individual bowls or glasses.

Equipment needed – **Menu 10**

Starter

1 small saucepan
1 savoury wooden spoon
1 fine sieve
1 measuring jug
1 tin opener
1 baking tray
1 sharp knife
1 wire rack
1 teaspoon

Main course

1 heatproof bowl
1 potato peeler
1 savoury chopping board
1 sharp knife
1 medium bowl
1 ovenproof casserole dish with lid
1 garlic crusher (or see Handy Tip 4, pxviii)
1 savoury wooden spoon
1 tablespoon
1 measuring jug
1 teaspoon
1 cheese grater
1 ovenproof casserole dish (no lid) or roasting tin

Dessert

1 sweet chopping board
1 sharp knife
1 lemon squeezer
3 mixing bowls
1 balloon whisk or hand–held electric mixer
1 tablespoon
1 glass serving bowl or 4 individual glass bowls or champagne flutes

Shopping list – **Menu 10**

Starter

*25g (1oz) cooking margarine
*25g (1oz) plain flour
100g (4oz) prawns (frozen or fresh)
*300ml (½ pint) milk
*salt and pepper
*1 teaspoon lemon juice
350g (12oz) tin asparagus spears
4 medium or 8 small (frozen or fresh) vol-au-vent cases
1 bunch watercress
1 tomato
1 lemon

Main course

12 small pickling onions
450g (1lb) carrots
225g (8oz) parsnips
900g (2lb) lamb fillet, shoulder of lamb or leg (boneless, if possible)
*25g (1oz) cooking margarine
*2 cloves garlic
*1 tablespoon vegetable oil
*50g (2oz) plain flour
*1 beef stock cube or 300ml (½ pint) fresh stock
300ml (½ pint) red wine
*1 tablespoon tomato purée
2 sprigs fresh rosemary or 1 tablespoon dried rosemary
675g (1½lb) old potatoes
225g (8oz) mild Cheddar cheese
*25g (1oz) table margarine or butter
*salt, pepper and nutmeg
*pinch mustard powder
*1 vegetable or chicken stock cube
½ fresh red cabbage

Dessert

1 lemon
1 orange
*50g (2oz) caster sugar
2 egg whites only
300ml (½pt) double cream
1 packet sweet biscuits (e.g. langues de chat)

*Check store cupboard

Countdown – **Menu 10**

If you want to prepare and cook the whole menu, you will need 150 minutes, including a 30-minute break. If you are a slow cook, add 5–10 minutes to each course to ensure that you do not run out of time. Remember that the times given are only a guide, as each cook will take different lengths of time to complete each task. The starter can be prepared in advance, then put together and heated up just before serving. The main course is cooked in the oven so it gives the cook a welcome break. The dessert should be made only a few hours before serving, otherwise the orange and lemon juice separates and sinks to the bottom.

If you are using frozen prawns, you must defrost them for at least 2 hours before using them.

Starter

Preparation time: 30 minutes
Cooking time: 25 minutes

Preheat the oven to 220°C/425°F/Gas mark 7. If you are making the sauce the night before, or even a few hours before, you will not need the oven until you are ready to cook the vol-au-vent cases. Cook the vol-au-vent cases from frozen only a few hours before serving – the pastry becomes soggy if left sitting around too long. Assemble all the equipment and ingredients you need for the starter. Set your timer for 30 minutes.

30 mins Measure out 25g/1oz (1 tablespoon) margarine and place in a small saucepan. Put the saucepan over a low to medium heat. When the margarine has melted, turn the heat off and add 25g/1oz (1 tablespoon) of plain flour. Stir well. Put the saucepan back over a low heat and cook the flour for 2 minutes to remove the starchy taste.

25 mins Turn the heat off and allow the flour mixture to cool. Take the prawns (which must be defrosted), place them in a fine sieve and run them under cold water to remove any excess salt. Leave them to drain.

20 mins Place the vol-au-vent cases on a baking tray 1cm (½ inch) apart so they have room to expand. Bake in the oven for 8 minutes, then turn the baking tray around and cook for a further 5–7 minutes. The timing will vary depending on how hot your oven is. The vol-au-vents are ready once they are well risen and golden brown.

PROBLEMS AND HANDY TIPS

Make sure you stir the margarine and flour together well so that there are no lumps.

Do not overcook the margarine and flour. Cook it for only a very short time. It must not change colour. If it burns, you will have to discard it and start again.

If the vol-au-vents lean over to one side this means that your oven is uneven. You can counteract this by turning the vol-au-vents right round and hope that they will lean the other way as they continue to cook.

17 mins Measure out 300ml (½ pint) of milk and slowly add to the flour mixture, stirring constantly to ensure that no lumps appear. Once all the milk has been added, bring the sauce gently to the boil, stirring all the time. Once the sauce is boiling, allow it to simmer for 2 minutes. If the sauce is very thick add a little extra milk. (Remember, you need a thick sauce, so add the milk only if really necessary.) Turn the sauce off.

Stir the milk very slowly into the flour and margarine. The slower you add the milk, the better, as this is the time when you can end up with a lumpy sauce.

12 mins Check the vol-au-vents and turn the baking tray around. Continue to cook for a further 5–7 minutes.

10 mins Season the sauce with ground black pepper, a teaspoon of lemon juice and a small pinch of salt. Allow the sauce to simmer on a very low heat for 2 minutes.

Make sure that the sauce does not burn. Keep stirring it.

8 mins Meanwhile, open the tin of asparagus and drain the liquid. Add all the asparagus tips and prawns to the sauce, stir well and allow to heat through.

Make sure you allow the prawns and asparagus to heat through properly before turning off the heat and replacing the saucepan lid.

5 mins Check the vol-au-vents as they should now be cooked. They should be well risen and golden brown. Remove them from the oven. Using a sharp knife, carefully remove the central part of each pastry case; it should come away easily. Keep these lids as you will use them to place on top of the filling.

3 mins If the vol-au-vents look rather soggy inside put them back in the oven to dry out for a further 2–3 minutes.

Sometimes the inside of the pastry is rather soft, so it is a good idea to put the vol-au-vents back in the oven, without their lids, just to dry them out slightly.

1 min Turn the sauce off and set the pan aside with a lid on until you are ready to fill the vol-au-vent cases. Take the vol-au-vents out of the oven and leave them to cool on a wire rack, if you have one, or on a plate. The vol-au-vents will be filled after your break, just before serving them.

0 mins Wash up and clear away.

Leave the oven on if you are going to make the Lamb Bourguignonne next, but turn it down to 180°C/350°F/Gas mark 4.

Main course

PROBLEMS AND HANDY TIPS

Preparation time: 50 minutes
Cooking time: 90 minutes

Preheat the oven to 180°C/350°F/Gas mark 4. Assemble all the ingredients and equipment you need for the main course. If you don't have a casserole that can be used on both the hob and in the oven, use a saucepan to prepare the bourguignonne and transfer it to the casserole when it is ready to go in the oven. Set your timer for 35 minutes.

35 mins Take approximately 12 pickling onions and place them in a heatproof bowl. Fill the kettle and bring it to the boil. Meanwhile, peel the carrots and parsnips and set aside. Pour the boiling water over the onions and leave them to stand for 5 minutes. Take the meat and cut away any excess fat and connecting tissue using a sharp knife. If the meat has a bone, remove it as carefully as possible and cut the meat up into even-sized 3.5cm (1½ inch) cubes. Place the meat in a bowl, cover and place in the fridge until required. (Preparing the meat can take some time; don't worry about the onions, they can sit in the hot water without spoiling.)

The pickling onions are put into boiling water to make it easier to peel them. Once they have sat in the hot water for some time the outer skin comes away quite easily.

20 mins Drain the onions, then one at a time, cut a small amount off the top and bottom. Cut a slit down the onion and peel off the outer skin. Repeat until all the onions are peeled.

Add some cold water to the onions in the bowl if they are too hot to handle.

15 mins Place 25g/1oz (1 tablespoon) cooking margarine in the casserole dish and add the onions. Place on a medium heat and cook, stirring occasionally. Meanwhile, peel and crush the garlic, then add to the onions and cook for a further 2 minutes. Add 1 tablespoon of vegetable oil to the casserole dish, then add all the meat. Turn up the heat and cook briskly until the meat is sealed and brown all over.

See Handy Tip 4, pxviii for an easy way to crush garlic if you don't have a garlic crusher.

The reason why the oil is added to the casserole is to increase the heat while cooking and sealing the meat.

10 mins Once the meat is sealed, turn the heat off, add 50g/2oz (2 tablespoons) of plain flour and stir well. If you are using a stock cube, crumble it into the casserole dish now. Do not add the fresh stock or liquid yet.

7 mins Put the casserole back over a low heat and cook for 2 minutes to remove the starchy floury flavour. Turn the heat off and allow to cool. Measure out 300ml (½ pint) of fresh stock, or 300ml (½ pint) of water if you are using a stock cube. Add 300ml (½ pint) of red wine. (This makes 600ml (1 pint) of liquid in total.)

It is important to cook the flour and margarine well to prevent it having a starchy taste.

Make sure you add the liquid very slowly, stirring all the time. If the sauce starts to go lumpy, stop adding liquid. Use a wooden spoon to beat the sauce very well, until the lumps have disappeared. Slowly continue to add the rest of the liquid.

5 mins With the heat still off add 1 tablespoon of tomato purée to the casserole. Now slowly add the liquid to the meat and flour mixture, stirring all the time. When all the liquid has been mixed in, put the casserole back over a low to medium heat and bring slowly to the boil. Once the sauce is boiling and has thickened, season it with a pinch of salt and pepper, 1 teaspoon of mustard powder and the rosemary. Simmer for 2 minutes.

Check the seasoning before putting the casserole into the oven.

1 min Cut the carrots and parsnips into long strips 5×1cm (2×½ inch) and add them to the casserole. Cover

and cook in the oven for approx. 90 minutes.
0 mins Wash up and clear away.

Potatoes au gratin

Preheat the oven to 180°C/350°F/Gas mark 4, if the oven isn't already on for the lamb, otherwise the potatoes will go into the same oven as the lamb.

Set your timer for 15 minutes. If you have a food processor, you will probably be quicker.

15 mins Peel all the potatoes and cut them into thin slices using either a sharp knife or a food processor with a thin slicer blade. Grate the cheese, using the food processor if you wish (it is not necessary to wash up the processor between slicing the potatoes and grating the cheese, but you will need to change the blade to a medium-sized grater). Place the cheese in a bowl.

A food processor will speed things up when making the potatoes au gratin, but they can quite easily be made without.

10 mins Grease an ovenproof dish or roasting tin using 12g/½oz (½ tablespooon) of margarine or butter.

8 mins Now it is time to put the potatoes au gratin together. Make a layer of potato slices at the bottom of the dish, sprinkle with some cheese and season with salt, ground black pepper, nutmeg and a good pinch of mustard powder. Continue layering the ingredients in this order, leaving enough cheese at the end to cover the top of the dish.

5 mins Dissolve 1 vegetable or chicken stock cube in 300ml (½ pint) of boiling water and pour over the potatoes. Cook in a preheated oven alongside the lamb bourguignonne for approximately 80 minutes.

Make sure the stock cube is well dissolved before adding it to the dish.

The potatoes and lamb can sit in a warm oven without spoiling if your guests are late or the starter takes extra time.

Dessert

PROBLEMS AND HANDY TIPS

Preparation time: 15 minutes
Cooking time: None

Assemble all the ingredients and equipment needed for the dessert. Set your timer for 15 minutes.

15 mins Take the lemon and orange and roll them under the palm of your hand on a work surface to release the flesh inside. Cut the lemon and orange in half and squeeze

ut the juice. Place it in a small mixing bowl and add
50g/2oz (2 tablespoons) caster sugar.

10 mins Carefully separate the eggs. Put the yolks into
a small bowl and set aside, as they will not be used in the
dessert. Place the whites in a mixing bowl ready to be
beaten.

7 mins Put the double cream into a separate mixing
bowl and, using an electric mixer or a balloon whisk,
beat until it holds its shape. Do not overbeat, and watch
out for curdling. Wash and dry the mixer blades or balloon whisk, then beat the egg whites until they stand up
on their own in peaks.

4 mins Now it is time to put all the ingredients
together. Add the lemon and orange mixture slowly to
the cream, stirring continuously to avoid creating
lumps. Fold the egg whites carefully into the mixture so
that it remains light and fluffy. Spoon the syllabub into a
large serving bowl or into individual bowls or tall
Champagne glasses and chill. Remember, this is a very
rich dessert so don't make the servings too large; there
should be enough syllabub to make 5 servings. Chill
until required.

0 mins Wash up and clear away.

Relax

Have a break for 30 minutes. When you return you will
only need to cook or reheat the vol-au-vent mixture and
fill the cases, prepare and cook the red cabbage, and
decorate the syllabub.

Welcome back

Feeling better after your break?

Last-minute tasks

Set your timer for 30 minutes.

30 mins Take the lamb out of the oven and stir it well.
Check that the potatoes are not browning too much;
move them down if they are. Put everything back in the
oven to continue cooking.

26 mins Take the saucepan of prawn and asparagus
sauce, and put it over a low heat to warm through
slowly.

If you loosen the flesh of oranges and lemons before squeezing them, you will find it much easier to squeeze them and you will get a lot more juice from them.

See Handy Tip 8 for an easy method of separating eggs. Don't forget, it is very important that no egg yolk slips into the egg white, otherwise they will not whip up properly.

Watch the cream when you are beating it, as soon as it starts to thicken, stop whipping and finish it off carefully and slowly by hand. If you curdle the cream now, there is little you can do.

When you are putting the syllabub together, try to incorporate as much air as possible. Do not beat the mixture – fold it with round movements.

24 mins Put the cooked vol-au-vent cases back onto a baking tray and place at the bottom of the oven to heat through. (You will probably have to juggle things around to make enough room.)

If you don't have enough room in the oven for all the food, take the casserole out and leave the lid on; you can put it back after the vol-au-vents are ready.

22 mins Check the sauce and stir well. Allow it to come to the boil, then turn it down to simmer.

20 mins Take the red cabbage, cut it up into thin shreds and place it in a saucepan ready to cook.

15 mins Fill the kettle and put it on to boil.

Be careful with the red cabbage as it can stain your chopping board and fingers. The colour should come out with a good wash.

14 mins Take the vol-au-vent cases out of the oven and turn off the asparagus and prawn sauce. Using a teaspoon, fill the vol-au-vents with the sauce, making sure that they all have enough filling. Put a pastry lid on the top of each vol-au-vent and put them back into the oven to heat through for approximately 10 minutes. Note: It is important that the asparagus and prawn filling is properly heated up if you are adding it to a hot vol-au-vent case. You can use a cold filling if the vol-au-vent is also cold, but you must be sure that both the pastry and filling are properly heated through before serving.

As you fill the vol-au-vents, give them a little shake to get rid of any air locks that could be at the bottom stopping you from filling them well.

9 mins Make the garnish for the vol-au-vents. Wash the watercress, if it hasn't been washed already, twist off the stalks and place a small amount on each starter plate. Cut the tomato into quarters and place a piece on each plate. Take 1 lemon and cut it in half lengthways. Cut one half into 4 wedges, and put a wedge on each starter plate.

If you don't have any green garnish, don't worry, just use the lemon wedges and tomato quarters.

5 mins Cut the other half of the lemon into 4 thin slices to decorate the top of the dessert. You can either lie the lemon slice down, stick it into the syllabub, or make a twist in it and place it on top of the syllabub.

You could also decorate the top of the syllabub with some grated chocolate or anything else suitable you have in store.

1 min Pour the boiling water over the red cabbage and put it on to a low heat to cook for approximately 10 minutes (very slowly).

0 mins Wash up and clear away.

Watch points

Once the meal has started, it is not possible to give specific times, so the following instructions should be used only as a guide.

Take the vol-au-vents out of the oven and place them on the starter plates with the garnish.

If you had to take the lamb out of the oven to make room for the vol-au-vents, replace it now and leave it to cook

If you feel that the starter might take some time, let the cabbage come to the boil and then turn it off. You can continue to cook it while you put out the main course.

while you eat the starter. Leave the oven at the correct temperature, 180°C/350°F/Gas mark 4.

Turn the oven down low before putting the main course plates and any serving dishes into it to warm through. You can only do this if the lamb is already cooked.

Serve the main course. Drain the red cabbage through the colander. Put it into a serving dish if you have one. Serve the lamb and potatoes from the dishes they were cooked in. Either serve your guests or place everything on the table for people to help themselves.

Everything can be served from the ovenproof dishes; the only thing that needs a serving dish is the red cabbage.

The dessert is served straight from the fridge with the biscuits of your choice. It is extremely rich, so you might like to have a break before serving it.

Vegan menu
Moderately difficult to prepare and cook
Cost level: inexpensive
Serves: 4

A 30-minute break is incorporated in this menu.

Starter	Artichoke and cucumber salad with croûtons	Preparation time = 25 minutes Cooking time = None

Main course	Stuffed spinach cannelloni baked in tomato and tofu sauce Glazed caramelized carrots	Preparation time = 55 minutes Cooking time = 40–50 minutes

Dessert	Mixed fruit crumble	Preparation time = 25 minutes Cooking time = 40–45 minutes

This menu is suitable for vegans – those who do not eat any meat, poultry, fish, eggs or dairy products. Don't forget, if you are preparing this menu, you must buy special vegan margarine.

The starter and main course are best made on the day to keep them fresh and moist, but the dessert can be made in advance and is easy and straightforward to prepare.

The countdown is set out so that you can have a break while everything is cooking in the oven. There are very few last-minute tasks, which means you can come back from your break and finish off the meal fairly quickly.

Don't forget you will need a French dressing for the starter. If you want to make one yourself, turn to page 196, otherwise use a bought one.

Equipment needed – **Menu 11**

Starter

1 tin opener
1 fine sieve
1 savoury chopping board
1 sharp knife
1 potato peeler
1 colander
1 lemon squeezer
1 pair of scissors
1 measuring jug

Main course

1 colander or fine sieve
1 large saucepan
1 measuring jug
1 garlic crusher (or see Handy Tip 4, pxviii)
1 mixing bowl
1 savoury wooden spoon
2 deep baking dishes or roasting tins
1 teaspoon
1 fork
1 tin opener
1 tablespoon
1 cheese grater
1 potato peeler
1 savoury chopping board

Desert

1 mixing bowl
1 potato peeler
1 sharp knife
1 ovenproof dish (preferably glass)
1 tin opener
1 tablespoon
1 sweet chopping board

Shopping list – **Menu 11**

Starter

175g (7oz) tin cooked and ready-to-serve artichoke hearts
8 cherry tomatoes
1/2 cucumber
1/4 iceberg lettuce
1 orange
225g (8oz) tin mandarins
1 punnet cress
150ml (1/4pt) French dressing
70g (3oz) packet croûtons
*salt and pepper

Main course

500g (11/4lb) fresh or frozen spinach
*2 cloves garlic
38g (11/2oz) vegan cooking margarine
1 packet Vegebanger/burger mix
*salt, pepper and nutmeg
16 cannelloni (4 per person)
225g (8oz) tofu (bean curd)
*425g (15oz) tin chopped plum tomatoes
*1 tablespoon tomato purée
100g (4oz) rennet-free vegetarian cheese (optional)
8 large carrots
2 teaspoons granulated or demerara sugar

Dessert

75g (3oz) vegan margarine
*75g (3oz) demerara sugar
*150g (6oz) wholemeal flour
450g (1lb) cooking apples
225g (8oz) tin peach slices or halves in syrup

*Check store cupboard

Countdown – **Menu 11**

If you want to prepare the whole menu you will need 145 minutes which includes a 30-minute break. If you are a slow cook, add 5–10 minutes to each course to ensure that you do not run out of time. Remember the times are only a guide as each cook will take different lengths of time to complete each task. The starter and main course should be made on the day as they are best served fresh. The dessert can be made the day before and heated up just before serving.

Dessert

Preparation time: 25 minutes
Cooking time: 40–45 minutes

Preheat the oven to 200°C/400°F/Gas mark 6. Assemble all the ingredients and equipment you need for the dessert. Set your timer for 25 minutes. If you haven't made the dessert in advance cook it while you are preparing the main course.

25 mins Measure out 75g (3oz) margarine, 75g (3oz) of demerara sugar and 150g (6oz) of wholemeal flour. Place all the ingredients in a mixing bowl. Using your fingers, rub the fat into the flour and sugar until the mixture resembles fine breadcrumbs. Set aside while you prepare the apples.

15 mins Peel the cooking apples and cut them into quarters. Remove the core in each quarter, then slice the fruit evenly. You should get approx. 3–4 slices out of each quarter. Place the sliced apple in an ovenproof (preferably glass) dish and spread out evenly.

7 mins Open the tin of peach slices and pour all the syrup into the dish. Arrange the peach slices on top of the apples.

4 mins Spread the crumble mixture evenly over the fruit, so that all the apples and peaches are well covered. Place in the preheated oven for 20 minutes, then turn down to 180°C/350°F/Gas mark 4 and cook for a further 20–25 minutes.

0 mins Wash up and clear away.

PROBLEMS AND HANDY TIPS

Try to ensure that you don't make the crumble mixture into a ball of pastry; work as lightly as possible. If your hands get warm, hold them under cold water, pat them dry, then continue.

Don't worry too much if the raw apple starts to go brown; once it is cooked it will not be noticeable.

Make sure you coat the apples well with the syrup as this will help stop the apples from going brown.

Cover the apples and peaches well so that they don't dry out.

Starter

Preparation time: 25 minutes
Cooking time: None

Assemble all the ingredients and equipment you need for the salad. Set your timer for 25 minutes.

25 mins If you have bought a tin of artichokes that must be cooked before being used, check the instructions on the side of the tin first. Cook them now so that they will be cool enough to add to the salad later on.

Different brands of tinned artichokes will have different cooking instructions, so read them well.

18 mins If you are using ready-cooked artichokes, open the tin and drain out the liquid. Wash the artichokes under cold running water and leaved to drain.

16 mins Take the tomatoes, cut them in half and place them in a serving bowl. Peel the ½ cucumber and cut it in half, and then half again. Dice it into bite-sized pieces. Take quarter of the iceberg lettuce and shred it into small pieces. Wash the lettuce and leave to drain.

Remember to keep all the salad ingredients as small as possible to make the starter easier to eat.

10 mins Take 1 orange and roll it under the palm of your hand on a work surface. This loosens the flesh and makes it easier to squeeze. Cut the orange in half and squeeze both halves. Place the juice in a bowl and set aside.

7 mins Open the tin of mandarins and drain off the juice (you will not be using this so you can set it aside and use it for something else). Mix the mandarin segments with the tomatoes and cucumber in the salad bowl.

5 mins Take the cress and snip it into the salad bowl using a sharp pair of scissors. Pat the shredded lettuce dry and mix it into the salad. Take the artichoke hearts, and if they are rather large, cut them in half. Place them in a mixing bowl. Pour over all the orange juice and then 150ml (¼ pint) of French dressing. (Don't forget to shake the dressing well first.) Leave to soak for 2 minutes.

If the artichoke hearts are very big, you might have to cut them into quarters instead of halves.

0 mins Wash up and clear away.

Watch points

If you are not going to serve the salad for over an hour, wait until you have prepared the main course before dressing it. The artichoke hearts can continue to soak up the dressing until you are ready to put the finishing touches to the salad. If you are serving the salad immediately, lift the artichokes out of the dressing, pour it over the salad and toss well. Place the artichoke hearts on top of the salad and season with a pinch of salt and some freshly ground black pepper. Chill until required.

Don't dress the salad too early as it will go soggy. Wait until approx. 30 minutes before serving.

Main course

PROBLEMS AND HANDY TIPS

reparation time: 55 minutes
Cooking time: 40 minutes

Assemble all the equipment and ingredients you need for the main course. Preheat the oven to 200°C/400°F/Gas Mark 6. Set your timer for 40 minutes. Put the crumble in to cook now if you haven't already cooked it.

0 mins Fill the kettle and put it on to boil.

8 mins If you are using fresh spinach, wash it well under cold running water to remove all the dirt and sand which is often present. Pick over the spinach, removing any large stalks or old-looking leaves. Place the washed spinach in a large saucepan and pour not more than 300ml (½ pint) of boiling water all over it. The spinach will cook down dramatically and if you use too much water, all the goodness is lost. Cook for 4–5 minutes on a medium to high heat. If you are using frozen spinach follow the instructions on the packet. It should take about the same length of time to cook as the fresh spinach.

You might find that you have to wash the spinach more than once to get rid of the sand and grit.

Frozen spinach needs no water as it has such a high water content already.

16 mins Peel and crush 2 cloves of garlic with a garlic crusher (or see handy tip 4, pxviii) and set aside.

12 mins Drain the spinach through a colander and leave until all the excess water runs out. Rinse out the spinach saucepan and add the crushed garlic and 12g/½oz (½ tablespoon) of cooking margarine. Cook over a medium heat for 2 minutes.

You might need to use a sieve instead of a colander if you are using frozen spinach. It is much finer than fresh spinach and could be lost through the holes of a colander.

8 mins Once the garlic has cooked, turn the heat off. Take the vegebanger mix and empty the whole packet into a mixing bowl. Measure out 170ml (6fl oz) of cold water and mix well. Leave to stand for 10 minutes. *Do not follow the instructions on the packet.*

The vegebanger mix needs to stand and soak up the water to increase its volume.

5 mins While you are waiting for the mixture, take the drained spinach and press out any excess water using a wooden spoon. Now add the spinach to the garlic in the saucepan. Mix well and season with salt, pepper and a pinch of nutmeg. Put the pan back over a medium heat and stir for a few minutes. Leave on a low heat.

2 mins Take out a baking dish or roasting tin and arrange the cannelloni inside. You will need approx. 16 (4 per person). Set aside. Turn off the spinach and garlic and add the vegebanger mix from the bowl. Stir well. Take a teaspoon and fill each cannelloni with the mixture. This is best done by placing a cannelloni shell over the saucepan and using the handle of the teaspoon to push in the mixture. You should have enough mixture to fill 16 cannelloni shells. If there is not enough, fill as many as

Make sure the baking dish you use is deep. You will need space for the sauce you add to cover all the cannelloni.

If you have problems filling the cannelloni, you might find it easier to use a different utensil; you will have to experiment. Make sure you fill them over the saucepan to catch any mixture that falls out.

possible, then fill leftover ones with the tomato and tofu sauce. (The filling of the cannelloni can take some time, so be patient.)

0 mins Wash up and clear away.

Tofu Sauce

Set your timer for 15 minutes.

15 mins Take 225g (8oz) of tofu, place it in a mixing bowl and mash well with a fork. Open the tin of tomatoes, pour the contents into the mixing bowl with the tofu, add 1 tablespoon of tomato purée and stir well. Pour the mixture all over the cannelloni, covering it well to prevent it drying out or burning. If you feel that there is not enough sauce, you can always add some extra plum tomatoes.

The tofu needs to be well mashed before using.

Make sure you mix the tofu and chopped tomatoes well before pouring them over the cannelloni.

10 mins Grate 100g (4oz) of vegetarian cheese and sprinkle it evenly all over the cannelloni (optional).

0 mins Wash up and clear away. The finished dish will be put in the oven after you have prepared the carrots.

Glazed carrots

8 mins Peel 8 large carrots, top and tail them and cut them into 5cm (2 inch) pieces. Then cut the pieces lengthways in half again. Place the carrot pieces flat side down in a baking dish or roasting tin. Take 25g/1oz (1 tablespoon) of margarine and spread it over the carrots, then sprinkle 2 teaspoons of granulated or demerara sugar on top.

Don't worry too much about the size of the carrots; as long as they are all roughly the same size, they will cook evenly.

1 min Place the carrots and cannelloni in the preheated oven. The cannelloni should be on the top shelf with the carrots underneath. Cook for 40–50 minutes.

0 mins If you have not yet dressed the salad, do so now. Lift the artichokes out of the dressing, then pour it over the salad and toss well. Arrange the artichoke hearts on top of the salad. Season with a pinch of salt and some freshly ground black pepper. Chill in the fridge until required. Wash up and clear away.

Relax

Have a 30-minute break. The main course is cooking in the oven now so when you return you will only have to put the finishing touches to the meal.

Welcome back

Feeling better after your break?

Last-minute tasks

Set your timer for 10 minutes. This is how long you have before serving the starter.

10 mins Check the cannelloni in the oven. If it looks well browned, move it down to the carrot shelf. Turn the carrots over and move the dish to the top shelf. If both the carrots and the cannelloni are well done, turn the oven down to 150°C/350°F/Gas mark 3.

To check whether the cannelloni is cooked, take a sharp knife and pierce one of the pasta tubes in the centre. If the knife goes through easily and comes out clean, the dish is ready.

5 mins If you are turning the oven down, you could put the plates in to warm for the main course.

4 mins Take the salad out of the fridge and garnish it with the croûtons. Place on the table ready to serve.

0 mins Serve the starter. Don't worry about the main course; it can sit quite happily in the oven without spoiling, as long as you have turned the heat down. Wash up and clear away.

The carrots can also be tested with a sharp knife. Push the knife into the middle of a carrot which is cooking in the centre of the baking tray. Again if the knife goes through easily, they are ready. The carrots are also delicious if they are slightly undercooked and still a little crunchy.

Watch points

Take the cannelloni and carrots out of the oven, and the plates if you have warmed them. Leave the oven on a low setting, 150°C/350°F/Gas mark 3. Put the fruit crumble in the oven to warm through, ready to serve after the main course. Serve the dessert as it is and don't forget to turn the oven off.

The crumble needs only to warm through, just to take the chill off it; it doesn't have to be piping hot.

ummer grill menu

Moderately difficult to prepare and cook
ost level: good value
erves: 4

30-minute break is incorporated in this menu.

| **Starter** | Chilled watercress and orange soup
Brown rolls and butter | Preparation time = 30 minutes
Cooking time = 15 minutes |

| **Main course** | Grilled trout or mackerel stuffed with mushrooms and tomatoes
New potatoes
Fresh mixed salad | Preparation time = 35 minutes
Cooking time = 30 minutes |

| **Dessert** | Fruit flan and cream | Preparation time = 20 minutes
Cooking time = None |

his menu is a light summer grill and would suit people
who don't eat meat, but enjoy eating fish.

he soup is served chilled and is refreshing and light. The
fish is stuffed with mushrooms and tomatoes, and makes
change from plain grilled fish. Remember that mackerel
a strong-tasting fish and is therefore not to everyone's
liking. Trout is a more subtle and delicate fish, and would
probably appeal to more people.

he fruit flan can be made with either tinned or fresh
fruit, depending on what is in season.

emember, you will need a French dressi..g for the
mixed salad. This is best made in advance if possible.
urn to page 196 for details. Alternatively buy a bottle of
ready-made.

Equipment needed – **Menu 12**

Starter

1 savoury chopping board
1 sharp knife
1 medium-to-large saucepan
1 lemon squeezer
1 bowl
1 savoury wooden spoon
1 measuring jug
1 teaspoon
1 fine sieve or liquidizer or food processor
1 tablespoon

Main course

1 ovenproof dish or baking tin lined with
  tin foil
1 pastry brush
1 savoury chopping board
1 sharp knife
1 medium saucepan
1 savoury wooden spoon
1 lemon squeezer
1 tin opener
1 pair of scissors
1 teaspoon
1 medium salad bowl
1 colander
1 bread basket

Dessert

1 plate or serving dish
1 tin opener
1 fine sieve or colander
1 measuring jug
1 small saucepan
1 sweet wooden spoon
1 pastry brush or tablespoon
1 sweet chopping board
1 sharp knife

Shopping list – **Menu 12**

Starter

2 bunches fresh watercress
*50g (2oz) cooking margarine
2 oranges
*38g (1½oz) plain flour
*1 chicken or vegetable stock cube or 300ml
  (½ pint) fresh stock
*salt and pepper
pinch of nutmeg
*1 teaspoon Worcestershire sauce
*Dried mustard powder
450ml (¾ pint) milk
4 brown rolls
100g (4oz) butter

Main course

4 gutted trout or mackerel (275g/10oz person)
oil for oiling fish
225g (8oz) mushrooms
*25g (1oz) margarine
1 lemon
*450g (16oz) tin chopped tomatoes
fesh chives or 1 bunch of fresh parsley
*salt and pepper
*2 slices brown or white bread
1 egg
16 small new potatoes or 8 medium to large
  potatoes
sprig of mint (optional)
2 little gem lettuces
½ cucumber
1 head chicory
1 bunch spring onions (optional)
1 red pepper or 1 yellow pepper
150ml (¼ pint) French dressing

Dessert

1 medium or large sponge flan case
*425g (15oz) tin of fruit such as: peach slices,
  mandarins, pineapple, pitted cherries OR
  450g (1lb) fresh strawberries
*38g (1½oz) sachet quick-setting gel mix
1 small tub vanilla ice cream or 300ml (½ pint,
  single cream

*Check store cupboard

Countdown – **Menu 12**

If you want to prepare the whole menu, you will need 145 minutes. This includes a 30-minute break. If you are a slow cook, add 5–10 minutes to each course to ensure that you do not run out of time. Remember that the times are only a guide as each cook will take different lengths of time to complete each task. You have the choice of leaving out a course if time is short. The soup can be made either the day or evening before required. It needs to have enough time to chill well before serving.

Starter

PROBLEMS AND HANDY TIPS

Preparation time: 30 minutes
Cooking time: 15 minutes

Assemble all the ingredients and equipment needed for the soup. Set your timer for 30 minutes.

30 mins Take both bunches of watercress and (if not already pre-washed) hold them by the stalks and wash well under cold running water. Remove the stalks using a sharp knife, or hold them with one hand, twist off the leaves at the top with the other hand. Place the watercress leaves in a medium-to-large saucepan, measure out 50g/2oz (2 tablespoons) of cooking margarine and place it in the saucepan. Put the pan over a medium heat to melt the margarine. Leave the watercress to cook down for approximately 5 minutes.

Today most shops stock pre-washed watercress, but always check the packet first.

20 mins Take 2 oranges and roll them hard under the palm of your hand on a work surface. This is done to release the flesh and make it easier to squeeze out the juice. Cut both the oranges in half and squeeze them, place the juice in a bowl and set aside. Stir the watercress every now and then.

18 mins Once the watercress has cooked down, measure out 38g/1½oz (1½ tablespoons) of plain flour. Turn the heat off from under the watercress and add the plain flour, turn the heat back on to low and cook the flour for 2 minutes, stirring continuously.

15 mins Remove the pan from the heat. Measure out 300ml (½ pint) of fresh stock or cold water and slowly add the liquid to the watercress, stirring as you do so. If you are not using fresh stock, take 1 chicken or vegetable stock cube and crumble it into the pan, stirring well. Put

Good stock makes the soup taste even better, you can buy fresh stock in plastic pots at the meat counter of some supermarkets.

back over a low heat to slowly thicken, stirring continuously.

10 mins Once the soup has thickened, allow it to boil for a few minutes and keep stirring. Turn the heat right down, add all the orange juice to the pan and allow the soup to simmer on a very low heat for a further 10 minutes.

The soup should be quite thin in consistency once it has boiled. It will thicken when it is cold.

7 mins Season the soup with salt, pepper, a good pinch of nutmeg and mustard powder and a teaspoon of Worcestershire sauce. Cook for a further 5 minutes. Check the seasoning and adjust if necessary.

You could put the soup into a serving bowl now and chill it. This would save you having to transfer it into another bowl later.

5 mins Use any extra time to wash up and clear away. Turn the soup off.

2 mins If you have a liquidizer, or food processor with a sharp chopping blade, liquidize or process the soup. If not, push the soup through a fine sieve with the back of a spoon and discard any large bits that are left in the sieve. Once all the soup has been sieved, add 450ml (¾ pint) of cold milk. Chill until required.

0 mins Wash up and clear away.

Dessert

PROBLEMS AND HANDY TIPS

Preparation time: 20 minutes
Cooking time: None

Assemble all the ingredients and equipment you need for the dessert. Set your timer for 20 minutes.

15 mins Take the sponge flan case and put it on to a plate or serving dish. Open the tin of fruit and drain well, reserving the juice in a measuring jug. If you are using fresh fruit, remove the stalks, then place the berries in a colander and wash them well. Put the fruit to one side.

The fresh or tinned fruit will need to be drained well to get rid of any excess water or juice. This avoids a soggy flan base.

11 mins Empty the packet of gel mix into a small saucepan and add the required amount of liquid (juice if you are using tinned fruit, or water if you are using fresh fruit). Check how much juice or water is needed by looking on the packet.

Ensure that you measure the liquid for the jelly very accurately, otherwise the jelly will not set.

9 mins Bring the jelly slowly to the boil, stirring all the time. Check to see if the jelly is very sweet. If so, add 1 teaspoon of lemon juice to make it less sweet. When the jelly has boiled for 1–2 minutes, turn off the heat. Using a pastry brush, if you have one, or the back of a spoon, pour a small amount of the jelly into the bottom of the flan. Spread the jelly out as thinly as possible (this is to seal the sponge so that it doesn't go soggy).

If the jelly is running everywhere, it is too thin. So stop and put the sponge into the fridge to chill and set the jelly before trying to continue.

6 mins Arrange the fruit in a circle in the flan case. If some pieces of fruit are too thick or too large, cut them in half (this applies to peaches, pineapples and strawberries). Arrange the fruit as neatly as possible so that the whole base of the flan is covered.

2 mins Reheat the remaining jelly, stir well and pour carefully all over the fruit. Do not make the layer of jelly too thick; it should just be a good covering. You might not need to use all the jelly, depending on the size of the flan and the type of fruit you are using. Discard any excess.

0 mins Chill the flan in the fridge until required. Wash up and clear away.

Main course

Preparation time: 35 minutes
Cooking time: 30 minutes

PROBLEMS AND HANDY TIPS

Assemble all the ingredients and equipment you will need for the main course. Set your timer for 35 minutes.

35 mins Take the fish, wash them well under cold running water, then place them in an ovenproof dish or baking tin. Oil the fish lightly all over with a pastry brush or your fingers. If you are using mackerel, this will not be necessary as they are very oily fish anyway.

25 mins To make the stuffing: wash the mushrooms well. Chop them as finely as possible. Take 25g/1oz (1 tablespoon) of margarine and put it into a medium saucepan. Turn the heat on to low and allow the margarine to melt. Add the chopped mushrooms to the saucepan and cook slowly, stirring occasionally.

20 mins Take the lemon and roll it hard under your hand on a work surface. This releases the flesh and enables you to get more juice out of the lemon. Cut the lemon in half lengthways and squeeze one half only in a lemon squeezer. Add the juice to the mushrooms and continue to cook.

The remaining half of the lemon will be used to make lemon wedges. This is why you cut the lemon lengthways.

16 mins Use the other half of the lemon to make 4 even-sized lemon wedges to serve with the fish. Set aside until required.

13 mins Open the tin of chopped tomatoes and add them to the mushrooms. Continue to cook slowly, stirring occasionally.

10 mins Wash the chives or parsley and snip them (using a sharp pair of scissors) into the saucepan with all the

The chives or parsley add colour and texture to the stuffing.

95

other ingredients. Stir well and allow the mixture to come to the boil. Remove the pan from the heat and season with salt and ground black pepper.

8 mins Take 2 slices of brown or white bread and break them up into very small pieces. Add them to the mixture in the saucepan. Take 1 egg and break it into the mixture, beating well to bind everything together.

Break the bread up as small as you can to make breadcrumbs.

6 mins Using a small spoon, stuff the fish with enough stuffing to make them look plump. Arrange the fish in the ovenproof dish, gutted side uppermost, so the stuffing can be seen. This is to enable the stuffing to set before turning the fish on to their side. If you have any extra stuffing, place it around the fish to cook and serve it separately.

0 mins Cover the fish and place them in the fridge if you are going to have a break. You can cook them when you get back. Take the butter out of the fridge to serve with the brown rolls and soup. Wash up and clear away.

Relax

Have a 30-minute break. When you come back, you will only have to prepare the salad and cook the new potatoes and fish. The soup and dessert are already finished.

Take your timer with you in case you forget how much time has passed.

Welcome back

Feeling better after your break?

Last minute tasks

Set your timer for 30 minutes. This is how long you have before serving the soup.

30 mins Put the new potatoes into a sink of warm water and wash them well. Place them in a medium-sized saucepan and add some fresh mint, if you have any. Fill the saucepan up with enough cold water just to cover the potatoes. Set aside.

Leave the new potatoes to soak in some warm water if they have a lot of excess soil on them. This will make it easier to wash them afterwards.

25 mins Assemble all the ingredients for the salad. Wash the lettuces, cucumber, chicory, spring onions and pepper. Chop the cucumber, chicory, spring onions and pepper into bite-sized pieces. Place them in a salad bowl. Shred the lettuce and leave it to drain in a colander to get rid of any excess water.

15 mins Put the potatoes over a medium heat to cook, adding a pinch of salt to the saucepan.

12 mins Turn the grill on to a high setting to heat up.

10 mins Take the brown rolls and place them in a bread basket or on individual plates on the table, ready to serve.

8 mins Remove the soup from the fridge and stir it well. Serve it straight into soup bowls and place on the table ready to eat.

Make sure you stir the watercress soup very well before serving.

4 mins Take the fish out of the fridge, remove the cover and place the dish under the pre-heated grill. Check the time as the fish will need 10 minutes with the stuffing uppermost, then 10 minutes on each side (30 minutes in total).

2 mins Add the lettuce to the salad bowl and mix well. Take the French dressing, shake it well, pour it all over the salad, then toss well and set aside until needed.

Dress the salad now, so the lettuce has time to absorb the flavour and will taste better.

0 mins Serve the chilled watercress and orange soup with rolls and butter. Wash up and clear away.

Watch points

Once the meal has started, it is impossible to give specific times, so the following checklist should be used only as a guide.

After 10 minutes the stuffing should have become firm. Turn the fish over on to their side and continue cooking for a further 10 minutes on each side.

If the stuffing hasn't quite set, wait a few more minutes, otherwise the stuffing will fall out when you turn the fish over.

Check the new potatoes. If they are almost done, turn them right down or even off until you are ready to serve.

The potatoes can sit in the boiling water, keeping hot while you are waiting for the fish to cook.

Check the fish again and turn it over for the last time on to the side which has not yet been exposed to the heat.

The fish is cooked when the eyes go white and stick out. Another test is to stick a knife into the flesh; if it goes in easily and you see some juice running out, it is ready.

Drain the potatoes, put them into a serving dish and place them on the table. Put the salad on the table. Check the fish, which should be ready by now. Serve at once, with the extra stuffing, if you have any. Don't forget the lemon wedges; serve them on a separate plate so that your guests can help themselves.

The dessert can either be served on its own or with cream or vanilla ice cream.

All seasons menu
Moderately difficult to prepare and cook
Cost level: good value
Serves: 4

A 30-minute break is incorporated in this menu.

| **Starter** | Cream of mushroom soup with French bread | Preparation time = 30 minutes
Cooking time = 10–15 minutes |

| **Main course** | Grilled lamb or pork chops
Cauliflower and onion cheese
Parsnip and potato cream | Preparation time = 40 minutes
Cooking time = 30 minutes |

| **Dessert** | Meringue baskets filled with fruit and cream | Preparation time = 15 minutes
Cooking time = None |

This menu can be made all year round and is a standard supper menu that you might make for friends if you don't have a lot of time to spare. You can leave out the starter or dessert or replace the dessert with fruit and cheese; this will depend on how much time and energy you have.

The soup can be made in advance, either the night before, or even earlier, and frozen. Allow at least 8 hours for the soup to defrost overnight in the fridge, or 3 hours at room temperature. By using a vegetable stock cube this course is suitable for vegetarians. (The main course is, of course, for meat-eaters only.)

The meringues should be filled only a few hours before serving, otherwise they will go soggy.

Equipment Needed – **Menu 13**

Starter

1 large saucepan with lid
1 savoury wooden spoon
1 savoury chopping board
1 sharp knife
1 bowl or plate
1 measuring jug
1 tablespoon
1 fine sieve or colander
1 food processor, liquidizer or sieve

Main course

1 grill pan
1 turning utensil
1 savoury chopping board
1 sharp knife
1 colander
1 medium saucepan
1 medium saucepan with lid
1 savoury wooden spoon
1 measuring jug
1 cheese grater
1 potato peeler
1 large saucepan
1 potato masher

Dessert

1 potato peeler and/or sharp knife
1 sweet chopping board
1 colander or sieve
1 tin opener
1 teaspoon
1 balloon whisk or hand–held electric
  mixer

Shopping list – **Menu 13**

Starter

450g (1lb) button mushrooms
*50g (2oz) cooking margarine
*50g (2oz) plain flour
*1 chicken stock cube or 1 vegetable stock cube
  (for vegetarians)
*salt and pepper
*1/2 teaspoon nutmeg
*1 tablespoon lemon juice
150ml (1/4 pint) single cream
1 French-bread stick
100g (4oz) butter

Main course

4 large pork chops or 8 small lamb chops
1 medium/large cauliflower
*1 large onion
*25g (1oz) cooking margarine
*25g (1oz) plain flour
*450ml (3/4 pint) milk
*salt, pepper and a pinch of mustard powder
50g (2oz) Cheddar cheese
8 old potatoes
2 parsnips
*50g (2oz) table margarine or butter
*1 pinch nutmeg
225g (8oz) jar apple sauce (for pork)
225g (8oz) jar redcurrant sauce (for lamb)
225g (8oz) jar mint sauce (for lamb)

Dessert

4 medium or 8 small meringue nests or baskets
fresh fruit in season, e.g. pears, bananas,
  apples, oranges in winter, or strawberries,
  raspberries and kiwi in summer or 425g
  (15oz) tin peaches, mandarins, pineapples
150ml (1/4 pint) double cream

*Check store cupboard

Countdown – **Menu 13**

If you want to prepare and cook the whole menu, you will need 145 minutes. This includes a 30-minute break. If you are a slow cook, add 5–10 minutes to each course to ensure that you do not run out of time. Remember, the times given are only a guide, as each cook will take different lengths of time to complete each task. The soup can be made in advance the day before, or even a few weeks before, and frozen. Don't forget that if you do freeze it, it must be properly de-frosted before serving it. The main course and dessert are made on the day. As with most of the other menus in this book, you have the option of leaving out a course if time or cost are not on your side.

PROBLEMS AND HANDY TIPS

Preparation time: 30 minutes
Cooking time: 10–15 minutes

Assemble all the ingredients and equipment you need for the soup. Add an extra 5–10 minutes if you are going to chop the mushrooms by hand and not use a food processor or liquidizer. You can use a food processor or liquidizer to finish off the soup if you prefer a smoother texture, otherwise you can sieve it. Set your timer for 30 minutes.

30 mins Take 450g (1lb) of button mushrooms and soak them in cold water to wash off the dirt. Meanwhile, measure out 50g/2oz (2 tablespoons) of margarine, place it in a large saucepan and put over a low heat to melt. Turn the heat off and add 50g/2oz (2 tablespoons) of plain flour. Put the pan back on a low heat for 2 minutes to cook out the starch in the flour. Turn the heat off and allow to cool.

20 mins Drain the mushrooms and pat dry on kitchen paper. Remove the stalks and chop the mushrooms as small as possible. Transfer to a bowl or a plate and set aside until required. If you have a food processor or liquidizer, you need not chop the mushrooms, as they will be blended in the machine later. (Keep a few slices of mushroom in a separate bowl to use as a garnish for the top of the soup just before serving.)

10 mins Crumble the stock cube into the flour mixture

You must make sure that the mushrooms are washed well to remove the soil. Soaking them can help to loosen any stubborn dirt.

It is important to cook the flour and margarine at this stage to get rid of the starchy flavour often found in soups and sauces.

If the mushrooms are very big and you are going to use a food processor, cut them in half or even into quarters to make cooking easier.

and add 1.2 litres (2 pints) of cold water. Stir well, put back on a medium heat and slowly bring to the boil. Once the sauce has thickened and boiled for a few minutes, add all the mushrooms, stir well and season with a pinch of salt, freshly ground black pepper, ½ teaspoon of nutmeg and 1 tablespoon of lemon juice.

5 mins Allow the soup to simmer on a very low heat for 10–15 minutes.

Be careful not to add the liquid too quickly, otherwise lumps might start forming. If it starts to go lumpy, stop adding the liquid and beat the sauce until it becomes smooth again, then continue to add the liquid.

Watch points

If you have used whole mushrooms, place the soup in a food processor or liquidizer and blend until you reach the desired consistency, i.e. large, medium or small pieces of mushroom. If you do not have a food processor or liquidizer, you can either serve the soup as it is, or pass it through a sieve.

Be careful when liquidizing the soup if you do it immediately after cooking; it will be boiling hot, so take care not to burn yourself.

If you decide to sieve the soup, you must allow enough time as this can be a lengthy process.

If you are going to freeze the soup, wait until it is cold before doing so. Don't forget to label the container with the date it was made, what it is and how many people it will serve. If you have made the soup a day ahead, there is no need to freeze it. Place it in a bowl, cover and put it in the fridge until required.

To serve the soup, heat it thoroughly and garnish with a few pieces of sliced mushroom scattered on the top. Check the seasoning before you serve as the soup will change on standing.

Main course

PROBLEMS AND HANDY TIPS

Preparation time: 40 minutes
Cooking time: 10 minutes

Cauliflower and Onion Cheese

Assemble all the ingredients and equipment you need for the main course. Set your timer for 40 minutes.

40 mins Take the cauliflower and using a sharp knife, cut it into small, even-sized pieces. Wash the sprigs in a colander and place in a saucepan ready to cook later.

32 mins Peel 1 large onion, chop it as small as possible and place it in a medium-sized saucepan. Add 25g/1oz (1 tablespoon) of margarine and put the pan over a medium heat to cook the onion. While the onion is cooking, check

When cutting the cauliflower, try to keep to the natural sprigs; this should be quite easy. When a sprig is too big, cut it in half. The soup is cooked when the mushrooms are soft. Try a piece of mushroom and if it is not hard or crunchy, the soup is ready. Don't forget the soup will be heated up again before serving.

the mushroom soup. If you feel it is ready, turn it off and leave to cool.

25 mins Measure out 25g/1oz (1 tablespoon) of plain flour. Turn the heat off, and add the flour to the onion and mix well. If the mixture is too thin, add a little extra flour.

22 mins Put the pan back over a low heat and cook for 2 minutes to remove the starchy flavour.

20 mins Measure out 300ml (½ pint) of cold milk. Turn the heat off and slowly add the milk to the mixture, stirring all the time. Make sure that no lumps appear; if they do, stop adding the milk and beat the sauce well with a wooden spoon until it is smooth again. Then continue to add the rest of the milk. Once all the milk has been added, put the saucepan back over a very low heat and bring it slowly to the boil.

15 mins Season the sauce with salt, pepper and a pinch of mustard powder. Once it has thickened and is boiling, allow it to simmer for a few minutes to get rid of the floury taste.

Make sure you season the sauce well as cauliflowers are quite bland vegetables.

13 mins Turn the heat off and grate 50g (2oz) of Cheddar cheese into the sauce. Mix well, replace the lid and leave to stand. You will heat the sauce up again and pour it over the cauliflower just before serving.

Parsnip and potato cream

10 mins Top and tail 2 parsnips, then peel them. Peel 6 old potatoes. Cut the potatoes and parsnips in half (quarters, if large) and place them in a saucepan. They all need to be roughly the same size to cook evenly.

The pieces of parsnip can be quite a bit bigger than the potatoes, as they tend to cook faster.

4 mins Fill the saucepan with enough cold water to cover all the vegetables, add a pinch of salt, replace the lid and set aside.

0 mins Wash up and clear away.

Relax

Have a break for 30 minutes. When you return you will only have to cook the vegetables and chops for the main course, and reheat the mushroom soup. The dessert can be made while you are waiting for everything else to cook.

Welcome back

Feeling better after your break?

Before starting to prepare the dessert, put the potatoes and parsnips on to a medium heat to cook, ready for mashing later.

Dessert

PROBLEMS AND HANDY TIPS

Preparation time: 15 minutes
Cooking time: None

Assemble all the ingredients and equipment you need for the dessert. Set your timer for 15 minutes.

15 mins Place the meringues on a serving plate. Prepare the fruit: winter fruits, such as pears, apples and bananas, must be peeled and cut into small thin slices; summer fruits need to be washed and left to drain. It is important to have some colour, so if you are using only winter fruits, you could decorate the top with some grated chocolate or slices of kiwi fruit. Tinned fruit must be drained well before being used, or the meringue will go soft and soggy.

Make sure the fruit is well drained before adding it to the meringue baskets, otherwise they will become soggy.

6 mins Whip the double cream with a balloon whisk or hand–held electric mixer until thick, but smooth. Place a small amount in the bottom of each meringue basket. Arrange the fruit in the baskets, overlapping one piece with another so that the meringues are well filled.

Be careful not to overwhip the double cream, or it will curdle. It should be thick and smooth.

2 mins Add a blob of cream to the top of each meringue and decorate with any remaining fruit, grated chocolate or anything you like. Place in the fridge until required.

0 mins Wash up and clear away.

Last-minute tasks

All you have to do is finish the last-minute tasks. Take the butter out of the fridge and put it on the table to soften.

Set your timer for 30 minutes. This is how long you need before you serve the soup. Preheat the oven to 150°C/ 300°F/Gas mark 3.

30 mins Put the soup bowls, dinner plates and serving dishes in to warm. Place the French bread near the top of the oven for a few minutes to crisp up.

25 mins Fill the kettle with water and put it on to boil. If

e potatoes and parsnips are boiling rapidly, turn them
n to a low setting and allow to simmer gently.

4 mins If you are cooking pork chops, heat the grill
ow, as pork must be well cooked. Lamb chops do not
ke as long. Allow 30 minutes for pork chops, and 20
inutes for lamb chops.

2 mins If you need to liquidize the soup, do so now.
eturn it to the saucepan to heat up slowly, ready to
rve.

7 mins Put the pork chops (if using) under the grill and
ave them to cook for about 15 minutes before turning
em over. Do not start cooking lamb chops yet.

5 mins Put the white sauce you made earlier on to a low
eat to warm through. Stir the soup well.

3 mins Pour the boiling water over the cauliflower
rigs, add a good pinch of salt and put over a medium
eat to cook.

2 mins Check the potatoes and parsnips to see if they
re ready. Test them by using a sharp knife to see whether
ey are soft all the way through. If they are ready, drain
em through a colander and leave for a minute.

0 mins Stir the white sauce and the soup, and make sure
ey are not burning.

mins Put the lamb chops (if using) under the grill and
ok for about 10 minutes before turning.

mins Put the potatoes and parsnips back into the
ucepan and mash well until you have a smooth purée.
dd 50g/2oz (2 tablespoons) of table margarine or butter
nd mix well before adding 150ml (¼ pint) of milk. Stir
ell and season with salt, pepper and a good pinch of
utmeg. Place in a serving dish and put it in the oven to
eep warm.

mins Check the cauliflower to see whether it is cooked;
sharp knife should go through a stalk easily. Drain it
rough a colander and place it in a serving dish.

mins Turn the chops and check how well they are
oking. Stir the white sauce and if it is hot enough, pour
all over the cauliflower. Put the whole dish back in the
ven.

mins Now everything is ready. If you are worried that
e chops might overcook or burn, turn the grill off while
ou eat the starter. You can always continue to cook
em once you have eaten the soup, or you could put the
ops in the oven to keep warm until required. Wash up
d clear away.

The potatoes and parsnips need to simmer slowly, not boil rapidly, otherwise they will start to fall apart and cook unevenly.

Check the seasoning in the mushroom soup, it might need readjusting after standing for some time.

If the potatoes and parsnips start to fall apart, turn off the heat and leave to stand until you have time to drain and mash them.

Undercook the cauliflower rather than overcook it, as it will continue to cook while keeping warm in the oven.

Make sure the soup is piping hot when you serve it. It always helps if you have warmed the soup bowls first as this retains the heat.

Watch points

Once the meal has started, it is not possible to give specific times, so the following instructions should be used only as a guide.

Take the French bread and the soup bowls out of the oven. Cut the bread up if you like and place it on the table.

Stir 1 teaspoon single cream into each bowl of mushroom soup, and garnish with 1 or 2 slices of mushroom scattered on top.

Serve the main course. Take the plates out of the oven and place the vegetable dishes on the table, and lastly serve the chops. Don't forget to serve any sauces you might have bought to go with the meat.

Serve the potato and cauliflow dishes on the table. The chops can either be served straight or to the plates or your guests car help themselves.

The meringue baskets are served just as they are.

Barbecue menu

Moderately difficult to prepare and cook
Cost level: good value
Serves: 4

There is no break incorporated in this menu.

Starter   Garlic bread

Preparation time = 20 minutes
Cooking time = 25–30 minutes

Main course   Chicken satay with peanut sauce
Home-made hamburgers
Mixed salad and new potatoes

Preparation time = 50 minutes
Cooking time = 30–40 minutes

Dessert   Fresh strawberry and raspberry
cream

Preparation time = 15 minutes
Cooking time = None

This is quite a standard barbecue menu. You can add some sausages to the menu if you like. Most of the preparation can be done on the day or the evening before, except the chicken satay, which must be marinated overnight. Prepare the chicken at least 12 hours before cooking it; this gives it time to soak up all the flavours in the marinade. You can also choose other meats if you prefer.

The garlic bread can be made in advance and frozen if time is short, or even bought ready prepared to save time.

The dessert is simple and can be adapted, according to the type of fruit available. I have not allowed for a break, as there are too many things to stop and start. In general, everything can be prepared in advance, which will leave only the cooking and last-minute tasks to do on the day or evening.

You will need a French dressing for the salad. Either buy a ready-made one, or turn to page 196 for details of how to make it yourself. The dressing is best made in advance.

If your barbecue is rained off, don't panic – everything can cook in the oven just as well. Set the oven at 200°C/400°F/ Gas mark 6. The chicken and hamburgers will need approximately 60 minutes in the oven.

Equipment needed – **Menu 14**

Starter

1 bowl (to mix the butter or margarine)
1 savoury chopping board
1 sharp knife
1 garlic crusher (or see Handy Tip 4, pxviii)
1 savoury wooden spoon
1 bread knife
tin foil
1 round–ended knife

Main course

1 medium bowl (large enough to hold the marinade and chicken and to fit in the fridge)
1 tablespoon
1 savoury chopping board
1 sharp knife
1 lemon squeezer
1 potato peeler
1 fine grater
1 plate
1 savoury wooden spoon
8 wooden satay sticks or 4 metal skewers
1 baking tray, tin or plate
1 small saucepan with lid
1 medium-sized mixing bowl
1 teaspoon
1 plate or clean work surface (for shaping hamburgers)
1 barbecue
1 pair scissors (to snip chives)
1 medium saucepan with lid
1 large tin or plate
1 colander or fine sieve

Dessert

1 colander or fine sieve
1 sharp knife
2 mixing bowls
1 fork
1 balloon whisk or hand–held electric mixer
1 tablespoon
1 plastic spatula

Shopping list – **Menu 14**

Starter

*100g (4oz) butter or margarine
*2 cloves garlic
1 long French loaf, brown or white

Main course

100g (4oz) jar satay sauce
3 tablespoons dark soy sauce
*3 tablespoons white wine vinegar
*2 tablespoons brown or white sugar
*1 orange
150g (5oz) crunchy peanut butter
1 small lemon or 2 teaspoons lemon juice
5cm (2 inch) piece fresh root ginger
*1 teaspoon Worcestershire sauce
8 chicken thighs, skinned and boned
450g (1lb) lean minced beef
*1 onion
*1 slice fresh brown or white bread
*1 egg
*1 pinch salt
*ground black pepper
*1 tablespoon mixed herbs (optional)
*2 tablespoons plain flour
50g (2oz) ready-made, dried breadcrumbs
1 lettuce (iceberg, cos or frisée)
1 cucumber
2 carrots
100g (4oz) button mushrooms
1 red pepper
*150ml (¼ pint) French dressing, bought or home-made (see p196 for recipe)
16 new potatoes
1–2 sprigs fresh mint
*Ready-made relishes, such as barbecue sauce, tomato sauce, sweetcorn relish, cucumber relish and mild mustard

Dessert

2 punnets strawberries
2 punnets raspberries (use 4 punnets of one fruit if both varieties are not available)
300ml (½ pint) double cream
*25g (1oz) caster sugar
1 packet langues de chat biscuits

*Check store cupboard

ountdown – **Menu 14**

you want to prepare and cook the whole menu, you
ill need 125 minutes. There is no break, as there is so
uch stopping and starting involved in this menu and
ou will probably make several things the day before. If
ou are a slow cook, add 5–10 minutes to each course, to
sure that you don't run out of time. Remember that the
nes given are only a guide, as each cook will take
fferent lengths of time to complete each task. The
arinade must be made the night before and left to soak
to the chicken overnight. The garlic bread and ham-
rgers can be made in advance or on the day. The garlic
ead can also be frozen; it will need approx. 4 hours to
frost. The rest of the menu is made on the day or
ening and is straightforward.

lain course – **Satay Marinade**

PROBLEMS AND HANDY TIPS

ssemble all the ingredients and equipment needed to
ake the marinade. Set your timer for 20 minutes

) mins Take a medium-sized bowl and add half a jar of
tay sauce. Then add 3 tablespoons of dark soy sauce, 3
blespoons of white wine vinegar and 2 tablespoons of
own or white sugar. Stir well.

As long as you use the same
sized tablespoon for all the
ingredients, you will have an
even-tasting marinade.

5 mins Take 1 orange and 1 lemon, cut them in half and
ueeze the juice from all four halves. Add the orange
ice and 2 teaspoons of lemon juice to the mixture in the
owl and stir well. Peel the root ginger using a sharp
ife or potato peeler. Grate it on to a plate, then add it to
e marinade and stir well. Set aside.

Roll the orange and lemon under
the palm of your hand on a hard
surface before squeezing. This
helps loosen the flesh and
makes squeezing easier, as well
as increasing the amount of
juice you can extract.

mins Take the pre-skinned and boned chicken thighs
d cut each into approx. 2.5cm (1 inch) strips or pieces.
Remember that the chicken will be cooked on satay
icks, so it must be a size that can be easily skewered.)

The chicken chunks should be
bite-sized pieces and roughly all
the same size.

mins Mix the chicken pieces into the marinade. Stir
ell and make sure all the chicken is covered with the
arinade. Cover and place in the fridge overnight.

mins Wash up and clear away.

amburgers

PROBLEMS AND HANDY TIPS

ssemble all the ingredients and equipment needed for
e hamburgers. Set your timer for 15 minutes.

5 mins Place the minced beef in a medium-sized mixing

bowl. Take 1 onion, and chop it as finely as possible and add it to the minced beef. Then take one slice of bread, crumble it into small pieces and add it to the mince and onions. Break 1 egg into the mixture and season with salt, ground black pepper, 1 tablespoon of mixed herbs (optional) and 1 teaspoon of Worcestershire sauce.

10 mins Using either your own hands or a spoon, mix the beef and other ingredients together well. Once the mixture forms a large lump, take a small handful and roll into a ball. Press flat to a thickness of approx. 1.5cm (½ inch). Using a mixture of flour and the dried, ready-made breadcrumbs, coat the meat until it is completely covered. The mixture should make 4 large hamburgers or 8 small ones. Place in a tin or on a plate ready for cooking on the barbecue later. Try to ensure that the hamburgers are all about the same size, so they will cook in roughly the same time.

1 min When you have made and coated all the hamburgers, place them in the fridge and chill until required.

0 mins Wash up and clear away.

The onion needs to be as small as possible to make a neat hamburger.

Make sure you mix the egg, meat and onion together well to bind the mixture.

The mixture can be very cold and slimy to mix with your hands, so use a wooden spoon if you prefer.

If the mixture won't come together, you need to work it harder, until the egg takes hold. Once you have a large ball of meat mixture, you are ready to make the individual burgers.

Cover the hamburgers with a plate or some cling film if you are going to leave them for several hours.

Starter

Preparation time: 20 minutes
Cooking time: 20–30 minutes

Assemble all the ingredients and equipment needed for the starter. Set your timer for 20 minutes.

20 mins Measure out 100g (4oz) butter or margarine and leave to soften at room temperature. Peel and crush 2 cloves of garlic and add to the butter. See Handy Tip 4 if you don't have a garlic crusher. If the butter or margarine is very hard, you can soften it in a microwave for a few seconds. If you don't have a microwave you will have to wait until it softens slightly before mixing in the garlic.

15 mins Mix the garlic and butter together well with a spoon or fork. Place the French bread on a chopping board and make diagonal cuts about 2.5cm (1 inch) apart that do not go right through the loaf.

10 mins Take a piece of tin foil large enough to be wrapped round the French stick at least once. Place the bread in the middle, but do not wrap up yet.

9 mins Using a round-ended knife, spread some garlic butter on each side of the diagonal cuts. (Each slice of bread should be buttered on both sides, except the end pieces.) Continue all the way along the loaf. Do not

PROBLEMS AND HANDY TIP

If the butter or margarine is ve hard and you don't have a microwave, beat it with a wooden spoon to soften it.

Cut through the bread diagonally, trying not to cut rig through to the bottom. This keeps the bread together and makes it easier to handle.

Make sure the slices of bread are roughly the same size.

The tin foil keeps the bread moist and stops it from drying out and burning while cooking.

butter too heavily at first; you should have enough for the whole french stick.

1 min Once all the bread has been buttered, wrap the loaf up in the foil. Make sure you seal both ends well. Leave in the fridge, or in the kitchen, until it is time to bake it.

0 mins Wash up and clear away.

Make sure you seal the foil well around the bread, especially if you are keeping it for a while. If you make the garlic bread the night before, put it in a deep freeze as this will keep it much fresher. Defrost 2–3 hours before cooking.

Dessert

PROBLEMS AND HANDY TIPS

Preparation time: 15 minutes
Cooking time: None

Assemble all the ingredients and equipment you need for the dessert. Set your timer for 15 minutes.

15 mins Wash the strawberries and raspberries in a colander and set aside any bruised or squashed ones. Cut the good strawberries in half and place them in a serving bowl. Add all the good raspberries to the same bowl and mix together well. Set the bowl aside.

You need about 5–6 strawberries and 8–10 raspberries to make a purée.

8 mins Take the bruised fruit, place in a bowl and mash with a fork to make a purée. (This mixture does not have to be completely smooth.)

5 mins Pour the double cream into a mixing bowl and whip until thick using a balloon whisk or an electric mixer. The cream should hold its shape. If you are using extra-thick double cream, you will not need to beat it at all.

Do not overbeat the cream, or it will curdle. It is better to underbeat it.

2 mins Once the cream is well beaten, add 25g/1oz (1 tablespoon) caster sugar. Add all the sweetened cream to the puréed fruit and mix together well, making a fruit cream.

Do not beat the mashed fruit into the cream: fold it gently to prevent it from curdling or separating.

1 min Pour the fruit cream over the fresh strawberries and raspberries. Place in the fridge to chill until required.

0 mins Serve in a clear bowl with fancy biscuits. Wash up and clear away.

This dessert will keep for 1–2 days, but it must be covered and kept in the fridge. Excess juice from the fruit sinks to the bottom of the bowl the longer it stands.

Mixed salad

Assemble all the ingredients you have bought for the salad. Set your timer for 15 minutes.

15 mins Take the lettuce and chop it up into bite-sized pieces so that it is easy to eat with a fork. Wash it well and leave it to drain in a colander.

All the salad ingredients need to be washed well and cut into bite-sized pieces.

10 mins If you are using a cucumber, wash it well under cold running water and either peel it or, if you would like a decorative effect, run a fork down the whole length of the cucumber through the skin. When you slice it up each piece will have a frilly edge. The other advantage of using this method is that you use the skin, which contains all the goodness and vitamins.

5 min Wash the other salad ingredients. Quarter the tomatoes and snip the chives. Put them into a salad bowl and place in the fridge, if you have room, otherwise set aside with a tea towel over the bowl. You will need a French dressing for the salad; either use a ready-made one, or make one yourself, as described on page 196.

0 mins Wash up and clear away.

A home-make French dressing is best made in advance so that all the ingredients can combine and mature. A French dressing can sit in a cool store cupboard in a bottle with a lid for 1–2 months.

Last-minute tasks

Set your timer for 15 minutes. Preheat the oven to 200°C/400°F/Gas mark 6 to cook the garlic bread; you could serve this while you are cooking the meat on the barbecue.

15 mins Take out the new potatoes. Allow 16 small potatoes in total or 2 to 3 per person if larger.

If the potatoes are very dirty, leave them to soak in some warm water to loosen the soil.

12 mins Wash the potatoes well under warm water to remove any soil. Place the potatoes in a saucepan with cold water and add a pinch of salt and 1 or 2 sprigs of fresh mint, if available. Set aside until you are ready to cook them.

10 mins Remove the chicken from the fridge and thread on to at least 8 satay sticks or 4 large metal skewers. Try to get the same amount of chicken on each stick or skewer. Set aside on a baking tray or plate. Place any marinade left in the bowl in a small saucepan and cover with a lid; you will use this to make the peanut sauce later on.

When you are threading the chicken on to the skewers, make sure that any excess marinade drips back into the bowl to be used later in the peanut sauce.

Light the barbecue and leave it to get hot. Put the garlic bread into the preheated oven near the top. Set your timer for 25 minutes. This is how long you have before the garlic bread is ready to serve, but you should be cooking the meat at the same time.

Put the garlic bread on to a baking tray to cook in case butter runs out. It also keeps the loaf together while it is cooking.

Now that all the food is prepared, all you have to do is put everything together and cook the meat. The barbecue is hot enough to cook on when the charcoal has gone white. The hamburgers will take about 15 minutes on each side, depending on their thickness and how well cooked you like them. Place the chicken satay on the barbecue with the hamburgers. It will take 10–15 minutes to cook on each side.

Put the potatoes on to cook. Have the heat high until they come to the boil, then turn them down to a very low heat with the lid half on. Allow to simmer gently for 20–25 minutes, depending on the size of the potatoes. If they are tiny they will only need 10–15 minutes.

If the potatoes are cooked before the meat is properly barbecued, drain the water away and leave them in a saucepan with a lid on, or in a serving dish in the bottom of the oven.

Watch points

Once you start the barbecue it is impossible to give exact times, so the following instructions are intended only as guidelines.

Pour the French dressing over the salad, toss well and place on the table. Put out the butter for the potatoes and any barbecue sauces you have bought for the meat. Check the garlic bread. It is ready once all the butter has melted and the bread is crisp.

Serve the garlic bread with some napkins, while people are still standing and the meat finishes cooking.

Just before serving the chicken, heat the marinade and allow it to boil for a few minutes. Add half a jar of crunchy peanut butter and continue to cook for a further 3 minutes. If the sauce is very thick, add a little cold water until you reach the right consistency.

Serve the sauce hot in small bowls on the table.

Curry menu
Moderately difficult to prepare and cook
Cost level: good value
Serves: 4

A 30-minute break is incorporated in this menu.

Starter   Poppadoms, onion bhajis or samosas with yogurt and cucumber sauce

Preparation time = 20 minutes
Cooking time = 10–15 minutes

Main course   Special chicken curry
Boiled rice
Mango chutney

Preparation time = 40 minutes
Cooking time = 60 minutes

Dessert   Mango water ice

Preparation time = 20 minutes
Freezing time = 8–10 hours

This curry menu is moderately difficult to prepare and cook. All the starter ideas can be bought ready-made from the supermarket or an Indian shop. Serve them with a delicious home-made yogurt and cucumber sauce.

The chicken curry can be made mild, medium or hot, depending on your preference. The recipe given is mild to medium, so add extra curry powder if you want it hotter. The mango water ice makes a refreshing end to the curry meal, but it must be made in advance, preferably the night before, so that it has time to set in the freezer.

If you do not have a freezer or would prefer not to make the water ice, you could serve tinned mango with cream as an alternative.

Equipment needed – **Menu 15**

Starter

1 mixing bowl
1 potato peeler
1 small bowl
1 fine sieve
1 sharp knife
1 cheese grater
1 tablespoon

Main course

1 savoury chopping board
1 sharp knife
1 medium or large ovenproof casserole
  dish
1 savoury wooden spoon
1 frying pan (optional)
1 tablespoon
1 teaspoon
1 measuring jug
1 medium saucepan
1 colander
1 ovenproof dish or roasting tin

Dessert

1 tin opener
1 fine sieve
2 mixing bowls
1 fork
1 metal spoon
1 plastic container for freezing
1 balloon whisk or hand–held electric
  mixer

Shopping list – **Menu 15**

Starter

100g (4oz) natural yogurt
½ cucumber
4 onion bhajis or 4 vegetable samosas
8 poppadoms
mango or peach chutney
lime pickle

Main course

2 large onions
*★50g (2oz) cooking margarine (85g (3½oz) if
  frying the chicken)*
8–10 chicken thighs
*★medium to hot curry powder (depending on
  taste)*
★37g (1½oz) plain flour
★2 tablespoons tomato purée
*★1 chicken stock cube or 600ml (1 pint) fresh
  chicken stock*
★100g (4oz) sultanas
★225g (8oz) long grain easy-cook rice

Dessert

425g (15oz) tin mangoes in syrup
350g (12oz) natural yogurt
★2 egg whites
★25g (1oz) caster sugar

★Check store cupboard

Countdown – **Menu 15**

If you want to prepare the whole menu, you will need 115 minutes. This includes a 30-minute break. If you are a slow cook, add 5–10 minutes to each course to ensure that you don't run out of time. Remember that the times given are only a rough guide, as each cook will take different lengths of time to complete each task. You have the choice of leaving out a course if you think it is too much, or if time is limited. The dessert must be made in advance to allow it time to freeze properly.

Dessert

PROBLEMS AND HANDY TIPS

Preparation time: 20 minutes
Freezing time: 8–10 hours

Assemble all the ingredients and equipment you need for the water ice. Set your timer for 20 minutes.

20 mins Open the tin of mangoes. Put a sieve over a mixing bowl and drain the fruit through it. Using a fork, mash the mangoes in the sieve until they look like a purée. Add them to the syrup. Measure out 350g (12oz) natural yogurt (approximately 12 tablespoons) and add it to the mangoes and syrup. Stir well.

The mango does not have to go through the sieve: it has to be well mashed.

12 mins Take 2 eggs and separate the whites from the yolks. If you are worried about this, use different bowls for the whites so that any broken yolk does not contaminate both whites.

See Handy Tip 8, pxix for an easy method of separating eggs.

8 mins Whisk the egg whites in a mixing bowl with a balloon whisk or a hand-held electric mixer, until they are stiff and hold their shape. Measure out 25g/1oz (1 tablespoon) of caster sugar and fold it into the egg whites. Slowly add all the mango purée and mix into the egg white, stirring but not beating, until all the mango purée is incorporated. Place in a covered plastic container and put straight into the deep-freeze to set.

Do not beat the mixture – fold it gently to incorporate as much air as possible. If you beat the air out, the water ice will be heavier.

0 mins Wash up and clear away.

The water ice must be made at least 8 hours before being served. Stir with a fork halfway through its setting time in case the mango has sunk to the bottom.

Main course

Preparation time: 40 minutes
Cooking time: 60 minutes

Assemble all the ingredients and equipment you need for the main course. Preheat the oven to 180°C/350°F/Gas mark 4. Set your timer for 40 minutes.

40 mins Peel 2 large onions and chop them into small pieces. Measure out 50g/2oz (2 tablespoons) cooking margarine and place in an ovenproof casserole dish with the onions. Put the casserole over a medium heat and cook the onions until light golden brown (this will take approx. 5 minutes). Stir the onions occasionally.

The onion does not have to be finely chopped as it will cook down in the sauce.

30 mins If you are using skinless chicken, leave out this section and add the raw chickens to the sauce as instructed later. If your chicken has the skin on, melt 12g/½oz (½ tablespoon) cooking margarine in a frying pan over a medium heat and fry the chicken, skinside down, until brown.

If you use chicken breasts, they will take less time to cook than thighs or legs.

26 mins While the chicken is browning, add 1 tablespoon of medium or hot curry powder to the casserole dish with the onions. If you are using a hot curry powder, this amount will make a medium curry. If you prefer a mild flavour use only 1 teaspoon of curry powder. Don't forget that different brands of curry powders differ in strength, so add a little at a time to reach the required strength.

22 mins Allow the curry powder to cook with the onions for at least 2 minutes.

20 mins Remove the casserole from the heat and stir 37g/1½oz (1½ tablespoons) plain flour into the mixture. Cook for a further 2 minutes to remove the starchy flavour.

Mix the flour well in to make a smooth paste.

18 mins Turn the heat off, add 2 tablespoons of tomato purée and mix well. Stir in 600ml (1 pint) of fresh stock, or crumble 1 chicken stock cube into the casserole and add 600ml (1 pint) water. Stir well.

Add the liquid very slowly, stirring it all the time so that you do not end up with a lumpy sauce.

14 mins Check the chicken and, if necessary, turn it over to brown on the other side.

12 mins Turn the curry sauce back on and allow it to come slowly to the boil, stirring constantly until thick. Lower the heat and simmer for 2 minutes. Check the chicken in the frying pan. If you are having to cook 2 batches, transfer the first batch into the casserole dish with the sauce. Try to leave as much fat as possible in the

Make sure when transferring the chicken from the frying pan to the casserole dish that as little fat as possible passes over. This will prevent the curry sauce from being greasy.

frying pan. Add the second batch of chicken and brown as before.

8 mins Stir the sauce occasionally and keep an eye on the chicken in the frying pan. If you are using skinless chicken, add it to the sauce now and stir well. Put the lid on the casserole and cook in the pre-heated oven to cook for 60 minutes.

5 mins Add the second batch of browned chicken to the casserole leaving as much fat in the pan as possible. Place the casserole in the preheated oven for 60 minutes.

0 mins Wash up and clear away.

The chicken curry can sit in the oven for a while without spoiling, so don't panic if you are running behind time.

Watch points

The consistency of the curry sauce should be thin rather than thick. If, at the end of cooking, you feel the sauce is too thin, you can thicken it with cornflour (see Handy Tip 6, pxviii).

The advantage of using chicken with skin is that it provides extra flavour, but at the end of the cooking time it is necessary to remove any excess fat from the top of the casserole with a tablespoon.

Relax

Have a break for 30 minutes. When you return you will only have to prepare the starter and cook the rice.

Welcome back

Feeling better after your break? You now have 25 minutes before you serve the starter.

Finishing the main course

Set your timer for 25 minutes.

25 mins Measure out 100g (4oz) of sultanas. Take the chicken curry out of the oven, remove the lid and stir in the sultanas. Replace in the oven for a further 20–30 minutes. (The cooking time varies, depending on how hot your oven is and what type of chicken you are using.)

Chicken must always be well cooked. If you are in any doubt, it is always better to overcook it.

Starter

Preparation time: 20 minutes
Cooking time: 10–15 minutes

20 mins If you are making the yogurt sauce, put 100g (4oz) of natural yogurt into a mixing bowl. Take half a cucumber, peel it with a sharp potato peeler and cut a small amount off the end and discard. Grate the cucumber over a separate bowl, then transfer to a sieve and drain off the liquid. Add the cucumber flesh to the yogurt and mix well. Clean up the bowl, or use a new bowl for serving. Chill in the fridge until required.

Do not add all the liquid that comes from the cucumber as it will make the sauce too thin. Try to add just the grated cucumber.

15 mins Place the onion bhajis or vegetable samosas on a baking tray and heat them up in the top of the oven for approx. 10–15 minutes.

The onion bhajis will sit in the oven alongside the chicken curry and heat up gradually.

11 mins Fill the kettle with water and put it on to boil. Measure out 225g (8oz) long grain, easy-cook rice and place it in a saucepan.

9 mins Add 25g/1oz (1 tablespoon) of margarine to the pan, then pour the boiling water over the rice. Stir well until all the margarine has melted. Add a pinch of salt. Place on a medium heat to cook for approximately 10–12 minutes. To have the rice ready before starting the meal, stop it cooking after 8 minutes. Drain it through a colander and pour some warm water over it to remove any excess starch. Line an ovenproof dish or roasting tin with tin foil. Spread the rice out on the foil and dot with a small amount of margarine or butter to prevent it from sticking. Fold up the foil to cover the rice and place the tin in the bottom of the oven.

Do not overcook the rice; once it is ready, turn the heat off and drain it. This will prevent it from continuing to cook and becoming soggy. You can always heat it up again in the oven, or by pouring boiling water over it. Drain again before serving.

6 mins The poppadoms should be served with the starter. Place them in the oven or under a hot grill for a few seconds on each side. Watch them closely as they can burn easily. They are ready when they bubble and become golden. Serve immediately while crisp and hot.

Poppadom cook very quickly and can burn easily, so do not leave them unattended.

2 mins Turn off the rice, drain it through a colander, but leave it over the pan with a lid on if you are not using the foil method described earlier.

0 mins Wash up and clear away.

Watch points

Once the meal has started, it is not possible to give specific times, so the following instructions are given as guidelines.

Remove the onion bhajis or samosas from the oven. Place the yogurt sauce and chutney on the table. Before serving, turn the oven down to 150°C/300°F/Gas mark 2. Serve the starter.

Serve the main course with the rice. Leave the chutney and yogurt sauce on the table in case any of your guests would like some with their main course.

The mango water ice is served just as it is. If the chicken curry was quite hot, it will be a welcome palate cleanser.

Stir the yogurt sauce well before serving it.

Before serving the curry, make sure that you remove any excess grease. This is best done by tipping the casserole and allowing the fat to run to one side. Skim it off with a tablespoon and discard.

Stir the curry well before serving.

Mexican taco menu
Moderately difficult to prepare and cook
Cost level: good value
Serves: 4

A 30-minute break is incorporated in this menu.

| **Starter** | Baked potato skins with sour cream | Preparation time = 10 minutes
Cooking time = 35 minutes |

| **Main course** | Taco shells with spicy Mexican mince, avocado, lettuce, cheese and sour cream | Preparation time = 30 minutes
Cooking time = 60 minutes |

| **Dessert** | Baked banana sponge with crème fraîche or cream | Preparation time = 25 minutes
Cooking time = 40–45 minutes |

This menu can be a lot of fun to make and eat. It is similar to a fondue, as you invite your guests to choose their own combination of fillings for their tacos.

The starter can either be eaten as a dip when your guests are standing up, or sitting down with a side plate and spoon for the sour cream.

The main course can be eaten with the fingers or with cutlery, it is up to you. There is quite a lot of preparation but once everything is on the table, it is up to individuals to select the combination of ingredients they want to fill their taco shells.

The dessert is very straightforward and can either be served hot or cold. It will also sit in the oven without spoiling while you eat the starter and main course. It should be served with crème fraîche or single cream.

Equipment needed – **Menu 16**

Starter

1 savoury chopping board
1 sharp knife
1 mixing bowl
1 colander
1 spatula
1 baking tray or roasting tin

Main course

1 savoury chopping board
1 sharp knife
1 fine grater or 1 food processor
1 garlic crusher (or see Handy Tip 4, pxviii)
1 savoury wooden spoon
1 potato peeler
1 measuring jug
1 lemon squeezer
1 tablespoon
1 teaspoon
4 small bowls (for chopped ingredients)
1 medium saucepan with lid or 1 hob-to-oven casserole dish
1 colander

Dessert

900g (2lb) loaf tin or 18cm (7 inch) round cake tin
2 mixing bowls
1 sweet wooden spoon or hand-held electric mixer
1 fine sieve
1 tablespoon
1 soft spatula
1 sweet chopping board
1 sharp knife
1 teaspoon

Starter

4 large old potatoes
★25g (1oz) cooking margarine
★salt and pepper
100g (4oz) sour cream

Main course

★1 large onion
★25g (1oz) cooking margarine
★2 cloves garlic
900g (2lb) minced beef
2.5cm (1 inch) piece fresh root ginger
2 eating apples
★1 beef stock cube
25g (1oz) packet Mexican spice mix or taco seasoning mix
100g (4oz) sultanas
2 oranges
★salt and pepper
★1 teaspoon chilli powder
★1 teaspoon of dried mustard powder
★1 tablespoon Worcestershire sauce
75g (3oz) pitted green olives (optional)
½ iceberg lettuce
2 fresh tomatoes
1 ripe avocado
100g (4oz) Cheddar cheese
100g (4oz) sour cream
1 packet taco shells

Dessert

★75g (3oz) margarine or butter
★75g (3oz) caster sugar
★75g (3oz) self-raising flour
★2 eggs
3 small or 2 large bananas
★1 teaspoon lemon juice
300ml (½ pint) single cream or crème fraîche

★Check store cupboard

Countdown – **Menu 16**

If you want to prepare the whole menu you will need 130 minutes. This includes a 30-minute break. If you are a slow cook, add 5–10 minutes to each course to ensure that you do not run out of time. Remember, the times given are only a guide, as each cook will take different lengths of time to complete each task. This is a fun menu and there is quite a lot of preparation to be done, but once the meal is under way your guests make up their own tacos and enjoy helping themselves to the various fillings. The Mexican mince and dessert can be made in advance if preferred.

If you have a food processor, you can save a great deal of time by chopping the onions, apples, cheese and olives using the thin slicer or fine grater. You do not need to wash the machine after each ingredient as they will all end up in the same dish.

Dessert

Preparation time: 25 minutes
Cooking time: 40–45 minutes

PROBLEMS AND HANDY TIPS

Assemble all the ingredients and equipment you need for the dessert. Set your timer for 25 minutes. Preheat the oven to 180°C/350°F/Gas mark 4.

25 mins Grease a loaf tin or round cake tin with a small amount of margarine. Set aside until required.

22 mins Measure out 75g (3oz) of margarine or butter and 75g (3oz) of caster sugar into a mixing bowl. Beat together with a wooden spoon or a hand-held electric mixer until the mixture is light and fluffy and has changed colour to a pale yellow.

A small hand-held mixer will speed up the process of making the dessert, but it can quite easily be done by hand.

15 mins Measure out 75g (3oz) of self-raising flour and sift it through a fine sieve into a bowl.

Remember to sieve the flour well as this helps to make a lighter sponge.

13 mins Break 1 egg into the sugar mixture, add 1 tablespoon of self-raising flour and stir well with a wooden spoon or electric mixer. Make sure the mixture is holding together before adding the second egg and 1 more tablespoon of flour. Beat well again. Fold in the remaining flour. Do not beat at this stage; try to incorporate as much air as possible using a metal tablespoon or a soft spatula.

Don't worry too much if the mixture starts to separate when you add the eggs, add a little extra flour and this should bring it back together again.

8 mins Peel and slice the bananas into 1cm (½ inch) slices and carefully stir them into the flour mixture. Add 1 teaspoon of lemon juice, mix well and pour the mixture into the well-greased loaf tin or cake tin.

3 mins Place the tin in the preheated oven as near to the top as possible, for 20 minutes. Then turn the temperature down to 160°C/325°F/Gas mark 3 and continue to cook for a further 20–25 minutes. The sponge is cooked when it has shrunk away from the sides of the tin and when a sharp knife pushed into the centre comes out clean.

0 mins Wash up and clear away.

Try not to break up the bananas when you mix them into the flour mixture; they should remain in slices if possible.

Once all the mixture is in the tin knock it gently on the work surface to release any air bubbles caught in the corners. This makes for a more even sponge.

This sponge is better slightly undercooked, as it tends to dry out otherwise.

Main course

PROBLEMS AND HANDY TIPS

Preparation time: 30 minutes
Cooking time: 60 minutes

Assemble all the ingredients and equipment you need for the main course. Set your timer for 30 minutes. If you are using the oven to cook the banana sponge, there is no need to set the oven. If you have not made the sponge and would like to cook the meat in the oven, preheat the oven to 160°C/325°F/Gas mark 3.

30 mins Peel and chop the onion as small as possible using a sharp knife or food processor. Place 25g/1oz (1 tablespoon) cooking margarine in the saucepan or casserole dish. Melt the margarine, then add the onion and cook over a low heat until soft and transparent.

22 mins While the onion is cooking, peel and crush the 2 cloves of garlic (see Handy Tip 4, pxviii for an easy method if you don't have a garlic crusher). Add the garlic to the onion and cook for a further 2 minutes.

16 mins Once the onion and garlic are cooked, add the mince to the pan and continue to cook on a low heat, stirring occasionally.

14 mins While the meat is cooking, peel the fresh root ginger with a sharp knife or potato peeler. Using a fine grater, grate all the ginger on to a plate or savoury chopping board (discard any long hairy pieces). Add the grated ginger to the meat and stir well. Do not wash the grater yet, as you will use it again for the apples and cheese, unless you are going to use a food processor.

10 mins Turn the oven down to 160°C/325°F/Gas mark 3 and check the banana sponge. Leave to cook for a further 20–25 minutes.

It is best to cook the mince in the oven if possible, as it is less likely to burn than on a hob. Also, if you are using the oven for the sponge and potato skins you will save energy.

Garlic should always be cooked as it takes the sharp edge off the taste.

Don't allow the onion and garlic to burn, just to colour lightly.

The ginger can be grated straight into the mince to save washing up.

9 mins While the meat is cooking, take 2 eating apples and wash them well under cold running water. Cut them into quarters and remove the cores. Do not peel as all the goodness is in the skin and it will soften during cooking. Grate the apples on a grater or in a food processor. Discard any large pieces of skin; this can take some time, so be patient.

You do not have to cut the apple up well if you are using a food processor; just take the core out and place the apple straight in the processor.

4 mins Stir the meat well and if it is cooking too fast, turn the heat down or off. Add all the grated apple and mix well. Take 1 beef stock cube, crumble it into the meat and stir in 300ml (½ pint) of cold water. Mix in the packet of Mexican spice mix or taco seasoning mix, stir well and put back on to the heat. Bring slowly to the boil. Measure out 100g (4oz) of sultanas, add them to the meat and stir well. Take 2 oranges, cut them in half and squeeze them on a lemon squeezer. Add all the juice to the meat and stir well.

The meat should be brown before any water is added.

Before cutting the oranges in half, roll them under the palm of your hand on a work surface. This releases the flesh inside the oranges and makes it easier to squeeze out the juice.

1 min Season with a pinch of salt (do not use too much, as the olives, to be added later, can be salty), ground black pepper, 1 teaspoon of dried mustard powder and 1 table-spoon of Worcestershire sauce. Stir well and leave to simmer on a low heat, or place in the oven for approx. 60 minutes at 160°C/325°/F/Gas mark 3.

Season the meat well, but you can season it again once it has cooked for a while.

0 mins Wash up and clear away.

Starter

Preparation time: 10 minutes
Cooking time: 35 minutes

Assemble all the ingredients and equipment you need for the starter. Set your timer for 10 minutes.

10 mins Wash 4 old potatoes and, using a sharp knife, slice them into pieces 5cm (2 inches) long and 2.5cm (1 inch) wide. Try to cut the strips as evenly as possible.

This recipe is better with old potatoes rather than new, but if you are stuck, new ones will do, although the end result will not be as crisp.

5 mins Place the potato slices in a bowl of hot water as you do them. The hot water removes the excess starch and makes for a better finish. The potatoes will sit quite happily in the water while you have a break. You will cook them when you return.

1 min Check the banana sponge to see if it is cooked. It is ready if it has shrunk away from the edges of the tin and a sharp knife or skewer pushed into the centre comes out clean. Remove it from the oven and set aside if you plan to reheat it later and serve it hot. If you want to serve it

Don't forget to take the banana sponge out of the oven before you go for your break.

cold, run a knife around the edges to loosen the sponge and turn it out on to a serving plate.

0 mins Wash up and clear away.

Relax

Have a 30-minute break. When you return you will only have to finish off the last-minute tasks.

Welcome back

Feeling better after your break?

Last-minute tasks

Set your timer for 35 minutes. This is how long you have before you serve the starter. Turn the oven up to 200°C/400°F/Gas mark 6.

35 mins Drain the potatoes through a colander and dry them on a clean tea towel. Place them on a baking tray or in a roasting tin and dot them evenly with 25g/1oz (1 tablespoon) of cooking margarine. Season with salt and pepper. Place the potatoes in the oven as near to the top as possible and cook for 35 minutes.

Try to dry the potatoes as well as possible; this makes them crispier.

31 mins Take the mince out of the oven and stir it well. You will need to put it near the bottom of the oven while the potatoes are cooking.

30 mins Take the olives, if using them, and cut them in half ready to add to the mince later on.

The olives can be cut into quarters, or chopped very finely.

28 mins Take out the lettuce, tomatoes, avocado and cheese. All these ingredients will be served in small bowls on the table so that your guests can help themselves.

25 mins Chop the lettuce finely, place in a colander and wash under cold running water. Leave to drain.

Try to chop all the ingredients quite small so that they fit into the taco shells.

20 mins Wash the tomatoes, then chop, slice or dice them, and place in a bowl ready to serve.

15 mins Cut right round the avocado from top to bottom. Twist the 2 halves in opposite directions and pull apart. Scoop out the stone with a spoon, then peel off the skin. Cut the flesh into small pieces and place in a small bowl ready to serve.

Add 1 teaspoon of lemon juice to the avocado before putting it into the serving bowl to prevent it turning black.

10 mins Grate the Cheddar cheese, using a large grater or food processor, then place it in a bowl ready to serve.

5 mins Dry the lettuce on kitchen paper, then place in a serving bowl. Put all the bowls to one side, covered with a tea towel until they are required.

mins Check the potatoes to see if they are crispy. If
ot, don't worry; heat up the grill and place the baking
ray of potatoes under it to crisp up. This should take
only a couple of minutes and gives the potatoes a lovely
golden brown finish.

min Take the sour cream out of the fridge and place it
n a serving bowl.

mins Turn the oven down to 150°C/350°F/Gas mark 3
o that the Mexican mince doesn't burn. Place the empty
aco shells on a baking tray and put them into the oven to
eat up. Place the banana sponge in the oven now if you
re going to serve it hot. Wash up and clear away.

The potato skins are finished
when they are golden brown
and crispy. If you would like to
make then a little crisper, pop
them under the grill for a few
minutes.

The taco shells heat up very
quickly. If you put them in the
oven when you begin the
starter, they will be ready by the
time you have finished.

Watch points

erve the hot potato skins with the sour cream. They can
e eaten as a snack before the meal, or as a first course at
he table.

erve the main course. Place the small bowls of lettuce,
omatoes, avocado and grated cheese on the table, along
vith the taco shells and the Mexican mince. You can
eave the sour cream on the table as it is also delicious
vith tacos.

It is a good idea to put an
assortment of cutlery on the
table for your guests to help
themselves, as the taco shells
sometimes fall apart while
trying to eat them.

How to fill a taco

Take a taco shell and place a small amount of the meat
mixture inside it. Then take small amounts of the
ngredients in the bowls. Top the meat with some chop-
ed lettuce, tomato and avocado, followed by some
heese. Lastly, if you like, add a small amount of sour
ream.

erve the dessert, hot or cold with crème fraîche or single
ream. Don't forget to turn the oven off if you have
varmed up the sponge.

Spring dinner party menu
Moderately difficult to prepare and cook
Cost level: good value
Serves: 4

A 30-minute break is incorporated in this menu.

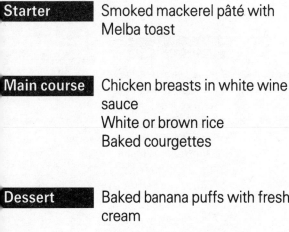

Starter

Smoked mackerel pâté with
Melba toast

Preparation time = 15 minutes
Cooking time = None

Main course

Chicken breasts in white wine
sauce
White or brown rice
Baked courgettes

Preparation time = 55 minutes
Cooking time = 50 minutes

Dessert

Baked banana puffs with fresh
cream

Preparation time = 25 minutes
Cooking time = 30 minutes

This menu would suit anyone who prefers not to eat red
meat. It has a wide variety of delicious flavours, from
smoked fish pâté, subtle chicken in a white sauce to
creamy, hot banana puffs.

The emphasis is on cooking as much as possible in the
oven in order to save time and energy. The starter and
dessert can be prepared in advance the day or night
before, or a few hours before the main course. This will
enable you to have more time on the night to spend with
your guests.

If you are going to use frozen pastry for the dessert, don't
forget to take it out of the deep freeze at least 90 minutes
before using it. Alternatively, leave it to defrost in the
fridge overnight.

Equipment needed – **Menu 17**

Starter

1 savoury chopping board
1 sharp knife
1 food processor with metal blade or
    bowl, a large fork and a wooden spoon
1 lemon squeezer

Main course

1 savoury chopping board
1 sharp knife
2 plates
1 medium hob-to-oven casserole dish
    with lid
1 savoury wooden spoon
1 colander or fine sieve
1 measuring jug
1 frying pan
1 ovenproof glass dish or roasting tin
    preferably with a lid
1 large saucepan
1 balloon whisk (optional)

Dessert

1 baking tray
1 small bowl
1 fork
1 tablespoon
1 rolling pin or wine bottle
1 sharp knife
1 pastry brush (optional)
1 spatula

Shopping list – **Menu 17**

Starter

2 smoked mackerel fillets
225g (8oz) cream cheese
100g (4oz) cottage cheese
2 lemons
★salt and pepper
parsley to garnish
100g (4oz) packet Melba toast
100g (4oz) butter

Main course

4 large courgettes, 900g (2lb) approx.
*4 boneless chicken breasts (with or without
    skin)*
★2 medium onions
★87g (3½oz) cooking margarine
450g (1lb) button mushrooms
★38g (1½oz) plain flour
*★1 chicken stock cube OR 300ml (½ pint) fresh
    chicken stock*
300ml (½ pint) dry white wine
*★salt, pepper, nutmeg and dried mustard
    powder*
★mixed dried herbs
225g (8oz) white or brown easy-cook rice

Dessert

★Knob of margarine
4 small or 2 large bananas
★1 egg
★1 tablespoon plain flour
225g (8oz) puff pastry
★4 tablespoons thick honey
50g (2oz) sour cream
300ml (½ pint) single cream to serve

★Check store cupboard

ountdown – **Menu 17**

f you want to prepare and cook the whole menu, you
eed 125 minutes. This includes a 30-minute break.
emember, the times given are only a guide. If you are a
low cook, add 5–10 minutes to each course to ensure that
ou don't run out of time. The starter and dessert can be
nade in advance, either the day or evening before. The
nain course is best made on the day or evening to keep it
resh and to stop the chicken breasts from drying out.

Don't forget, if you are using frozen puff pastry, it must
e defrosted for at least 90 minutes at room temperature,
r overnight in the fridge.

Starter

PROBLEMS AND HANDY TIPS

reparation time: 15 minutes
Cooking time: None

Assemble all the ingredients and equipment you need for
he starter. Set your timer for 15 minutes. If you have a
ood processor, you will be able to save time and have a
ner pâte.

5 mins Take the skin off the mackerel, then place the
sh in a food processor or mixing bowl.

To skin the fish, start at the tail
end and pull the skin towards
the head. If this doesn't work,
use a sharp knife to ease it off.

2 mins Add 225g (8oz) of cream cheese and 100g (4oz)
f cottage cheese to the fish and mix until smooth. Take 1
emon and roll it under the palm of your hand on a work
urface to release the flesh. Cut the lemon in half and
queeze both halves over a lemon squeezer. Add ½ the
uice to the fish mixture and season with ground pepper.
Check the seasoning as you might need more lemon or
epper. Mix really well. Don't use any salt as the
nackerel will already be salty.

If this mixture is very stiff, add
all the lemon juice at once. This
should help break down the
cream cheese.

mins Spoon the mixture into a serving dish and gar-
ish with parsley. Take the second lemon and cut it
ngthways to make 4 wedges. Put them on a plate ready
o serve, or place in the fridge alongside the pâté until
equired.

mins Wash up and clear away.

Dessert

Preparation time: 25 minutes
Cooking time: 30 minutes

Preheat the oven to 200°C/400°F/Gas mark 6 if you are going to cook the banana puffs straight away. If using frozen puff pastry, it must be defrosted before you can use it. Do not set the oven if you are going to cook the puffs just before you sit down to eat the main course. Assemble all the ingredients and equipment you need for the dessert. Set your timer for 25 minutes.

25 mins Grease a baking tray with a small amount of margarine.

Grease the baking tray with either a piece of greaseproof paper or your fingers.

22 mins Peel the 4 small bananas. If you are using 2 large bananas instead, peel them and cut them in half.

20 mins Break the egg into a bowl and beat well with a fork.

18 mins Take 1 tablespoon of plain flour and sprinkle it over a clean work surface. Take the puff pastry and roll it into a large, thin rectangle. Place the bananas on the rolled-out pastry to see whether the rectangle is large enough to be cut into 4 pieces, which can be wrapped around each banana like a sausage roll.

Use a clean bottle if you do not have a rolling pin.

If the pastry won't stick together, pinch it hard with your fingertips to ensure a good seal. Use some extra flour if the pastry has become too wet with the egg; this will help you to seal the pastry.

11 mins Once you are sure the pastry will fit, cut the pastry around each banana. Take half the beaten egg and, using a pastry brush or your fingers, brush it on to the exposed pastry.

8 mins Spread 1 tablespoon of thick honey and 1 tablespoon of sour cream over each banana. You must be quick as the honey and sour cream can ooze out over the edges. Roll the pastry up around the bananas, like a sausage roll. The egg should help to stick the pastry together.

Don't worry too much if you cannot seal the puffs well as they will probably burst open during the cooking time anyway.

6 mins Place the banana puffs on the greased baking tray and brush them with the remaining egg to give a shiny finish when baked. Chill the puffs until you are ready to bake them.

0 mins Wash up and clear away.

Main course

Preparation time: 45 minutes
Cooking time: 50 minutes

Preheat the oven to 200°C/400°F/Gas mark 6. Assemble all the ingredients and equipment you need for the main course. Set your timer for 45 minutes.

5 mins Wash the courgettes under cold water, top and ·il them and cut them in half lengthways. Lie them down ı a plate flesh upwards and sprinkle liberally with salt. This process, called 'degorging', removes the bitterness ·hich is often found in courgettes.)

7 mins Wash the chicken breasts under cold running ·ater and set aside on a plate.

5 mins Peel and chop 2 medium onions as finely as ·ossible.

0 mins Place a hob-to-oven casserole dish over the heat ·ıd melt 50g/2oz (2 tablespoons) of margarine. Add the ·ıopped onion and leave to cook on a medium heat for 5 ·ınutes, stirring occasionally. While the onions are cook-·ıg, take the mushrooms and wash well under cold run-·ıng water. Discard the stalks and cut the mushrooms ·ıto quarters. Leave to drain in a colander or sieve. Check ·ıe onions and turn them off if soft and lightly coloured.

5 mins Take the butter for the starter out of the fridge ·ıd place it on a plate or butter dish to soften.

4 mins Add 38g/1½oz (1½ tablespoons) of plain flour ·ıd 1 crumbled chicken stock cube to the onions. (If you ·ıe using fresh stock, you do not need to use the stock ·ıbe.) Stir well. If the mixture is very stiff, add a small ·ınount of extra margarine to make it less dry. Put the ·ıixture (which is called a roux) back on a low heat and ·ıok for 2 minutes. Turn off the heat and leave to cool.

0 mins Measure out 300ml (½ pint) of white wine and ·ı0ml (½ pint) of cold water or fresh stock. Slowly add ·ıe liquid to the roux, stirring all the time. Once all the ·ıquid has been added, turn the heat on very low and ·ıring the sauce slowly to the boil, stirring constantly, ·ıntil it thickens. Season well with salt, pepper and a pinch ·ıf nutmeg and mustard powder. Taste and adjust the ·ıasoning as necessary.

6 mins Leave the sauce to simmer for 10 minutes on a ·ıry low heat.

5 mins Wash the courgettes really well under cold ·ınning water to remove all the salt. Leave them to drain.

2 mins Melt 12g/½oz (½ tablespoon) of margarine in a ·ıying pan, add the chicken breasts and fry them quickly ·ır 2½ minutes on each side to seal the meat. Transfer the ·hicken to the sauce, which should still be simmering. ·ıurn the heat off, cover the casserole and place in the ·ıreheated oven for 50 minutes.

mins Lay the courgettes, skin-side down, in an oven-·ıoof dish. Season with pepper and a pinch of mixed

If the courgette skins look old and tough, you might need to peel them.

Don't cook the onions too fast while you are washing and cutting up the mushrooms in case they burn.

If the sauce goes lumpy, stop at once. Turn the heat off and beat the mixture thoroughly with a wooden spoon or balloon whisk. Once all the lumps have gone, return the sauce to the heat.

If the sauce is still lumpy after beating it, don't worry, you can always sieve it. Wait until the sauce comes back to the boil and has simmered for at least 2 minutes before sieving.

herbs. Take 25g/1oz (1 tablespoon) of margarine and dot it over the courgettes. Place the dish in the bottom of the oven or on the shelf below the chicken and cook for approximately 45 minutes.

0 mins Wash up and clear away.

Relax

Everything, except the dessert, is in the oven, so have a 30-minute break. Take your timer with you; when you return you will have only a few last-minute tasks to complete.

Welcome back

Feeling better after your break?

Last-minute tasks

Once the meal has started, it is difficult to predict how long each course will take. The following instructions are given only as a guide. Set your timer for 10 minutes. This is how long you have before you sit down and eat the starter.

10 mins Fill the kettle and put it on to boil.
8 mins Measure out 225g (8oz) of easy-cook rice and place it in a large saucepan with a knob of margarine and a pinch of salt. (The margarine prevents the rice from sticking together while cooking.)
6 mins Set the table. Take the chicken out of the oven and stir in the mushrooms. Check the courgettes. Return both dishes to the oven and continue cooking.

Check the chicken and courgettes in the oven. Stir the chicken well and continue to cook.

2 mins Just before you sit down to eat the starter, pour the boiling water over the rice and leave it to cook on a very low heat.

0 mins Wash up and clear away.

Watch points

If you have a facility for warming the dinner plates and serving dish for the rice, put them in now.

You can place 1 or 2 courgette on top of each other if you don have enough room in the dish for them all to lie down.

If you are not using easy-cook rice, you will need to put it on earlier as it will take longer to cook.

.ace the smoked mackerel pâté on the table with the .elba toast and lemon wedges.

Place the melba toast on the table at the same time as the butter so you do not forget it.

eset your timer for a further 10 minutes. This is how ng it will take to finish cooking the chicken while you t the starter. If you feel that the chicken is already)oked or that the starter will take longer than 10 minutes eat, turn the oven down to 140°C/275°F/Gas mark 1. If .e rice is cooked, turn it off and leave it in the boiling ater to keep hot.

If you are not sure whether the chicken is cooked, push a sharp knife into the flesh; if no red juices appear and the chicken has shrunk, it is ready.

rain the rice and run it quickly under hot water to ·move any excess starch. Place in the warmed serving .sh.

Allow the rice to drain for a few seconds to get rid of any excess water.

[ow you are ready to serve the main course. Take the ιicken and courgettes out of the oven and place them on heatproof mat. Turn the oven up to 220°C/425°F/Gas ιark 7 and put the banana puffs into the oven.

:t your timer for 30 minutes. This is the approximate ιne the dessert will need to cook.

.ake the plates out of the warming oven and serve the ιain course.

˙ the main course takes longer than 30 minutes to eat, or ɔu would like to take a break before eating the dessert, ɔn't worry. Check the pastry and if it looks golden ɾown, turn the oven off and leave the puffs in the oven ɔ keep warm until you are ready to serve them with fresh eam.

The banana puffs are ready when they have risen and are golden brown. Turn the oven down and leave them to keep warm until you are ready to serve them.

Summer buffet menu
Difficult to prepare and cook
Cost level: good value
Serves: 4

A break is incorporated in this menu.

| **Starter** | Smoked haddock mousse with brown rolls and butter | Preparation time = 40 minutes
Cooking time = 10–15 minutes |

| **Main course** | Coronation chicken
Mixed rice salad
Bean salad with yogurt dressing
Tomato and chive salad | Preparation time = 40 minutes
Cooking time = 60 minutes |

| **Dessert** | Rich chocolate mousse with wafer biscuits and strawberries
Selection of cheeses
Fresh fruit | Preparation time = 30 minutes
Cooking time = None |

This is a good summer lunch or dinner menu. Everything can be eaten with a fork, which means that people don't have to sit down formally. Most of the food can be made the day before.

There is quite a lot of preparation, but as everything is served cold there are very few last-minute tasks, which gives you time to relax and prepare yourself for the party. If you have some friends who are vegetarian, it would be a good idea to make up a vegetarian dish from another menu so that they have something to eat with the salads.

The chocolate mousse is deliciously rich. It is best made in advance, either the day before or on the day, leaving it enough time to chill and set. You could serve some fresh fruit alongside the mousse in case people are watching their figures or would prefer to eat something lighter. You could also serve a selection of cheeses if you feel that some guests might prefer them to a dessert.

Don't forget, you will need a French dressing to serve with the salads. See page 196 if you want to make your own, or buy a ready-made one.

If you are having more than 4 guests to the buffet, it is easy to double or treble the quantities to serve 8, or even 12 people.

Equipment needed – **Menu 18**

Starter

1 savoury chopping board
1 sharp knife
1 medium saucepan with lid
1 measuring jug
1 lemon squeezer
1 small saucepan
1 tablespoon
1 dessertspoon
1 fine sieve
1 savoury wooden spoon

Main course

1 potato peeler
1 savoury chopping board
1 sharp knife
1 savoury wooden spoon
1 small saucepan with lid
1 tablespoon
1 large wine glass
1 large plate or roasting tin
1 carving fork or 2 large spoons
2 large or 3 medium mixing bowls
1 medium saucepan
1 large saucepan
1 tin opener
1 colander
1 bowl
1 fine sieve
1 pair scissors
1 teaspoon

Dessert

1 heatproof bowl that fits inside the saucepan
1 saucepan
2 mixing bowls
1 sweet wooden spoon
1 balloon whisk or hand-held electric mixer
1 plastic spatula
1 colander
1 sharp knife

*Check store cupboard

Shopping list – **Menu 18**

Starter

450g (1lb) raw smoked haddock
*450ml (¾ pint) milk
*ground black pepper
1 lemon
*1 tablespoon water
*1 level dessertspoon powdered gelatine
*25g (1oz) cooking margarine
*25g (1oz) plain flour
*2 tablespoons mayonnaise
1 small bunch parsley to garnish

Main course

1 medium 1–1.5kg (3½–4lb) chicken
*2 onions
1 carrot
*6 peppercorns
*1 teaspoon salt
*4 bay leaves
*38g (1½oz) margarine
*½ level tablespoon curry powder
*1 tablespoon tomato purée
1 large glass red wine
*1 teaspoon sugar
*salt and pepper
*2 tablespoons apricot jam
*4 tablespoons mayonnaise
*225g (8oz) easy-cook rice
225g (8oz) tin sweetcorn
100g (4oz) frozen peas
900g (2lb) French beans
425g (15oz) tin kidney beans
425g (15oz) tin butter beans
300ml (½ pint) French dressing
50g (2oz) natural yogurt
4 large or 8 small tomatoes
1 bunch chives
1 bunch watercress to garnish

Dessert

150g (6oz) plain chocolate
*3 eggs
*2–3 drops of vanilla essence
*knob of butter or margarine
wafer biscuits to serve
fresh strawberries
flaked almonds to decorate
selection of cheeses and cheese biscuits
*225g (8oz) butter

Countdown – **Menu 18**

If you want to prepare and cook the whole menu, you will need 180 minutes. There is time to have a break between the stages of preparation, but a specific length of time for this is not given. If you are a slow cook, add 5–10 minutes to each course to ensure that you do not run out of time. Remember, the times given are only a guide, as each cook takes different lengths of time to complete each task. Most of this menu should be prepared and cooked in advance, then left to chill in the fridge until required. This leaves you with fewer last-minute tasks and more time to enjoy the party with your guests.

Main course

PROBLEMS AND HANDY TIPS

Preparation time: 40 minutes
Cooking time: 60 minutes

The chicken dish is best made in advance, preferably the day before, so that the chicken can absorb the coronation sauce.

Assemble all the ingredients and equipment you need for the chicken and sauce. Set your timer for 40 minutes. If you are cooking the chicken yourself, follow the instructions given below. If you have bought a ready-cooked chicken, you will only need to take the meat off the bone (see page 143).

40 mins Wash the uncooked chicken under cold water, then place it in a saucepan large enough to hold it comfortably. Add enough cold water just to reach the top of the breast. Half cover with a lid and place the pan over a medium heat. Slowly bring the chicken to the boil.

It is always a good idea to wash chicken before cooking it.

Make sure the saucepan is big enough before you start.

35 mins Peel and chop 1 onion. Add it to the chicken in the saucepan. Peel and thinly slice 1 carrot and add to the chicken. Add 6 peppercorns, 1 teaspoon of salt and 2 bay leaves. Stir the vegetables and seasoning around, and leave the chicken on a medium heat until it comes to the boil. Once boiling, turn the heat down to the lowest setting, half cover with a lid and simmer for approximately 60 minutes. Do not allow the chicken to boil rapidly or the flesh will become tough. While the chicken is cooking, make the coronation sauce.

The vegetables need only be roughly chopped; no precision is needed.

The chicken breast doesn't need to be completely covered as it tends to cook faster than the rest of the chicken.

25 mins Peel 1 medium-sized onion and chop it as finely as possible. Place it in a small saucepan, add 25g/1oz (1 tablespoon) of cooking margarine and cook over a medium heat. Stir well.

20 mins While the onion is cooking, assemble all the ingredients you need for the sauce. Once the onion has started to brown, add ½ tablespoon of curry powder and cook for a further 2 to 3 minutes, stirring all the time.

Cooking the curry powder removes its taste and makes it less strong. If you prefer a spicier sauce, add an extra ½ tablespoon of curry powder.

16 mins Now add 1 tablespoon of tomato purée and mix well. Measure out 1 large glass of red wine and add it to the sauce. Bring back to the boil and add 2 tablespoons of lemon juice, 2 bay leaves, 1 teaspoon of sugar, a pinch of salt and a small amount of pepper.

Use a standard size wine glass; the measurement doesn't have to be very accurate.

10 mins Put the saucepan over a low heat and allow all the ingredients to come back to the boil. Once boiling, keep the sauce on a very low heat to stop it from burning. Half cover the saucepan, as the sauce can spit and cause burns. Allow the sauce to simmer for at least 10 minutes.

8 mins While waiting for the sauce to cook, stir the chicken. Half cover and continue to cook for a further 25–30 minutes.

5 mins Fill the kettle with water and put it on to boil. Measure out 225g (8oz) of easy-cook rice and place in a medium-sized saucepan. Add a pinch of salt, 12g/½oz (½ tablespoon) of margarine and pour the boiling water over the rice. Stir well to coat all the rice with the margarine. Leave to cook for 10–15 minutes.

Margarine added to the rice stops it sticking together while it is cooking.

0 mins Once the sauce is cooked, turn the heat off and add 2 tablespoons of apricot jam and stir well. The heat should melt the jam into the sauce. Wash up and clear away.

Adding the jam now gives it time to melt into the sauce.

While you are waiting for the chicken to cook, make the chocolate mousse. This can also be made the day before and kept in the fridge, covered with clingfilm, until you are ready to serve it.

Dessert

Preparation time: 30 minutes
Cooking time: None

Assemble all the ingredients and equipment you need for the dessert. Set your timer for 30 minutes.

30 mins Break the chocolate up and place it in a heatproof bowl. Find a saucepan that the bowl can sit over without touching the bottom. Pour about 2.5cm (1 inch) of cold

The chocolate must not be in direct contact with the source of heat or it will become grainy.

water into the pan and place the bowl of chocolate over it. Put the saucepan over a medium heat and allow the water to boil; this will then melt the chocolate.

22 mins While the chocolate is melting take 3 eggs and separate the yolks from the whites. You will need to have 2 mixing bowls ready. The whites bowl must be big enough to whip the whites up later. Once you have separated the eggs, set them aside.

Make sure that none of the water from the saucepan splashes into the chocolate, as this can make the chocolate become hard.

If you are nervous about separating the eggs, see handy Tip 8, pxix for an easy method.

16 mins Test the rice by biting into a grain to see if it is soft. If cooked, drain the rice in a colander and pour some warm water through it to remove any excess starch. Leave it to drain.

14 mins Check the chicken. If a leg comes away easily and is not red inside, it is cooked. Turn off the heat and remove the chicken from the liquid using a carving fork or 2 large spoons. Place on a large plate or in a roasting tin and leave to cool. Remember, undercooked chicken can be a health hazard, so be on the side of caution and overcook it rather than undercook.

Be very careful when removing the chicken from the saucepan, as it will be boiling hot and could burn you.

12 mins Once the chocolate has melted to a smooth paste, remove the bowl from the saucepan. Be careful not to burn yourself on the steam. Add a knob of butter or margarine to the chocolate, stir well and leave to cool.

10 mins Beat the egg whites with a balloon whisk or a hand-held electric mixer until they become stiff and hold their own shape, i.e. they stand in peaks on their own.

6 mins It is now time to put the whole mousse together. Carefully add the egg yolks to the melted chocolate and beat well. Then pour the chocolate into the whisked egg whites and fold the mixture together, trying to keep as much air as possible in the mixture. Do not beat. Add 2–3 drops of vanilla essence and stir carefully.

Make sure you add the chocolate to the egg whites in the larger bowl, so you have room to fold the mixture thoroughly.

2 mins When all the egg white has disappeared and you are sure that all the ingredients are well mixed, pour the mousse into individual ramekins or into a medium-sized serving bowl. Chill in the fridge until required. If the mousse is going to sit in the fridge for a long time, cover it with clingfilm.

Do not make the individual mousses too big as they are extremely rich.

0 mins Wash up and clear away.

Boning the chicken

Set your timer for 30 minutes. This is how long it will take to remove the flesh from the chicken and to finish off the sauce.

30 mins Remove all the chicken skin and discard it. Carefully cut the flesh off the chicken. Chop it into bite-sized pieces so that your guests can eat it with a fork. Once you have de-boned the chicken, you can use the carcass to make stock. Put the bones back in the pan of liquid that the chicken cooked in. Turn the heat on low and cook the bones for approximately 40 minutes. At the end of this time you will have a good home-made stock. If, however, you do not want to make stock, simply discard the bones.

15 mins Place the chicken pieces in a bowl ready to be mixed with the sauce.

12 mins Take the coronation sauce, which should be cool by now, and pour it into a mixing bowl. Discard the bay leaves. Measure out 4 tablespoons of mayonnaise and add it to the sauce. Mix well and check the seasoning, adding extra salt or pepper as required. Mix all the chicken into the sauce and stir well. Cover the bowl and place in the fridge to chill and soak up all the flavours.

2 mins Place the cooked rice in a bowl, cover it and place in the fridge. The sweetcorn and peas will be added just before serving.

0 mins Wash up and clear away.

Relax

Have a break for as long as you like, depending on your timing and arrangements. The chicken and chocolate mousse are complete, so you have only the starter and salads left to make. They can either be made in advance or a few hours before serving.

Welcome back

Feeling better after your break?

Preparation time: 40 minutes
Cooking time: 10–15 minutes

Assemble all the ingredients and equipment needed for the starter. Set your timer for 40 minutes.

40 mins Take the smoked haddock and, if it still has its skin on, remove it, using a sharp knife. Start at the tail end and lift the skin with the knife. Hold the skin in one

Make sure that there are no bones among the chicken pieces.

Stock can be easily made from the chicken bones. It can be frozen or used for a sauce or casserole within the next few days.

If you like a rather spicy chicken, add some extra curry powder or paste, but be careful not to overspice the sauce.

PROBLEMS AND HANDY TIPS

Cover your chopping board with clingfilm to protect it from absorbing the smell of the fish.

hand and with the knife, make a gentle sawing action towards the head end of the fish. The skin should come away easily. If you come across any bones, discard them. Throw the skin away and place the fish in a medium-sized saucepan – it may need to be cut in half if it is too big for the pan.

35 mins Pour 300ml (½ pint) of cold milk over the fish and put on a low heat. Add a little ground black pepper, half cover with a lid and cook slowly for 10–15 minutes.

32 mins While waiting for the fish to cook, take the lemon and cut it in half lengthways. Cut 1 half into 4 wedges and set aside to use later. Squeeze the other half over a lemon squeezer.

28 mins Pour the juice into a very small saucepan and add 1 tablespoon of cold water. Measure out 1 level dessertspoon of gelatine and sprinkle it over the liquid in the pan. Leave to stand.

23 mins The fish should now be cooked. Pour the milk into a measuring jug, using a fine sieve to catch the fish. Leave the fish to stand as it will be very hot. Meanwhile, make a white sauce to go with the fish.

21 mins Take 25g/1oz (1 tablespoon) of cooking margarine, place it in the saucepan previously used to cook the fish and put over a low heat to melt. When the margarine has melted, turn the heat off and add 25g/1oz (1 tablespoon) plain flour and stir well. Put back over a low heat and cook for 2 minutes to remove the starchy flavour. Remove from the heat and leave to stand.

16 mins Make the hot milk from the fish up to 300ml (½ pint) by adding extra cold milk, if necessary.

14 mins Slowly add the milk to the flour and margarine, stirring all the time so that no lumps form. Once all the liquid has been added, put the sauce over a very low heat, and slowly bring to the boil, stirring constantly. When the sauce thickens, allow to boil for several minutes. Stir well and season with ground black pepper (no salt, as the smoked haddock is already very salty). Allow to simmer for a further 5 minutes.

10 mins Meanwhile, take the now cooled haddock and remove any bones. Turn the sauce off and add the fish, stirring well. Set aside.

7 mins Take the gelatine in the saucepan, which should now look like a thin jelly, and dissolve it over a very low heat. Do not let the gelatine get too hot as it will lose its setting properties and therefore be no good for the recipe. The best way of ensuring this doesn't happen is to stir the

If the fish is very fresh the skin might come off by pulling it hard and prizing it off along the body; this is the simplest method.

Make sure you measure the gelatine well: too much will give a very stiff mousse, and too little will give a runny consistency.

Do not allow the flour and margarine to get too hot or to change colour.

Make sure you add all the liquid to the flour and margarine very slowly, stirring all the time. Remember, this should be done off the heat.

If the sauce becomes lumpy, stop adding the milk and beat the mixture well. Continue to add the liquid very slowly. If the sauce is really lumpy, you might have to sieve it before bringing it to the boil.

gelatine with a clean finger. When your finger gets too hot, turn the heat off.

4 mins Once the gelatine is clear and smooth, remove it from the heat and pour it straight into the haddock and white sauce mixture. Stir well and adjust the seasoning to suit your taste; you might need to add more lemon juice or black pepper.

2 mins Add 2 tablespoons of mayonnaise to the haddock mixture and stir well. Pour the mousse into a serving dish and place it in the fridge to set for at least 2 hours.

0 mins Wash up and clear away.

You can now decide what kind of mousse you would like, either smooth or coarse. For a smooth mousse you will need to break down the fish with a spoon or fork. For a coarse consistency leave it as it is.

Last-minute tasks

Assemble all the ingredients and equipment you need for the salads and fruit. Set your timer for 40 minutes. These preparations can be done a few hours before the buffet party begins and do not have to wait until the last moment.

40 mins Fill the kettle and put it on to boil.

38 mins Top and tail the French beans, then place them in a saucepan ready to cook.

The fresh fruit needs to be washed under cold running water and left to drain.

30 mins Cover the beans with boiling water, add a pinch of salt and place them on a medium heat to cook.

28 mins Open the tins of kidney beans and butter beans, drain in a colander and rinse with cold water. Place the beans in a salad bowl. Mix together well.

25 mins Wash the tomatoes under cold water, then slice them as thinly as possible and place in a serving dish. Wash the bunch of chives, pat dry and using a sharp pair of scissors, snip them on top of the tomatoes.

20 mins Shake the ready-made French dressing and spoon 4 tablespoons of it over the tomatoes. Cover the dish and place it in the fridge until required.

If you haven't made a French dressing and would like to, turn to page 196 for details. Alternatively use a bought dressing instead.

17 mins Check the French beans. They should be crunchy, not soft and overcooked. Drain the beans and run some cold water over them to stop them cooking and help them cool down more quickly. Leave to stand.

14 mins Take the rice out of the fridge. Open the tin of sweetcorn and drain it through a sieve. Discard the liquid and mix the corn into the rice. Measure out 100g (4oz) of frozen peas and put them in a saucepan. Add a pinch of salt and 1 teaspoon of sugar, add just enough boiling water to cover, and cook the peas on a medium heat for approximately 5 minutes.

If you add a teaspoon of sugar to the peas, it gives them a fresher, sweeter taste.

12 mins Take the strawberries, or whatever fruit you are using, place them in a colander, and wash them well under cold running water. Remove the stalks and place the strawberries in a serving dish or bowl. They will be served alongside the chocolate mousse, just as they are.

9 mins Turn off the peas and drain them through a colander. Pour some cold water over them to stop them cooking and leave to drain.

7 mins Finish off the bean salad. Add the French beans to the other beans already in the salad bowl and mix well. Take the French dressing and place 150ml (¼ pint) in a bowl, add 50g (2oz) of natural yogurt and mix well. Pour the mixture all over the beans. Toss well, cover and set aside until you are ready to serve.

The beans need to be well mixed. Toss them well in the dressing and place in the fridge to chill until required.

4 mins Add the peas to the rice and corn and stir well. The rice salad is now finished. Cover it and set aside ready to serve with the main course.

Make sure your rice salad is well mixed; the corn and peas add colour.

2 mins Everything is now finished. Don't forget to put the brown rolls and butter on the table to serve with the Haddock Mousse.

0 mins Wash up and clear away.

Garnishes and Watch points

Before serving, you need to garnish the food.

Top the starter with a sprig of parsley placed in the middle of the serving bowl. The lemon wedges should be placed around the outside of the dish or on a separate plate.

Remember that colour and freshness are very important in garnishes. Choose unblemished watercress, and add a slice of tomato, if you like, for a little extra colour.

The Coronation Chicken should be spread out along a platter with a bunch of watercress placed at one end.

The various salads are served as they are; no extras need to be added.

The chocolate mousse could be garnished with either a few fresh strawberries or some flaked almonds, or anything else you feel appropriate. Serve extra cream and sugar with the strawberries, and some wafer biscuits.

As this menu is for a buffet, you can serve the chocolate mousse, strawberries and cheese and biscuits at the same time.

Cheese and biscuits can be served at the same time as the dessert, or after it.

MENU

19

All season menu
Moderately difficult to prepare and cook
Cost level: inexpensive
Serves: 4

A 40-minute break is incorporated in this menu.

Starter　Avocado and prawn salad with brown rolls and butter

Preparation time = 15 minutes
Cooking time = None

Main course　Sweet and sour meatloaf
Baked potatoes with sour cream
Fresh broccoli

Preparation time = 35 minutes
Cooking time = 80 minutes

Dessert　Apple and pear tumble with fresh cream

Preparation time = 35 minutes
Cooking time = 35 minutes

This menu is quick to prepare; it is also quite filling, so would suit hungry young friends. This is a good winter menu which involves very few last-minute tasks. Most dishes can be taken straight from the oven to the table, cutting down on time and energy.

The starter needs a French dressing, which can either be homemade or bought. If you want to make it yourself, turn to page 196 for instructions. Remember that the French dressing is best made in advance. See also Handy Tip 12 on page xx for an easy way of ripening avocados in advance.

The meatloaf, cooked in the oven, has a rich and spicy sauce which keeps it moist and tender.

The dessert can be made in advance and warmed through in the oven while you are eating the starter and main course.

If you are using frozen prawns, don't forget to defrost them at room temperature either the night before or 2 hours before using them.

Equipment needed – **Menu 19**

Starter

1 savoury chopping board
1 sharp knife
2 small mixing bowls
1 fine sieve
1 measuring jug
1 small mixing bowl
1 lemon squeezer
1 tablespoon

Main course

1 savoury chopping board
1 sharp knife
1 large mixing bowl
1 tablespoon
1 deep-sided roasting tin 30×20cm
    (12×8 inches)
1 garlic crusher (or see Handy Tip 4,
    pxviii)
1 small saucepan
1 medium-sized saucepan
1 savoury wooden spoon

Dessert

1 grater
1 medium-sized bowl
1 sharp knife
1 lemon squeezer
1 potato peeler
1 sweet chopping board
1 tablespoon
1 ovenproof dish, preferably glass
1 small saucepan

Shopping list – **Menu 19**

Starter

4 cherry tomatoes
¼ iceberg lettuce
½ green pepper
½ red pepper
250g (8oz) peeled prawns
★150ml (¼ pint) French dressing
50g (2oz) natural yogurt
1 lemon
1 ripe avocado (see Handy Tip 12, pxx)
★salt and pepper
4 brown rolls
★100g (4oz) butter

Main course

★1 large onion
★2 slices brown bread
900g (2lb) minced beef
★1 egg
★salt and ground pepper
★1 tablespoon mixed herbs
★4 tablespoons white wine vinegar
★4 tablespoons tomato purée
★3 tablespoons Worcestershire sauce
★4 tablespoons chutney
★3 teaspoons French mustard
★4 tablespoons brown sugar
★3 cloves garlic (optional)
300ml (½ pint) dry cider
4 large potatoes for baking
100g (4oz) sour cream
900g (2lb) broccoli or other green vegetable

Dessert

1 lemon
2 large cooking apples
2 Williams or Conference pears
★4 slices brown bread
★100g (4oz) demerara sugar
★100g (4oz) sultanas
50g (2oz) ground almonds
★75g (3oz) butter or margarine
★pinch cinnamon
300ml (½ pint) single cream for serving

★Check store cupboard

Countdown – **Menu 19**

If you want to prepare and cook the whole menu, you need 145 minutes, which includes a 40-minute break. If you are a slow cook, add 5–10 minutes to each course to ensure that you don't run out of time. Remember that the times given are only a guide, as each cook will take different lengths of time to complete each task. The starter is served cold and, apart from the avocados which discolour, can be prepared in advance. The dessert can also be prepared in advance and warmed through before serving. The main course is cooked in the oven, which gives you time to relax before serving.

Don't forget, if you are using frozen prawns, they must be defrosted for at least 2 hours before you are going to use them.

Starter

Preparation time: 15 minutes
Cooking time: None

Assemble all the ingredients and equipment you need for the starter. Set your timer for 15 minutes.

15 mins Wash the cherry tomatoes and the iceberg lettuce in cold water. Cut the tomatoes in half and shred the lettuce into small pieces so that it can be easily eaten with a teaspoon or a small fish knife and fork.

12 mins Take the green and red peppers, cut them in half lengthways and discard the stalks and pips. Wash them under cold running water, slice them into bite-sized pieces and set aside in a bowl.

8 mins Take the defrosted prawns, place them in a fine sieve and rinse them under cold running water. Leave to drain.

7 mins Measure out 150ml (¼ pint) of French dressing. (See page 196 if you want to make your own dressing; for the best results it should be made in advance.) Mix the dressing in a bowl with 50g/2oz (2 tablespoons) natural yogurt. Leave to chill until required.

5 mins Take the lemon and cut it in half lengthways. Cut half into 4 wedges to serve with the salad; squeeze the other half and keep the juice to pour over the prawns and lettuce later.

3 mins You can now combine all the starter ingredients, except the avocado which should be peeled and chopped

PROBLEMS AND HANDY TIPS

Use very cold water to freshen up the iceberg lettuce if it looks rather limp.

Washing the peppers under cold running water will help remove all the tiny seeds stuck inside.

Avocados discolour, so they must be prepared at the last minute.

at the last moment. Mix the peppers, prawns, tomatoes and lettuce, add the lemon juice and toss well. Season with salt and pepper to taste.

0 mins Wash up and clear away.

Dessert

Preparation time: 35 minutes
Cooking time: 35 minutes

This dessert can be made in advance and left to chill in the fridge overnight, or cooked after the meatloaf on the night itself. The dessert will need warming through before serving. Assemble all the ingredients and equipment you need for the dessert. Preheat the oven to 200°C/400°F/Gas mark 6 if you want to cook the dessert in advance. Set your timer for 35 minutes.

35 mins Take 1 lemon, wash it well under cold water and dry it. Roll the lemon under the palm of your hand on a work surface to release the flesh. Grate the lemon rind on a fine grater into a bowl. Use a knife to scrape all the rind off the grater into the bowl.

Make sure you grate only the yellow rind and not the white pith, which can be bitter.

30 mins Cut the lemon in half and squeeze out all the juice using a lemon squeezer. Add the juice to the bowl with the rind. Take the apples and pears, peel and quarter them, discard the core and cut the fruit into bite-sized pieces.

If you think the pears are too hard, don't worry – they will soften during cooking.

25 mins Place the apples and pears in the bowl of the lemon juice and stir well so that the fruit is well coated. This will prevent it discolouring.

15 mins Break the 4 pieces of brown bread into small pieces and place in the bowl with the fruit.

12 mins Measure out 100g (4oz) demerara sugar, 100g (4oz) sultanas, 50g (2oz) ground almonds and put all these ingredients into the bowl with the fruit and the bread. Mix well.

Don't worry too much how large you cut up the apples and pears. What matters is that all the pieces are roughly the same size so that they cook evenly. Try to cut each fruit into at least 8 pieces.

10 mins Take 75g (3oz) of butter or margarine and melt it in a saucepan (or in a microwave if you have one). Use some of the melted butter or margarine to grease a medium-size ovenproof dish; this prevents the apple and pear mixture from sticking to it. Add the remaining butter or margarine to the apple and pear mixture in the bowl and mix well.

The breadcrumbs will soak up the butter or margarine, adding extra flavour to the dish.

The mixture should at least half fill the ovenproof dish, but will shrink during cooking.

7 mins Spoon the mixture into the greased dish, pressing it into the corners and lightly smoothing it out. (Don't press too hard.) Lastly, take a good pinch of cinnamon and sprinkle it all over the top of the 'tumble'.

1 min The 'tumble' can either be cooked now, allowed to cool then reheated just before serving, or set aside covered in the fridge and cooked just before serving the main course. It will need 35 minutes in a preheated oven.

0 mins Wash up and clear away.

Main course

PROBLEMS AND HANDY TIPS

Preparation time: 35 minutes
Cooking time: 80 minutes

Assemble all the ingredients and equipment you need for the main course. Preheat the oven to 200°C/400°F/Gas mark 6. Set your timer for 35 minutes.

35 mins Soak the baking potatoes for a few minutes in warm water to loosen any soil stuck to them. Peel and chop 1 large onion as finely as possible, then place it in a large mixing bowl.

Specially prepared baking potatoes need little or no washing.

The onion needs to be chopped as fine as possible.

27 mins Break bread up into small pieces and place it in the bowl with the onion. Mix in the 900g (2lb) of minced meat; this is best done with your hands, but can be done with a wooden spoon if you prefer.

20 mins Break 1 egg into the bowl of meat, add a pinch of salt, some ground pepper and 1 tablespoon of mixed herbs and mix well. Form the mixture into a large ball and set aside.

You must mix the ingredients together very well. If the meat keeps falling apart, it is usually due to the egg not being mixed in well enough. Return the mixture to the bowl and work it really well until it comes back together again and holds its shape.

18 mins Finish washing the potatoes and dry them. Using a sharp knife, make a shallow cut all the way round each potato; this helps them to cook more evenly.

16 mins Put the potatoes straight on to the middle shelf of the oven. (The top shelf will be used for the meatloaf.)

As the potatoes start to cook, they open up, which makes it easier to fill them later on.

15 mins Scatter 1 tablespoon of plain flour on a clean work surface, take the ball of meat out of the mixing bowl and place it on the flour. Flour your hands well so that they do not stick to the meat and pat the mixture into a loaf shape approx. 25×10×10cm (10×4×4 inches). Make sure the meatloaf will fit into your roasting tin and that there will be enough room around it for the sauce – at least 1.5cm (½ inch).

The mixture should be quite firm.

12 mins Once you are happy with the size of the meatloaf, put it in the roasting tin and cook at the top of the preheated oven while you prepare the sauce.

10 mins Place the 4 tablespoons of white wine vinegar, 4 tablespoons of tomato purée, 3 tablespoons of Worcestershire sauce, 4 tablespoons of chutney, 3 heaped teaspoons

If the meatloaf falls apart when you try to move it into the tin, make the loaf in the tin itself, which means that you don't have to move it again. The meat will stick together again once it starts to cook.

of French mustard, 4 tablespoons of brown sugar, 3 cloves, crushed garlic, if using, and 300ml (½ pint) dry cider in a saucepan.

4 mins Stir all the ingredients together really well and leave them to come to the boil. Once the sauce is boiling, turn the heat down and simmer for 3–4 minutes.

3 mins While the sauce is simmering, wash and cut the broccoli into sprigs and place them in a saucepan ready to cook later.

Make sure the broccoli sprigs are all roughly the same size so that they cook evenly.

1 min Take the meatloaf out of the oven and pour the sweet and sour sauce all over it. You should end up with most of the sauce around the meatloaf. Return to the oven and cook for a further 60 minutes.

If you have too much sauce for the tin, add the remainder half way through the cooking time, when the meatloaf has shrunk a bit.

0 mins Wash up and clear away.

Relax

Have a 40–minute break. Take your timer with you. When you return you will cook the dessert, if you haven't done so already, and finish preparing the starter and main course.

Welcome Back

Feeling better after your break?

Last-minute Tasks

Set your timer for 20 minutes. This is how long you need before sitting down to eat the starter.

20 mins Place the prepared dessert in the preheated oven at 190°C/375°F/Gas mark 5. If the meatloaf is still cooking, put the dessert near the bottom of the oven. Cook for 35 minutes. This dessert will not spoil if left in a warm oven once cooked; turn the oven right down or even off. (Fruit can get extremely hot, so it is always a good idea to let it cool a little before serving.)

If you do not have enough room in the oven for both the dessert and the meatloaf, you can cook the dessert after the main course comes out of the oven. You will still have enough time.

18 mins Take the butter out of the fridge and place it on the table to soften. Turn the baked potatoes over and move them down a shelf if they are getting too brown. Check the meatloaf and spoon some of the sauce over it to keep it moist.

Remember to spoon the sauce over the meat at regular intervals so that it remains moist and does not dry out.

16 mins Take the avocado, cut it in half and discard the stone. Peel off the skin; a ripe avocado will peel easily. Cut the flesh into small chunks and mix them together with all the other salad ingredients. If you have the facility, put the

If the avocado is rock hard, make the salad without it. If you cannot remove the stone or peel, the fruit is not ripe enough to use and would be best left out.

rown rolls into a warming oven to heat through.

mins Stir the yogurt dressing, then spoon it over the alad, toss well and place a portion in each serving bowl. ou can pour the dressing over the salad before serving as his enhances the flavours; it also means you can have the alad finished in advance. Be sure to cover the avocado vell with the dressing, or it will discolour.

mins The starter is now ready to serve. Depending on he time, either put the starter on the table ready to serve r into the fridge until required.

mins Fill the kettle and put it on to boil for the roccoli.

mins Put the sour cream into a bowl or jug, ready to erve with the main course.

mins Test the dessert before sitting down to eat the tarter: push a sharp knife into several pieces of apple or ear; if it enters easily and comes out clean, the dessert is ooked. If this is not the case, return the 'tumble' to the ven and cook further.

min Pour the boiling water over the broccoli and put it n a very low heat to cook for about 5 minutes.

mins Reset your timer for 10 minutes as a reminder of vhen the broccoli and meatloaf are cooked. Wash up and lear away.

Watch points

Once the meal has started, it is difficult to predict how ong each course will take. The following instructions are ;iven only as a guide.

'ut the main course plates and dessert bowls in to warm if ou have the facility.

Now serve the starter with lemon wedges, brown rolls nd butter. If you have warmed the brown rolls, take hem out of the oven and place them on the table with the utter.

Drain the broccoli, place it in a serving dish and put it on he table. When you are ready to eat the main course, emove the baked potatoes from the oven and put them in bowl or basket lined with a napkin. Place the potatoes nd the sour cream on the table.

The 'tumble' should now be cooked, so turn the oven

If you cannot peel the avocado but feel it is ripe enough to use, scoop out the flesh with a teaspoon. Make the pieces quite small so that everyone has some in the salad.

If the 'tumble' is cooked, turn the oven right down to keep just warm.

The meatloaf and potatoes will sit quite happily in a warm oven without spoiling.

down low to keep it warm whilst you eat the main course.

Take the meatloaf out of the oven and cut it into 1.5cm (½ inch) slices. Serve a slice to each person with some of the sweet and sour sauce. Put some extra sauce on the table in a gravy boat if you wish.

There is no hurry to finish the main course at the dessert will not spoil in the oven. Don't forget to serve the dessert with fresh cream.

Cocktail or drinks party menu

Difficult to prepare and cook
Cost level: good value
Serves: 12

There is no break incorporated in this menu.

Dips	Avocado dip or blue cheese dip with crudités	Preparation time = 50 minutes Cooking time = None
Cold canapes	Smoked salmon rolls Asparagus rolls Ham and cream cheese rolls	Preparation time = 50 minutes Cooking time = None
Hot canapes	Devils on horseback Honey-roast cocktail sausages Chicken nuggets with mayonnaise	Preparation time = 35 minutes Cooking time = 20–30 minutes

Here are some recipes and ideas for a cocktail party. It is not necessary to do them all; you can make one dip, 2 or 3 cold canapés and 2 or 3 hot canapés, depending on how much time and money you have available and how many guests have been invited. Remember, many of these snacks can be made in advance.

The cold canapés will benefit from being made the day before. Check the countdown instructions to see what would suit the time available. Remember, you can always mix bought things with home-made to fill out the menu. Buy some pâté and biscuits or French bread, plus crisps and nuts as fillers.

Crudités are raw vegetables which have been cut into slices or sticks so you can dunk them into a dip.

Ready-made canapés, such as sausage rolls and mini pizzas, are widely available and useful if you anticipate a lot of hungry guests.

The recipes are for 12 people, which means you can easily double or halve the amounts depending on the number of guests you are expecting. Check your budget carefully as salmon can be very expensive, and you will have to buy a lot of drinks for 12 people.

Finger food can be messy to eat, so don't forget to buy cocktail sticks and napkins.

Equipment needed – **Menu 20**

Dips

1 savoury chopping board
1 small sharp knife
1 medium mixing bowl
1 teaspoon
1 food processor, blender or fork
1 savoury wooden spoon
1 tablespoon
1 plastic spatula
1 platter or tray for the crudités

Cold canapes

greaseproof paper
1 sharp knife
1 large roasting tin or deep baking tray
1 savoury chopping board
1 round-ended knife
1 lemon squeezer
1 pastry brush or teaspoon
1 tin opener
1 fine sieve
clingfilm

Hot canapes

1 tin opener
1 fine sieve
1 pair scissors
1 savoury chopping board
1 sharp knife
1 grill and grill pan
2 roasting tins or deep baking trays
1 mixing bowl
1 tablespoon
1 plate
Kitchen paper
Cocktail sticks
Napkins
Cling film
Tin foil

*Check store cupboard

Shopping list – **Menu 20**

Dips

Avocado Dip
    ★1 small onion
    1 ripe avocado
    225g (8oz) soft cream cheese
    225g (8oz) cottage cheese
    ★3 teaspoons lemon juice
    ★3 tablespoons mayonnaise
    ★salt and ground black pepper
    parsley to garnish
Blue Cheese Dip
    225g (8oz) blue cheese, such as Danish blue or
        Stilton
    100g (4oz) cream cheese
    100g (4oz) sour cream
    ★1 tablespoon port (optional)
Crudités
    fresh vegetables, such as carrots, celery and
        cauliflower, for crudités
    tortilla chips (optional)
    Assorted crisps and nuts

Cold canapes

Smoked Salmon Rolls
    225g (8oz) sliced smoked salmon
    6 slices brown bread
    ★100g (4oz) butter
    1 lemon
    ★ground black pepper
Asparagus Rolls
    175g (6oz) tin asparagus tips
    8 slices brown bread
    ★4 tablespoons mayonnaise
Ham and Cream Cheese Rolls
    8 slices honey-roast ham
    100g (4oz) packet cream cheese flavoured with
        garlic and herbs
Garnishes
    1 bunch watercress or parsley
    12 cherry tomatoes

Hot canapes

24 cocktail sausages (frozen or fresh)
★2 tablespoons clear honey
★2 tablespoons mango chutney
8 slices streaky bacon
1 225g (8oz) tin prunes
24 chicken nuggets (frozen or fresh)
1 bunch fresh chives or parsley
★225g (8oz) mayonnaise
★1 teaspoon lemon juice
★salt and pepper

Countdown –**Menu 20**

Canapés can be very time-consuming to make, so choose carefully and keep in mind your budget. If you are a slow cook, add 5–10 minutes to each course to ensure you don't run out of time. Remember, the times given are only a guide, as each cook will take different lengths of time to complete each task. Make as much as possible the day or evening before to give yourself enough time on the night to finish off all the last-minute tasks.

Smoked Salmon Rolls

PROBLEMS AND HANDY TIPS

Preparation time: 20 minutes
Cooking time: None

All the rolls are best made in advance, either the day or night before. Place them in a tin tightly packed together, and chill them in the fridge for a minimum of 8 hours. One piece of bread should make 4 rolls (allow 2 rolls per person).

Be careful if you are using an old roasting tin as it might be rusty and discolour the rolls. Wash and dry it well.

Assemble the ingredients and equipment you need for the rolls. Set your timer for 20 minutes.

20 mins Allow the salmon to 'breathe' before using it, i.e. put it on a plate and set aside.

8 mins Take a sheet of greaseproof paper and fold it into 18cm (7 inch) strips, making an accordion shape. Then, using a sharp knife, cut along the creases. Cut these strips in half again to double the quantity. Make 16 pieces in all (enough to do the asparagus rolls as well).

If you are confused over measuring the paper, just cut some strips that will be large enough to fit the length of each roll. Place the paper in the water bath.

15 mins Place all the paper in a roasting tin, pour some warm water over it and allow it to soak.

14 mins Arrange 8 slices of bread on a chopping board. Spread evenly with butter. If the butter is very hard, soften it in a microwave or by placing it in a bowl and beating it with a wooden spoon. Stack the bread butter side up and cut off all the crusts.

The bread needs to be as fresh as possible, or you will have problems rolling it up. Freezing it overnight and defrosting it for a few hours before making the rolls makes it easier to use.

10 mins Spread the bread out again and cover each piece with slices of smoked salmon. (Make sure you have enough salmon for all the bread.)

4 mins Take 1 lemon and roll it under the palm of your hand on a work surface to release the flesh inside. Cut the lemon in half and squeeze one half over a lemon squeezer. Using a pastry brush, if you have one, brush a small

If you don't have a pastry brush, use a teaspoon, but be careful not to use too much lemon juice.

amount of lemon juice over the salmon, then grind some fresh black pepper over the top. (Do not use too much pepper.) Cut the other half of lemon into thin wedges to be served alongside the finished salmon rolls.

2 mins Take 1 piece of the wet greaseproof paper and pat dry with kitchen paper so that it is only damp. Roll up a slice of bread and salmon as tightly as possible, then roll it up in the damp greaseproof paper. Prepare all the rolls in this way, then place in a roasting tin or a baking tray. Make sure you pack them tightly together; this will ensure that they hold their shape.

0 mins Cover and chill the rolls for at least 8 hours or overnight. Wash up and clear away.

Make sure you don't roll the greaseproof paper inside the salmon rolls. It must be rolled around the bread.

Asparagus Rolls

Preparation time: 20 minutes
Cooking time: None

These rolls are best made the day before the party, as they need to be well chilled. One piece of bread should make 3 rolls. Allow 2 rolls per person. Make them at the same time as the smoked salmon rolls to save time.

Assemble all the ingredients and equipment needed to make the asparagus rolls. Set your timer for 20 minutes.

20 mins Open the tin of asparagus, discard the liquid and leave the asparagus to drain in a sieve.

18 mins Prepare some greaseproof paper as described in the recipe for smoked salmon rolls.

12 mins Arrange 8 slice of bread on a chopping board. Spread each slice with approximately ½ a tablespoon of mayonnaise.

8 mins Stack the bread mayonnaise up and cut off all the crusts.

6 mins Take a piece of wet greaseproof paper and pat dry on kitchen paper so that it is only damp. Place a slice of bread on the greaseproof paper. Place 1 or 2 pieces of asparagus at one end of the bread, than roll up the bread from that end. Hold the asparagus tightly, so that it remains in the same place. Roll the greaseproof paper around the asparagus roll as tightly as possible. (You will find you get better the more you do.) Prepare all the rolls in this way, then place in a roasting tin or on a baking tray. Pack them firmly together to ensure that they hold their shape.

0 mins Wash up and clear away.

Some asparagus spears or tips are large and thick, whereas others are very thin. If they are too thin, it will be necessary to use 2 in each roll.

Make sure you don't roll the greaseproof paper inside the asparagus rolls. It must be rolled around the bread.

If your first attempts at making the rolls are not very successful, unroll them and try again as your technique improves.

Ham and Cream Cheese with Garlic Rolls

Preparation time: 10 minutes
Cooking time: None

These are best made in advance, at least 8 hours before being served. They will benefit from being packed tightly together in a tin and chilled in the fridge. The cream cheese should be allowed to reach room temperature before use, as this makes it easier to spread over the ham. The quantities given will make 24–32 rolls, depending on their size.

If the ham is rather wet, pat it dry on kitchen paper to remove some of the excess moisture, otherwise spreading the cream cheese can prove difficult.

10 mins Arrange the 8 slices of ham on a chopping board. Using a round-ended knife, spread the cream cheese thinly over the ham, making sure you go right to the edges. Roll up each slice of ham and set them seam side down so that they can't unroll.

5 mins Take some clingfilm and wrap up each ham and cream cheese roll separately. Pack them tightly into a tin alongside or on top of the salmon and/or asparagus rolls, and chill overnight.

Make sure you seal the ends of the clingfilm around the rolls to prevent them from drying out.

0 mins Wash up and clear away.

Serving the cold canapés

Take the rolls out of the fridge and carefully unwrap them, discarding the greaseproof paper and clingfilm. Place the rolls on a clean, dry chopping board. Cut the smoked salmon rolls and the ham and cream cheese rolls into 4 slices, and the asparagus rolls into 3 slices. Arrange all the slices on a platter so that the spirals of filling can be seen, and garnish with sprigs of watercress, cherry tomatoes and lemon wedges. Cover with clingfilm to keep moist if you are not serving immediately.

Use a very sharp knife to cut up the rolls. This will prevent them from falling apart or the filling spilling out.

Avocado Dip

Preparation time: 20 minutes
Cooking time: None

This dip is best made in advance to give the ingredients time to settle and chill. Make it the day before or at least a few hours before the party. The vegetables to accompany the dip should be prepared at the last minute to keep them fresh.

Assemble all the ingredients and equipment you need for the dip. Set your timer for 20 minutes. If you use a food processor or blender, you will need only 15 minutes.

20 mins Peel 1 small onion and chop it as finely as possible. Place it in a mixing bowl or food processor.

12 mins Cut 1 ripe avocado in half lengthways and discard the stone. Spoon the flesh into the mixing bowl or food processor.

8 mins Process the avocado, or mash it with a fork, until it becomes a fine paste. Add the 225g (8oz) of cream cheese and mix well, then add 225g (8oz) of cottage cheese and beat using a wooden spoon if working by hand.

5 mins Mix in 3 teaspoons of lemon juice, 3 tablespoons of mayonnaise and season well with salt and fresh black pepper. Taste and adjust the seasoning, if necessary. Place the avocado dip in a glass or china bowl, cover with clingfilm and chill until required.

0 mins Wash up and clear away.

When you come to serve the avocado dip you might find that the top has become discoloured. This is quite normal – the result of the avocado being exposed to the air. Stirring it just before serving will give it a fresh appearance.

Blue Cheese Dip

Preparation time: 10 minutes
Cooking time: None

This dip is best made in advance to give the ingredients time to settle and chill. Make it either the day before or at least a few hours before needed. The vegetables to accompany the dip should be prepared at the last minute to keep them fresh.

Assemble all the ingredients and equipment you need for the dip. Set your timer for 10 minutes. If you use a food processor or blender, you will need only 5 minutes.

10 mins Place 225g (8oz) of blue cheese in a bowl and break it up with a wooden spoon. Alternatively, place in a food processor and process until smooth. Mix in 100g (4oz) cream cheese, then slowly add 100g (4oz) of sour cream. If you have some port, add 1 tablespoon and mix well.

If you prefer a smooth dip, you can grate the onion instead of chopping it, or even leave the onion out.

Make sure you mix all the ingredients together really well.

The seasoning is very important. If you decide you would like a stronger flavoured dip, add a tiny amount of Tabasco sauce to give it a 'kick'.

PROBLEMS AND HANDY TIPS

The blue cheese should be well mixed with the cream cheese before you add the sour cream and port as these last 2 ingredients make the dip very thin. Add them slowly so that you keep the right consistency.

mins Once the dip is smooth and well blended, place it 1 a glass or china serving dish. Cover and chill until equired.

mins Wash up and clear away.

Devils on Horseback

Preparation time: 15 minutes
Cooking time: 10 minutes

PROBLEMS AND HANDY TIPS

These should be prepared and cooked on the day they are needed. You can prepare them early, but cook them just efore your guests arrive, as they tend to dry out.

Assemble all the ingredients and equipment you need. Set our timer for 15 minutes.

5 mins Open the tin of prunes, drain them through a ne sieve and set aside.

3 mins Take 6 slices of streaky bacon and remove any ind with some scissors or a sharp knife.

mins Place the bacon on a chopping board and stretch ach slice by running a knife along it. Cut the bacon in alf widthways. Take 12 prunes and, using a sharp knife, nake a small incision and remove the stone. Take a half lice of bacon, place a prune at one end roll the bacon ightly around it. Make the other 'devils' in the same vay.

Stretching the bacon before using it helps it to shrink around the prune during cooking and thus make a strong parcel.

mins Place the finished 'devils' on a grill pan or, if you re not going to cook them immediately, put them on a late and cover and chill in the fridge until required.

mins Wash up and clear away.

Honey-roast cocktail sausages

Preparation time: 10 minutes
Cooking time: 20–30 minutes

PROBLEMS AND HANDY TIPS

The sausages should be prepared, cooked and served at nce for the best results. Preheat the oven to 200°C/ 00°F/Gas mark 6. Assemble all the ingredients and quipment you need. Set your timer for 10 minutes.

10 mins Whether you are using frozen or fresh sausages, nip them apart (if necessary) and place them in a roasting in or deep baking tray.

Cocktail sausages may be cooked from frozen. They take the same time to cook as fresh sausages.

mins Place the sausages in the oven to start cooking.

mins Take a mixing bowl and measure out

2 tablespoons of clear honey and 2 tablespoons of mango chutney. Mix together well.

2 mins Take the sausages out of the oven and pour the honey mixture all over them. Put them back into the oven to cook for 20–30 minutes.

0 mins Wash up and clear away.

Remember that the sausages might take less time to cook if they are very small and thin. Check the instructions on the packet so that they do not burn

Chicken Nuggets with Mayonnaise

PROBLEMS AND HANDY TIP

Preparation time: 10 minutes
Cooking time: 15–20 minutes

The chicken nuggets, simple to prepare and cook, are best served immediately to prevent them from drying out. They may be served just as they are, but the mayonnaise sauce is a tasty accompaniment. Preheat the oven to 200°C/400°F/Gas mark 6. Assemble all the ingredients and equipment you need. Set your timer for 10 minutes.

10 mins Place all the nuggets, frozen or fresh, in a roasting tin or deep baking tray.

Chicken nuggets can usually be cooked from frozen.

8 mins Cook the nuggets in the oven according to the packet instructions while you prepare the mayonnaise sauce.

6 mins Chop up the chives or parsley and place in a mixing bowl. Add 225g (8oz) of mayonnaise to the bowl and mix well. Add 1 teaspoon of lemon juice, if you like. Season to taste with salt and freshly ground black pepper. Mix well. Place the finished mayonnaise in a serving bowl, ready for your guests to dip the chicken nuggets in to.

0 mins Wash up and clear away.

Crudités

PROBLEMS AND HANDY TIP

Preparation time: 20 minutes
Cooking time: None

Crudités are raw vegetables prepared to serve with the dips. Set your timer for 20 minutes. If you are making the vegetables a few hours in advance of the party, place them in a bowl of cold water to keep crisp and fresh. Assemble all the ingredients and equipment you need for the crudités.

If you are having the party during the summer months it might be a good idea to add some ice cubes to the water to keep the vegetables crisp.

20 mins The carrots should be peeled and cut into thin strips approx. 2cm (2 inches) long.

13 mins The celery should be washed well and broken

into separate stalks. Cut them into 5cm (2 inch) pieces, discarding any old or damaged pieces.

8 mins The cauliflower should be washed and cut into bite-sized sprigs.

4 mins Place the finished vegetables in a bowl of cold water if you are not going to serve them immediately. Otherwise, take a large platter or tray and cover it with foil, if necessary. Place the bowl(s) of dip in the centre and arrange the crudités in small piles around the edges.

0 mins Wash up and clear away. Check the sausages and nuggets in the oven and turn them over if necessary. If they are cooked, remove them from the oven and cover with tin foil to keep warm. Once all the hot food is ready, you can turn the oven down to 150°C/300°F/Gas mark 2 and leave it to keep warm until you are ready to serve.

Now cook the devils on horseback. Set your timer for 10 minutes. Preheat the grill on a high setting.

10 mins Take the ready-prepared devils out of the fridge and place them on the grill pan. Once the grill is hot, place the devils under it and allow them to brown on one side.

5 mins After 5 minutes turn them over and cook them on the other side. They are ready to eat when the bacon has became crispy. Place them on a serving platter with some cocktail sticks so that your guests can help themselves. Remember to warn your guests that they are very hot.

Serving the hot canapés

Arrange each type of canapé on a separate platter, placing the bowl of mayonnaise in the centre of the chicken nuggets, and an eggcup containing cocktail sticks in the centre of the sausages and devils on horseback. Garnish each platter with sprigs of watercress or parsley and some cherry tomatoes to add colour.

If you are also serving ready-made sausage rolls, mini pizzas or vol-au-vents, cook them according to the instructions on the packets and arrange them on platters with any garnishes you may have.

Keep in mind the size of the vegetables; there is nothing worse than having too much vegetable and not enough dip on it!

The time the 'devils' take to cook depends on how hot the grill is and on the thickness of the bacon. They devils should be crisp and golden brown when they are ready.

PROBLEMS AND HANDY TIPS

Remember to put out some extra nibbles such as crisps and nuts. These will help to fill out the menu.

Hungry winter menu

Difficult to prepare and cook
Cost level: good value
Serves: 4

A 30-minute break is incorporated in this menu.

| **Starter** | Chicken liver pâté with Melba toast | Preparation time = 40 minutes
Cooking time = 12 minutes |

| **Main course** | Pork fillet Normandy
Fresh green tagliatelle
Brussels sprouts | Preparation time = 45 minutes
Cooking time = 50 minutes |

| **Dessert** | Lemon cheesecake | Preparation time = 35 minutes
Cooking time = None |

This winter menu is rich and filling and needs quite a lot of preparation. The starter is a delicious pâté with a subtle orange flavour. It can be made in advance, either the night before or a few hours before serving. It should be served with Melba toast or hot toast.

The main course uses pork fillets, so do make sure that your guests eat this meat before you make this dish. The pork is cooked with apples and cider, and is extremely tender. It is best served with green tagliatelle as this gives the dish more colour.

The dessert can either be made in advance the night before, or as the first thing to prepare on the day.

Equipment needed – **Menu 21**

Starter

1 savoury chopping board
1 sharp knife
1 medium-sized saucepan with lid
1 garlic crusher (or see Handy Tip 4, pxviii)
1 savoury wooden spoon
1 fine sieve
1 lemon squeezer
1 wine glass
1 heatproof bowl
1 tablespoon
1 food processor or liquidizer (optional)

Main course

1 savoury chopping board
1 sharp knife
1 medium-size casserole dish with lid
1 savoury wooden spoon
1 potato peeler
1 measuring jug
1 frying pan
2 medium saucepans

Dessert

1 small saucepan
2 mixing bowls (1 plastic)
1 rolling pin or clean bottle
1 sweet wooden spoon
1 loose-bottomed 20cm (8 inch) flan or quiche tin about 4cm (1½ inches) deep, or a deep-sided cake tin or spring release mould
1 tablespoon
1 grater (fine)
1 sharp knife
1 lemon squeezer

Shopping list – **Menu 21**

Starter

*1 onion
*2 cloves garlic
*50g (2oz) cooking margarine
450g (1lb) chicken livers
1 small orange or tangerine
*½ a glass red wine
*salt and pepper
*pinch nutmeg
2 tablespoons double cream
1 bunch parsley to garnish
*100g (4oz) butter to serve with the toast
100g (4oz) packet Melba toast

Main course

*2 onions
*62g (2½oz) cooking margarine
1 large cooking apple
300ml (½ pint) dry cider
*50g (2oz) plain flour
*1 beef stock cube OR 150ml (¼ pint) fresh stock
675–900g (1½–2lb) pork fillets
*salt and pepper
*pinch dried mustard powder
900g (2lb) Brussels sprouts
225g (8oz) dried green tagliatelle

Dessert

*75g (3oz) butter
150g (6oz) chocolate digestive biscuits
100g (4oz) cottage cheese
100g (4oz) crème fraîche
1 lemon
*50g (2oz) caster sugar
2 tablespoons double or extra thick cream
*1 level tablespoon gelatine
50g (2oz) flaked almonds to decorate

*check store cupboard

Countdown – **Menu 21**

If you want to prepare and cook the whole menu you will need 150 minutes, which includes a 30-minute break. If you are a slow cook, add 5–10 minutes to each course to ensure that you do not run out of time. Remember that the times given are only a guide, as each cook will take different lengths of time to complete each task. The starter and dessert should be made in advance, giving them time to set and chill. The main course is best made on the day and is cooked in the oven.

Dessert

Preparation time: 35 minutes
Cooking time: None

Assemble all the ingredients and equipment needed for the dessert. Set your timer for 35 minutes.

35 mins Measure out 75g (3oz) butter and place it in a small saucepan. Put over a low heat to melt. Watch the butter carefully to stop it from burning or browning.

31 mins While the butter is melting, measure out 150g (6oz) (approximately 10) chocolate digestive biscuits.

30 mins Check the butter. If it is bubbling too fast, turn it off and leave the remaining butter to melt from the heat of the pan.

29 mins Place the biscuits in a bowl (preferably plastic) and crush them using a rolling pin or a glass bottle until they resemble fine breadcrumbs. Another method is to place the biscuits in a strong plastic bag, tie it well and crush the biscuits with a rolling pin or any other suitable utensil.

26 mins Take the warm butter and mix it into the crushed biscuits with a wooden spoon. Tip the mixture into the loose bottom tin and press the biscuits flat with the back of the wooden spoon to form a base for the cheesecake. Place in the fridge to set.

21 mins Wipe out the biscuit crumbs bowl and measure 100g (4oz) of cottage cheese and of crème fraîche (approximately 4 tablespoons) of each into it. Mix together well.

17 mins Take 1 lemon and wash it well under cold running water. Dry the lemon and roll it under the palm of your hand on a work surface to release the flesh inside. Take a fine grater and grate the lemon rind straight into the bowl with the cream mixture. Make sure you grate only

PROBLEMS AND HANDY TIPS

Do not allow the butter to burn; keep it on a very low heat. If the butter does burn, it is best to discard it and start again.

A plastic bowl makes it easier to crush the biscuits and makes less noise.

If you crush the biscuits in a plastic bag, you will have to take them out of the bag and place them in a mixing bowl before adding the melted butter.

Press the biscuits down firmly to ensure a solid base, using either the back of a spoon or the end of a rolling pin or bottle.

Make sure you use only the outer yellow skin of the lemon, not the bitter white pith. If you have grated too far into the lemon, use only the rind that has fallen into the mixture and not any left on the grater.

the yellow surface of the lemon. Scrape down the grater with a knife to release all the lemon. Mix all the ingredients together well.

13 mins Measure out 50g/2oz (2 tablespoons) of caster sugar and place it in the bowl with the rest of the ingredients. Stir in 2 tablespoons of extra thick cream. (If you are using double cream, you will need to whip it first until it holds its shape.)

Do not overwhip the cream; it is best to have it thinner rather than curdled.

10 mins Cut the lemon in half and squeeze both halves over a lemon squeezer.

8 mins Wash up the small saucepan that you used for melting the butter. Pour the lemon juice into it and sprinkle 1 level tablespoon of gelatine over it. Set aside for 2 minutes to allow the gelatine to be absorbed by the lemon juice.

6 mins Meanwhile, clear up the work surface and wash any dirty utensils.

4 mins Put the pan of gelatine over a very low heat to dissolve. Do not use a spoon or any utensils. The best method to ensure that the gelatine does not overheat is to stir it with your finger. Once the liquid becomes too hot for your finger, remove the gelatine from the heat. It is ready to use once all the granules have dissolved.

If you let the gelatine get too hot, it will lose its setting properties. If the gelatine starts to boil, you will have to discard it and start again with a fresh batch.

2 mins Pour the gelatine into the cream mixture and stir vigorously.

1 mins Take the biscuit base out of the fridge and run a sharp knife around the edge to loosen it. pour the cream mixture over the biscuit base, using a plastic spatula to smooth the top. Chill until required.

0 mins Wash up and clear away.

Starter

Preparation time: 40 minutes
Cooking time: 12 minutes

PROBLEMS AND HANDY TIPS

To make your own Melba toast, follow the recipe on p193. Assemble all the ingredients and equipment you need for the starter. Set your timer for 40 minutes.

40 mins Peel and chop the onion as finely as possible and place it in a saucepan. Peel and crush 2 cloves of garlic and add them to the saucepan.

See Handy Tip 4 on page xviii for an easy way to crush garlic without a garlic crusher.

36 mins Place 50g/2oz (2 tablespoons) of cooking margarine, put over a medium heat and cook the onion and garlic slowly until they become transparent. Do not allow them to brown. Stir occasionally to stop them from

If the onion *does* brown, don't panic, as long as it has not burnt, you can still use it. If, however, it has burnt, discard it and start again.

burning. Turn heat right down. Place the chicken livers in a fine sieve and wash them well under cold running water. Leave to drain. (You do not need to remove any of the connecting tissue from the livers as they will be sieved later on.)

30 mins Take 1 small orange and roll it under the palm of your hand on a work surface to release the flesh. Cut the orange in half and squeeze both halves, setting the juice aside to be used later. Add the chicken livers to the onion and garlic, stir well and cook for 5 minutes. Be careful to ensure that the livers don't stick to the bottom of the pan. Mash the livers down as they cook, as this will save time and work later on.

25 mins Turn the heat on to low and add the orange juice and half a glass of red wine. Place the lid half on the pan and leave the livers to cook on a very low heat for a further 7 minutes. While the livers are cooking, wash up and clear away.

18 mins Turn the livers off and place them in a food processor or liquidizer, if you have one. Blend for a couple of minutes until smooth. Alternatively, take a fine sieve and place it over a heatproof bowl. Empty the livers into the sieve and work them through it using a wooden or metal spoon. (This is quite hard work.) Discard any connecting tissue or white stringy pieces you find after blending or sieving.

11 mins Take a sharp knife and run it all over the underside of the sieve so as not to waste any of the liver. Stir the sieved mixture well and season with black pepper, a pinch of salt and a pinch of nutmeg.

7 mins Check that the mixture is only warm before adding 2 tablespoons of double cream. Mix well, then spoon the pâté into 4 ramekins or 1 small serving bowl. Chill until required.

0 mins Wash up and clear away.

If the livers stick to the saucepan and start to burn, quickly take a new saucepan and salvage as much as possible, discarding any burnt pieces.

You should stop sieving the livers when you have approx. 1 tablespoon left in the sieve and you feel you can't get any more through. Discard anything left in the sieve.

Garnish the pâté with parsley before serving it.

Main course

PROBLEMS AND HANDY TIPS

Preparation time: 30 minutes
Cooking time: 50 minutes

Preheat the oven to 200°C/400°F/Gas mark 6. Assemble all the ingredients and equipment you need for the main course. Set your timer for 30 minutes.

30 mins Take 2 onions and peel and chop them roughly. Place the chopped onion in the casserole dish and add

50g/2oz (2 tablespoons) of cooking margarine. Place over a medium heat to soften the onion, stirring occaionally.

25 mins While the onion is cooking, take 1 large cooking apple and peel it. Cut the apple into quarters, remove the core, then cut each quarter lengthways into approx. 4 slices.

The apple slices should all be about the same size.

21 mins Place the sliced apple in the casserole with the onion. Cook for a further 2 minutes.

Do not allow the apple to turn to a purée, it should remain firm and in slices.

19 mins Turn the heat off and leave the apple and onion to cool down. Measure out 300ml (½ pint) of dry cider and add 150ml (¼ pint) of fresh stock to it. (Use cold water if using a stock cube.) Take 50g/2oz (2 tablespoons) of plain flour and stir it into the onion and apple mixture using a wooden spoon. Crumble the beef stock cube (if using) into the mixture and cook for a few minutes to remove the starchy taste. Turn the heat off.

16 mins Slowly add the cider and water to the pan, stirring all the time. Make sure no lumps form in the sauce. Once all the liquid has been added, place the casserole back over a low heat and bring the sauce slowly to the boil, stirring occasionally.

Add all the liquid very slowly so that the sauce does not become lumpy.

13 mins Meanwhile, melt 12g/½oz (½ tablespoon) of cooking margarine in a frying pan. When it is foaming, add the pork fillets and brown them on all sides to seal the meat. Don't forget to stir the apple and onion sauce occasionally. This should have come up to the boil by now; allow it to simmer for a few minutes.

9 mins Once the meat is brown all over (this should take no more than 4 minutes), put it in the casserole dish with the apple and onion sauce. Season with freshly ground black pepper, a pinch of salt and a good pinch of dried mustard powder. Stir well and make sure the meat is covered with the sauce.

After cooking the meat, leave as much fat as possible in the pan as you don't want a greasy sauce. The meat must be covered with the sauce or it will dry out during cooking.

2 mins Cover the casserole and place in a preheated oven to cook for 50 minutes.

Nothing will spoil in the oven if you turn it right down.

0 mins Wash up and clear away.

Relax

Have a 30-minute break. Before leaving the kitchen set your timer for 30 minutes and turn the oven down to 180°C/350°F/Gas mark 4.

Welcome back

Feeling better after your break? All that is left to do are the last-minute tasks, and then you will be ready to serve the starter.

Last-minute tasks

Set your timer for 15 minutes. This is how long you have before you serve the starter.

15 mins Fill the kettle and put it on to boil.

14 mins Check the pork in the oven, stir it well and leave it to cook.

12 mins Take a sharp knife and prepare the Brussels sprouts by cutting off a few of the outer leaves. The sprouts should look shiny and have no brown marks on them. Cut a cross on the base of each sprout, but do not cut too deeply or they will fall apart during cooking. Place the finished sprouts in a saucepan.

Do not cut too far down into the sprout otherwise it will fall apart while cooling. Cutting a cross on each Brussels sprout helps them to cook more evenly. This method really does work and improves the taste of the sprouts.

7 mins Pour the boiling water over the sprouts in the saucepan, add a pinch of salt and put them on to a medium heat to come to the boil. They will take approximately 10 minutes to cook.

6 mins Put the Melba toast on the table, or make some ordinary toast if you prefer.

5 mins Refill the kettle and put it on to boil for the tagliatelle.

4 mins Garnish the pâté with a sprig of parsley and place it on the table with the toast.

If you do not have any parsley for garnishing, you can fork the top of the pâté to make it look more attractive.

3 mins Decorate the cheesecake with a handful of flaked almonds, then put it back into the fridge until required.

If you do not have any flaked almonds for the cheesecake, use any other bits you might have in store, such as grated chocolate or lemon and orange pieces.

2 mins Place the tagliatelle in a saucepan and pour the boiling water over it. Add a pinch of salt and a knob of margarine and mix well so that the pasta is coated by the fat. Cook over a medium heat for about 3 minutes if using fresh pasta and 10 minutes if using dried. Do not allow the sprouts or pasta to boil too vigorously; turn them down so that they simmer.

Adding a knob of cooking margarine to the pasta at the beginning of the cooking time prevents the pasta from sticking together.

0 mins Wash up and clear away. It is now time to serve the starter as everything is ready.

Watch points

Once the meal has started, it is difficult to give specific timings, so the following instructions are intended only as a guide.

Serve the starter with the Melba toast or hot toast. Put some butter on the table in case anyone wants it.

Leave the Brussels sprouts and pasta on a very low heat or turn them off completely. You don't want them to over-cook while you are eating the pâté. They can both continue cooking while you clear away the starter and serve the main course.

The vegetables should be undercooked, i.e. slightly crunchy. If you are doubtful of achieving this, leave cooking the sprouts until last. They will take only a few minutes.

Take the pork out of the oven and place it on a heatproof mat. Take the pork fillets out of the casserole, place them on a chopping board and slice them diagonally into 1cm (½ inch) slices. Return the sliced meat to the casserole and stir well so that it is covered with sauce. Replace the lid to keep hot.

Take out the serving dishes for the pasta and vegetables. Check the Brussels sprouts and the pasta to see if they are cooked. Drain them if they are ready, and put them into their serving dishes. Take out the dinner plates if you haven't already done so.

You are now ready to serve the main course. Put any extra sauce on the table in a gravy boat if you like. Don't forget to turn the oven down to 140°C/275°F/Gas mark 1 if you want to keep any remaining pork hot for second helpings.

The dessert is served straight from the fridge and needs no extras. Remove the cheesecake from the tin and transfer it to a serving plate.

Summer fish menu
Difficult to prepare and cook
Cost level: expensive
Serves: 4

A 30-minute break is incorporated in this menu.

| **Starter** | Stuffed mushrooms with brown rolls | Preparation time = 25 minutes
Cooking time = 30 minutes |

| **Main course** | Baked salmon trout with hollandaise sauce or mayonnaise
New potatoes
Mixed salad with French dressing | Preparation time = 55 minutes
Cooking time = 30 minutes |

| **Dessert** | Old English trifle with cream | Preparation time = 25 minutes
Setting time = 1½ hours |

This menu would suit those who prefer not to eat meat, but who eat fish. You have the option of leaving out a course if time or money are in short supply. The starter can be made a few hours before serving. The first half of the trifle is best made the night before; this will take approximately 15 minutes and eliminate the problem of having to wait for the jelly to set.

Both the mushrooms and the fish can sit in a warm oven for 15–20 minutes without spoiling. This is a great advantage and takes the pressure off the cook if guests are late or problems arise.

You will need a French dressing for the salad and mayonnaise or hollandaise sauce for the fish. Both can be bought ready-made, but if you prefer to make your own turn to pages 196 and 195 for instructions. Don't forget, you will need extra time if you decide to make them yourself.

Make this menu during the summer months when salmon trout are readily available and not so expensive. If you try to buy a salmon during the winter months, it can prove difficult and expensive.

Equipment needed – **Menu 22**

Starter

1 colander or sieve
1 savoury chopping board
1 sharp knife
1 garlic crusher (or see Handy Tip 4, pxviii)
1 saucepan
1 savoury wooden spoon
1 grater
1 tablespoon
1 deep-sided baking tray or tin
1 teaspoon

Main course

1 large baking tray or tin
1 roll of aluminium foil
1 savoury chopping board
1 sharp knife
1 wine glass
1 lemon squeezer
1 saucepan
1 measuring jug
1 large oval serving plate
kitchen paper

Dessert

1 sharp knife
1 medium-sized glass serving bowl
1 tin opener
1 mixing bowl
1 fine sieve
1 tablespoon
1 sweet chopping board
1 measuring jug
1 electric mixer or balloon whisk
1 grater

Shopping list – **Menu 22**

Starter

16 medium-sized mushrooms
★1 small onion
★1 clove garlic (optional)
★25g (1oz) cooking margarine
100g (4oz) Cheddar cheese
★1 slice brown bread
★1 tablespoon lemon juice
100g (4oz) sour cream
★salt and pepper
★pinch nutmeg
4 brown rolls
100g (4oz) butter

Main course

1½kg (2½–3lb) salmon, gutted, head and tail still on
★50g (2oz) margarine
1 iceberg lettuce
★1 small onion
★1 glass white wine
150ml (¼ pint) French dressing
1 cucumber
4 tomatoes
★2 bay leaves
★salt and pepper
2 lemons
parsley to garnish
16 new potatoes
mint sprig (optional)
25g (1oz) packet Hollandaise sauce, or see page 195 for recipe

Dessert

4 trifle sponges
425g (15oz) tin fruit in natural juice (peaches, fruit cocktail, strawberries, etc.), or a selection of fresh fruit (avoid those with small pips)
★2 tablespoons dry sherry
425g (15oz) strawberry-flavoured jelly or any other to suit your fruit
100g (4oz) instant custard powder
300ml (½ pint) whipping, double or extra thick cream
50g (2oz) plain chocolate to decorate

★Check store cupboard

Countdown – **Menu 22**

If you want to prepare and cook the whole menu, you will need 135 minutes, which includes a 30-minute break. If you are a slow cook, add 5–10 minutes to each course to ensure that you don't run out of time. Remember that the times given are only a guide, as each cook will take different lengths of time to complete each task. The starter and main course have a certain amount of flexibility and can sit in a warm oven for some time without spoiling.

Start with the dessert as this needs to set and chill before serving. Prepared half the trifle the night before if possible, and leave it in the fridge. The stuffed mushrooms can also be prepared in advance.

Dessert

PROBLEMS AND HANDY TIPS

Preparation time: 15 minutes
Cooking time: None

Assemble all the ingredients and equipment you need for the dessert. Set your timer for 15 minutes.

15 mins Take the 4 trifle sponges, slice them through the middle and lay them on and around the bottom of the serving bowl.

A glass bowl will help you to see that the sponge is sitting evenly at the bottom of the dish.

12 mins Fill the kettle and put it on to boil.
11 mins Open the tin of fruit and drain the juice through a sieve into a bowl. Set the fruit aside. Take 2 tablespoons of dry sherry and mix it with the fruit juice. (If you are using fresh fruit, you could squeeze 2 or 3 oranges and mix the juice with the sherry.)
9 mins Spoon the juice mixture over the sponges as evenly as possible, so that they become moist.

Press the sponge down with a tablespoon.

7 mins Take the fruit, which should be in bite-sized pieces, and spoon it over the sponge.

If the sponges start to float up into the jelly, take a spoon and carefully press them down again. They should absorb more of the liquid and therefore become heavier and sink back down again.

5 mins Read the instructions on the jelly packet; they should say something like, 'put the jelly into a measuring jug, pour in 300ml (½ pint) of boiling water and stir until all the jelly dissolves.' A crafty way of speeding up the setting time is to use only 300ml (½ pint) of boiling water, and when all the jelly has dissolved, bring it up to 600ml (1 pint) with 300ml (½ pint) of cold water.

If the jelly will not set and you need it in a hurry put it in the deep freeze for 5–10 minutes to speed up the process. Don't forget to set your timer for 10 minutes so that you remember to remove the jelly from the freezer.

1 min Pour the jelly over the fruit and sponge and leave it to set in the fridge for a minimum of 1½ hours. (You will finish it off with the custard and cream when the jelly has set.)

0 mins Wash up and clear away.

Starter

PROBLEMS AND HANDY TIPS

Preparation time: 25 minutes
Cooking time: 30 minutes

Preheat the oven to 400°F/200°C/Gas mark 6 if you intend cooking the mushrooms immediately. Assemble all the ingredients and equipment you need for the starter. Set your timer for 25 minutes.

25 mins Wash the mushrooms well and pull out the stalks. Leave the mushrooms to drain in a colander.

21 mins Peel and chop 1 onion as finely as possible. If you are using the garlic, peel and crush it (see Handy Tip 4 on page xviii for a method of crushing garlic without a crusher).

If the stalks are difficult to remove, leave them to soak in the water a little longer, then take the handle of a teaspoon and prise the stalks out carefully. It is essential that the mushroom caps remain whole.

16 mins Melt 25g/1oz (1 tablespoon) of cooking margarine in a heavy saucepan, add the onion and garlic, and cook on a low to medium heat. Meanwhile, grate 100g (4oz) of Cheddar cheese into a bowl. Stir the onion and garlic, and when golden brown, set aside to cool.

Watch that the onion and garlic don't burn; keep stirring them. Turn them down if they are cooking too fast.

10 mins Take 1 piece of bread and crumble it into the saucepan with the onion and garlic.

8 mins Add 1 tablespoon of lemon juice to the saucepan, then add 100g (4oz) of sour cream and season with salt, pepper and a good pinch of nutmeg. Stir well.

5 mins Take the deep baking tray or tin and place the mushrooms, rounded side downwards, in it.

If the mushrooms will not sit evenly on the baking tray, take a sharp knife and cut a thin sliver off the bottom of the mushroom.

4 mins Place a teaspoonful of the onion mixture in each mushroom. Do not overfill them as you must have enough mixture to fill all 16 mushrooms. Sprinkle a small amount of grated cheese on to each mushroom to cover the filling.

If the cheese will not stick to the filling, press it down lightly with your fingers.

1 min If you have made the starter in advance, put the mushrooms into the fridge until they are required. Otherwise, cook them in the preheated oven for 30 minutes.

0 mins Take the butter out of the fridge and put it on the table to soften, ready to serve with the starter. Wash up and clear away.

Relax

Take a 30-minute break – don't forget your timer. When you return you will finish off the trifle and prepare the main course.

Welcome back

Feeling better after your break?

Dessert

Set your timer for 10 minutes. This is how long you will need to finish off the dessert.

10 mins As you have made half the trifle in advance, you have only to make the custard and spread whipped cream over the top.

9 mins Fill the kettle and put it on to boil.

8 mins Read the instructions on the instant custard packet; they should tell you to add water to the powder and stir well. Make sure you achieve a good pouring consistency.

The custard should coat the back of the spoon if you have the correct consistency.

6 mins Take the trifle base out of the fridge and pour the custard over the top. Place in the fridge to set.

If the jelly hasn't set properly and the custard sinks into the fruit, don't worry. This will go unnoticed once the trifle is covered with cream and decorated.

5 mins Whip the cream carefully until it is thick. (If you are using extra thick cream, it will not be necessary to whip it.)

2 mins Spoon the cream over the top of the trifle. Take 50g (2oz) plain chocolate and grate it roughly over the top of the cream to decorate. The trifle is now finished and can be put back into the fridge until you are ready to serve it.

Do not overwhip the cream or it will curdle. As soon as the cream starts to thicken, stop whipping it. If it has separated, you will have to serve the trifle without the cream, but still decorate the top.

0 mins Wash up and clear away.

Main course

Preparation time: 30 minutes
Cooking time: 30 minutes

Preheat the oven to 350°F/170°C/Gas mark 4. Assemble all the ingredients and equipment you need for the main course. Set your timer for 30 minutes. If you have the facility, put the main course plates in to warm.

30 mins Take the new potatoes and put them to soak in warm water; this will help to remove any soil on them.

28 mins Wash the fish under cold running water, then pat dry with kitchen paper.

26 mins Take a deep baking tray or tin and line it with aluminium foil. Make sure the foil is long enough to cover the fish completely.

You will make a parcel out of the foil to wrap around the fish.

24 mins Grease the foil with 25g/1oz (1 tablespoon) of margarine, especially where the head and tail of the fish

If the margarine won't spread on the foil, melt a small amount in a saucepan and pour it over.

will lie, this will prevent the fish from sticking.

23 mins Place the fish on the foil. Peel and chop 1 small onion as finely as possible. Sprinkle the onion over the fish, then add 1 glass of white wine, 2 bay leaves, a pinch of salt and some ground black pepper. Take 1 lemon and roll it under the palm of your hand on a work surface to release the flesh inside. Cut the lemon in half and squeeze both halves over a lemon squeezer. Pour the juice all over the fish.

18 mins Grease the top of the fish with 25g/1oz (1 tablespoon) of margarine. Now wrap the fish up in the foil to make a parcel that will keep all the juices inside and keep the fish moist. Place the fish in the preheated oven and cook for approx. 25–30 minutes.

14 mins Meanwhile, prepare the salad. Wash and chop the lettuce, slice the cucumber thinly and chop the tomatoes into quarters or halves, depending on how large they are. Leave everything to drain.

9 mins Place the new potatoes and fresh mint (if you have any) in a saucepan of cold water and set aside.

5 mins Set aside a few slices of cucumber and tomato for garnishing the salmon, just before serving. Take a large salad bowl and place all the salad ingredients in it. Measure out 150ml (¼ pint) of French dressing, make sure it is well mixed, then pour it over the salad and toss well. Set aside until required.

3 mins Turn the oven up to 400°F/200°C/Gas mark 6, take the mushrooms out of the fridge and put them on the top shelf to cook. The fish should be moved down, as near to the bottom of the oven as possible.

0 mins Wash up and clear away.

If the fish is too big for the oven, try fitting it in at an angle, so that the tin is square, but the fish is lying diagonally across it.

Make sure all the salad ingredients are cut into bite-sized pieces.

A general rule is that vegetables that grow below the ground should go into cold water and be brought slowly to the boil; vegetables that grow above the ground should be cooked in boiling water from the start.

See page 196 for home-made French dressing. It is best made in advance.

The mushrooms will need approx. 30 minutes to cook.

Last-minute tasks

Set your timer for 25 minutes. This is how long you have before serving the starter.

25 mins Make up the packet of hollandaise sauce, or turn to the recipe on page 195. You will need an extra 15 minutes if you are making it yourself.

20 mins Cook the potatoes on a high heat until the water starts to boil. Simmer for about 20 minutes. (This time will vary depending on the size of the potatoes.)

19 mins Take the salmon out of the oven to test whether it is cooked: the eyeballs should be white and firm, and the skin should lift off easily, taking no flesh with it. If you are in any doubt, put the fish back into the oven for a further

5–10 minutes. It will not spoil the salmon, and will put your mind at ease.

16 mins Put the brown rolls into the bottom of the oven to warm through.

15 mins When the fish is cooked, unwrap it carefully, and pour away the juice, which is very bitter. Discard the onions and bay leaves. Take a sharp knife and, starting at the tail end of the fish, remove the skin. This should come away easily. Leave the head and tail on for decoration; this also keeps the fish in one piece. Take a large oval serving plate and place it over the fish. Turn the whole thing upside down, and you should be left with the fish on the serving plate. Now take the skin off the top side of the fish in the same way as before.

5 mins Turn the oven down to 150°C/300°F/Gas mark 2 and put the fish back in. (Take the mushrooms out if there isn't enough space.)

3 mins Drain the new potatoes and then put them into a serving dish. Place them in the oven to keep warm.

0 mins Wash up and clear away.

If you are not sure whether the fish is cooked, push a sharp knife into the flesh: it should come out clean. Don't worry if it is not quite ready. Turn the heat up, and by the time you have finished the starter it will be cooked.

If the fish starts to fall apart, this probably means you have overcooked it. Keep calm. Take the fish out of the oven at once. You can patch it up by using some of the cucumber and tomato slices as a garnish.

Drain the potatoes carefully so that they do not break up.

Watch points

Once the meal has started, it is difficult to specify exact times, so the following instructions are given only as a guide.

Serve the starter – don't forget the warmed rolls and butter.

Take the salmon and the potatoes out of the oven, garnish the fish with cucumber, tomato and lemon slices down the whole length of the body, and cover the eye with parsley. Don't forget to turn the oven off.

The fish looks very pretty once it is garnished with the cucumber and tomato slices. You can serve it at the table to show off your skills.

Serve the main course with the new potatoes, hollandaise sauce or mayonnaise, and tossed mixed salad. There is no need to hurry the main course as the dessert is cold and ready to serve.

The hollandaise sauce or mayonnaise should be served separately, not on the fish itself.

Formal dinner party menu
Difficult to prepare and cook
Cost level: expensive
Serves: 4

A 30-minute break is incorporated in this menu.

Starter   Haddock au gratin with French bread

Preparation time = 30 minutes
Cooking time = 20–25 minutes

Main course   Stuffed beef olives
Mange-tout or French beans
Potato and parsnip castles

Preparation time = 100 minutes
Cooking time = 50 minutes

Dessert   Lemon soufflé with water biscuits

Preparation time = 45 minutes
Cooking time = None

This formal menu is time–consuming, but worth the effort. Everything can be made in advance, so the work can be spread out over 2 days.

You have the option of leaving out a course if you feel it is too much. You could also serve cheese and fruit instead of the dessert to save time.

Equipment needed – **Menu 23**

Starter

1 savoury chopping board
1 sharp knife or food processor
1 small saucepan
4 individual ramekins or 1 ovenproof dish
1 savoury wooden spoon
1 lemon squeezer
1 grater
1 measuring jug

Main course

1 savoury chopping board
1 sharp knife
1 savoury wooden spoon
1 colander
1 teaspoon
1 mixing bowl
1 meat mallet or rolling pin
1 large carving knife
1 roasting tin
1 potato peeler
2 medium saucepans
1 potato masher
1 baking sheet
1 tablespoon
1 fork
1 small saucepan
1 measuring jug

Dessert

1 heatproof bowl (to fit over the saucepan)
2 mixing bowls
1 saucepan, preferably with a lid
1 grater
1 balloon whisk or a hand-held electric
    mixer
1 tablespoon
1 sharp knife
1 lemon squeezer
1 small saucepan
1 dessertspoon
1 plastic spatula

*Check store cupboard

Shopping list – **Menu 23**

Starter

*1 small onion
*25g (1oz) cooking margarine
225g (8oz) fresh haddock fillet
*25g (1oz) plain flour
1 lemon
50g (2oz) Cheddar cheese
*150ml (¼ pint) milk
*salt, pepper and nutmeg
*50g (1oz) dried breadcrumbs
1 French loaf to serve
100g (4oz) butter to serve with bread

Main course

8 thin slices topside or top rump of beef, 100g
    (4oz) each
*2 medium onions
*25g (1oz) cooking margarine
225g (8oz) button mushrooms
100g (4oz) back bacon
*ground black pepper
*pinch nutmeg
*1 teaspoon lemon juice
50g (2oz) shredded beef suet
*2 slices fresh bread
*25g (1oz) cooking margarine
*25g (1oz) plain flour
300ml (½ pint) fresh beef stock or 1 beef stock
    cube
900g (2lb) old potatoes
1 large parsnip
*50g (2oz) butter or table margarine
*1 beaten egg
*salt and pepper
450g (1lb) mange-tout or French beans

Dessert

*3 eggs
300ml (½ pint) double cream
*75g (3oz) caster sugar
1 large lemon
*1 dessertspoon gelatine
*flaked almonds or grated chocolate to decorate
wafer biscuits
150ml (¼ pint) single cream (optional)

Countdown – **Menu 23**

If you want to prepare and cook the whole menu, you will need 205 minutes, which includes a 30-minute break. If you are a slow cook, add 5–10 minutes to each course to ensure that you do not run out of time. Remember, the times given are only a guide, as each cook will take different lengths of time to complete each task. The starter is best made on the day to keep it fresh. The main course can be prepared in advance but should not be cooked until the day. The dessert is best made the day or evening before to give it time to set.

Dessert

PROBLEMS AND HANDY TIPS

Preparation time: 45 minutes
Cooking time: None

Assemble all the ingredients and equipment you need for the dessert. Set your timer for 45 minutes.

45 mins Take 3 eggs and separate them carefully, making sure that no egg yolk falls into the egg white. The egg yolks should be placed in a heatproof bowl, which will fit over a saucepan of hot water. The egg whites should be put into a mixing bowl large enough to accommodate them once they have been whisked and increased in volume.

Remember, this is a long and difficult menu to prepare. Read the whole method before starting.

If you are worried about separating the eggs, see Handy Tip 8 on page xix for an easy method. Remember, it is very important not to get any yolk in the whites or they will not whip up.

40 mins Half fill the saucepan with cold water, place it over a medium heat and bring to the boil. Cover the pan with a lid as this will make the water come to the boil more quickly.

35 mins Take a third bowl and pour 300ml (½ pint) of double cream into it. Set it aside in a cool place to be whipped later. Measure out 75g (3oz) of caster sugar and put it into the bowl with the egg yolks.

30 mins Take 1 lemon and roll it under the palm of your hand on a work surface to release the flesh inside. Wash the lemon under cold running water, dry it and grate the rind straight into the bowl with the egg yolks and sugar. When you grate the lemon make sure that you use only the yellow rind and not the white pith which is very bitter. Scrape the grater well to remove all the lemon rind.

As so many chemicals are used on fruits nowadays, it is a good idea to wash them well if you are going to use the rind.

25 mins Place the bowl containing the egg yolks, sugar and lemon rind over the saucepan of boiling water, turn

The longer you beat the egg and sugar mixture, the better, as this will make a lighter, airier soufflé.

the heat down very low and whisk the mixture until it becomes thick and much paler in colour. Test the mixture for readiness by writing your initials on the surface with a spoon; if the impression remains for a few seconds the mixture is thick enough.

20 mins Carefully remove the bowl from the saucepan so that you do not burn yourself on the steam. Leave the mixture to cool.

18 mins Cut the lemon in half and squeeze both halves over a lemon squeezer. Measure out 1 dessertspoon of gelatine and sprinkle it all over the lemon juice. Leave it to stand and soak up the juice.

If the lemon juice has pips in it, pour it through a fine sieve into the saucepan.

14 mins Take the bowl of double cream and whip it with a balloon whisk or a hand-held electric mixer until it holds its shape. Do not overbeat the cream or it will curdle. If in doubt, stop whipping as soon as the mixture starts to thicken.

The cream needs to thicken only slightly.

9 mins Place the pan of lemon juice and gelatine over a very low heat. As soon as the gelatine starts to melt, stir it with your finger. If your finger gets too hot, remove the gelatine from the heat at once. (If gelatine gets too hot it loses its setting properties.) Once all the granules have dissolved and the liquid is clear, the gelatine is ready to use.

Do not allow the gelatine to get too hot; if in doubt, move it away from the heat.

6 mins Pour the dissolved gelatine into the bowl with the beaten egg yolks and fold it in gently to incorporate air. Do not beat it.

4 mins Once the mixture is well folded, carefully fold in all the whipped cream.

When you are putting the soufflé together, remember that you want it as light and airy as possible, so fold everything in carefully, do not beat.

2 mins Wash and dry the balloon whisk or beating attachment of your mixer and whip the egg whites until they form peaks and stand up on their own. When they have reached this stage, carefully fold them into the egg and cream mixture. Pour the finished mixture into a glass serving bowl or 4 ramekin dishes. Chill until required.

The soufflé will take a minimum of 2 hours to set.

0 mins Wash up and clear away.

Main course

PROBLEMS AND HANDY TIPS

Preparation time: 40 minutes
Cooking time: 60 minutes

Preheat the oven to 200°C/400°F/Gas mark 6, but only if you plan to cook the beef immediately. Assemble all the ingredients and equipment you need for the main course. (All the chopping can be done in a food processor, if you have one.) Set your timer for 40 minutes.

40 mins Peel and chop 2 medium onions as finely as possible. Place them in a saucepan with 25g/1oz (1 tablespoon) of cooking margarine and cook over a low heat until the onion is transparent.

35 mins Wash 225g (8oz) of button mushrooms and leave them to drain. Chop the bacon into small pieces, discarding any rind. Chop the mushrooms as finely as possible. Add the bacon to the onion and continue to cook for a few minutes.

30 mins Add the mushrooms to the onion and bacon and cook for a further 2–3 minutes.

28 mins Season the mixture with ground black pepper, nutmeg and a teaspoon of lemon juice.

25 mins When the mixture is well cooked, remove it from the heat and allow to cool.

23 mins While the mixture is cooling, place 50g (2oz) of shredded beef suet in a mixing bowl. Take 2 pieces of bread and crumble them up into breadcrumbs. Add the crumbs to the suet, then add the onion and mushroom mixture. Break 1 whole egg into the bowl and mix well. Set aside.

16 mins If the beef is not sliced already, slice it now into about 8 thin pieces. If you make more, it doesn't matter. If the beef slices are very small, it is a good idea to beat them with a meat mallet or the end of a rolling pin. This means that the beef will be thinner but larger, which will make it easier to stuff.

10 mins Place a small amount of stuffing in the centre of each piece of meat, and roll the meat up to make a parcel. Place the rolls seam side down in a roasting tin. It doesn't matter if you cannot seal the meat very well; as long as the join is underneath, the mixture will stick together and bind to the meat quite successfully.

2 mins Place all the beef olives in the roasting tin and put in the fridge to chill for 30 minutes (this helps to set the stuffing). If you have a lot of stuffing left over, place it in a bowl to be used in the sauce that you will make later to accompany the beef olives.

0 mins Wash up and clear away.

If you are making the beef olives in advance, you must cover them and put them in the fridge until it is time to cook them.

The bacon can be left out if you know that some of your guests do not eat it.

The beef suet will expand when it soaks up the moisture in the mixture and during the cooking time.

You should make at least 8 parcels so that each guest will have 2 olives.

The beef slices should be roughly the same size so that all the finished olives look equal. Beating the slices of beef can help to make them all the same size.

Lay out all the beef slices and put stuffing on each one before wrapping them up. This way you will know whether you have enough stuffing for all the beef.

Watch points

If you are making the beef olives the night before, this is as far as you can go. You will cook them on the night.

If you are only cooking the beef olives and you are not having a break, you can cook the main course at once.

Relax

Have a 30-minute break, or stop completely until tomorrow when you will finish off the menu.

Welcome back

Feeling better after your break?

Starter

PROBLEMS AND HANDY TIPS

Preparation time: 30 minutes
Cooking time: 20–25 minutes

Preheat oven to 160°C/325°F/Gas mark 3. Assemble all the ingredients and equipment you need for the starter. Set your timer for 30 minutes.

30 mins Peel and chop 1 small onion as finely as possible. Place it in a small saucepan with 25g/1oz (1 tablespoon) of cooking margarine and put it over a medium heat to brown.

25 mins Take the fish, insert a sharp knife under the skin at the tail, and use a sawing action to work the skin away from the flesh. Do this on both sides of the fish, removing any bones that you see. Cut the fish into portions so that it fills 4 individual ramekins or, if you prefer, 1 large ovenproof dish.

When preparing the fish, cover your chopping board with clingfilm to prevent it absorbing the fishy smell.

If the fish is very fresh, you might find that the skin will come away easily just by pulling it hard with your fingers; you might not have to use the knife.

20 mins Return to the onions. Stir them well, and if they look golden brown, turn the heat off. Add 25g/1oz (1 tablespoon) of plain flour and mix well. If the mixture is too thin, add a little extra flour. If the mixture looks too dry, add a little more margarine. Cook the mixture for 2 minutes, stirring continuously. Remove from the heat and allow it to cool.

It is important to have the right consistency for the sauce, so make sure you are happy with the flour and margarine mixture before cooking it and adding the liquid.

15 mins Take 1 lemon and cut in half lengthways. Cut one half into 4 wedges and squeeze the other half over a lemon squeezer. Place the wedges on a plate and keep in the fridge to be used later.

12 mins Grate 50g (2oz) of Cheddar cheese on to a plate or into a bowl and set aside.

8 mins Return to the flour mixture and add 150ml (¼ pint) of milk. Place over a low heat and slowly bring to the boil, stirring constantly. Season the sauce with ground black pepper, a pinch of salt and a good pinch of nutmeg.

If you think the sauce is too thick, add some extra milk to thin it, but remember that it is meant to be a thick binding sauce.

6 mins Once the sauce has thickened, add all the lemon

juice. Don't worry if the sauce looks very thick – it is supposed to be. Allow the sauce to boil for 2 minutes, then set aside.

2 mins Season the haddock portions with ground black pepper and nutmeg, then pour a small amount of the sauce over each, ensuring you have enough to cover all 4 portions. Sprinkle the grated cheese on top of the sauce, then sprinkle some dried, ready-made breadcrumbs over the top. Cook immediately in a preheated oven at 160°C/325°F/Gas mark 3 for 20–25 minutes, or cover and place in the fridge until required for cooking.

0 mins Wash up and clear away.

It is a good idea to put the ramekins on a baking tray in case they overflow while cooking.

Potato and Parsnip Castles

Preparation time: 30 minutes
Cooking time: 30 minutes

Preheat the oven to 200°C/400°F/Gas mark 6. Assemble all the ingredients and equipment you need. Set your timer for 30 minutes.

30 mins Peel 3 medium to large potatoes and 1 parsnip, cutting a small amount off the top and bottom of the parsnip. Cut the vegetables into even-sized pieces (i.e. halves or quarters). Place them in a saucepan of cold water, add a pinch of salt and bring to the boil on a high heat. Once boiling, turn down the heat and simmer for 20–25 minutes.

Try to keep all the potatoes and parsnips roughly the same size so that they cook evenly.

20 mins Top and tail the mange-tout or French beans, wash them in a colander and place them in a saucepan. Set aside.

12 mins Stir the potatoes and parsnip to ensure they cook evenly. They should need another 10 minutes.

10 mins Take the beef olives out of the fridge and place them as near the top of the oven as possible. Cook for 50 minutes.

Turn the potatoes and parsnip down as soon as they come to the boil. If they do not simmer, they will fall apart.

8 mins Start the sauce now. Place 25g/1oz (1 tablespoon) of cooking margarine in a small saucepan and place over a low heat to melt. Add 25g/1oz (1 tablespoon) of plain flour to the melted margarine, off the heat, and stir well. Put the pan back over a medium heat and cook for 2 minutes. Turn off the heat and set the pan aside. If you are not using fresh stock, crumble 1 stock cube into the flour and margarine mixture. Set aside.

0 mins Wash up and clear away.

Last-minute tasks

Set your timer for 30 minutes. This is how long you have before you serve the starter.

30 mins Check the potatoes and parsnip, which should be cooked by now, and drain them well in a colander. Put them back into the saucepan, or place in a food processor, and mash or process until smooth. Once you have reached this stage, add 50g/2oz (2 tablespoons) of butter or table margarine and 1 egg, and beat the mixture to a smooth cream. Season well with salt and pepper and set aside.

Do not add any margarine to the potatoes and parsnip until the mixture is smooth and lump-free.

The beaten egg helps to bind the mixture together and thus keep the shape of the 'castles'.

22 mins Take the dish(es) of haddock and place in the oven on the shelf underneath the beef. Leave to cook for 20–25 minutes.

20 mins Fill the kettle and put it on to boil.

19 mins Grease a baking sheet with margarine using your fingers or some greaseproof paper. Take a table-spoon and place generous spoonfuls of the potato mixture on the baking sheet. Make at least 3 or 4 per guest.

14 mins Shape the mounds of potato into even-sized shapes using a fork. Put in the oven to cook for 30 minutes, or until they are crisp and golden brown.

Don't worry if you haven't quite understood what is meant by 'castles': just make little peaks on the baking sheet and rough them up using a fork.

10 mins If you have the facility to warm the plates and serving dishes, put them in now. Put the French bread into the bottom of the oven to warm through.

8 mins Measure out 300ml (½ pint) of beef stock, or 300ml (½ pint) of cold water if you have used a stock cube. Slowly add the liquid to the flour mixture, stirring all the time. Put the sauce back over the heat and bring it slowly to the boil. If you have any extra stuffing, you can add it now to the sauce.

Be careful when adding the liquid to the sauce, and make sure there are no lumps before you start to cook it. If you are worried, you can sieve it before bringing it to the boil.

4 mins While waiting for the sauce to come to the boil and thicken, take the starter out of the oven. Check the beef olives and move them down in the oven if they are browning too quickly.

3 mins Stir the beef sauce and allow it to boil for 2 minutes before turning it off. Check to see the fish is cooked by inserting a sharp knife and pulling a small piece of fish away from the side of the dish. If you see a clear liquid and the fish looks white and flaky, it is cooked.

1 min Before serving the starter, pour boiling water over the vegetables and put them on to cook very slowly.

0 mins Serve the starter with the French bread, butter and lemon wedges. Wash up and clear away.

Mangetout takes 5 minutes to cook once the water is boiling, whereas French beans take approx. 10 minutes.

Watch points

Once the meal has started, it is difficult to predict how long each course will take. The following instructions are intended only as a guide.

If the starter takes more than 10 minutes to eat, check the vegetables and turn them off if you think they might overcook. You can continue to cook them while you serve the main course.

If the potato and parsnip castles are not golden brown when you are ready to serve them, put them under a hot grill for a couple of minutes until they are crisp.

The sauce to accompany the beef olives needs to be brought slowly to the boil.

Drain the green vegetables and put them in a serving dish. Stir the sauce and place half of it in a sauce boat. Leave the other half in the saucepan to heat up later.

Serve the main course. You can either put everything on the table for guests to help themselves, or you can serve the beef and potatoes yourself and just put the vegetables and sauce on the table.

The dessert may be served as it is with wafer biscuits, or decorated with flaked almonds or finely grated chocolate. You can offer extra cream if you like, but the soufflé already has a lot of cream in it.

Appendix
Additional recipes

Serves: 4

Equipment

1 grill and grill pan
1 bread board or plate
1 bread knife
1 baking tray

Ingredients

6 medium slices of fresh brown or white bread

Countdown method

Preparation time: 15 minutes
Cooking time: 15 minutes

Preheat the oven to 190°C/380°F/Gas mark 5. Melba toast will keep crisp and fresh for a few days in an airtight tin or container. Assemble all the ingredients and equipment you need. Set your timer for 15 minutes.

15 mins Place the bread under the grill on a very low setting. Allow the bread to heat through, do not allow it to brown.

10 mins Remove the toast from the grill and cut off the crusts. Holding the toast down with one hand take a sharp bread knife and with a sawing motion slice the piece of toast in half through the middle, i.e. 1 piece of toast becomes 2 thin pieces. Repeat until you have sliced all the pieces in half.

Don't worry too much if the bread falls apart, it will be allright once it has cooked and dried out.

3 mins Put all the pieces of bread toasted side down on a baking tray and place in the preheated oven for 15 mins to dry out. After 7–8 minutes check the toast, as you might need to turn it over. The Melba toast should curl up and become golden brown in colour when it is ready.

If you like the toast really crisp then leave it in the oven a little longer.

1 min Serve the Melba toast with your starter or allow it to cool before storing it.

0 mins Wash up and clear away.

Basic white sauce

Serves: 4

Equipment

1 small saucepan
1 savoury wooden spoon
1 measuring jug
1 balloon whisk, if necessary
1 fine sieve

Ingredients

*25g (1oz) cooking margarine
*25g (1oz) plain flour
*600ml (1 pint) milk
*salt, pepper, nutmeg and dried mustard
  powder
Cheese sauce: Add 100g (4oz) Cheddar cheese,
  grated

*Check store cupboard

Countdown method

Preparation time: 15 minutes
Cooking time: 10 minutes

Assemble all the ingredients and equipment you need for the sauce. Set the timer for 15 minutes. Keep calm and think positively and you shouldn't have any problems.

15 mins Measure out 25g/1oz (1 tablespoon) of cooking margarine and place it in a small saucepan. Place over a low heat to melt.

If the margarine and flour are too thick you can add a small amount of extra margarine to form a soft paste.

12 mins Once the margarine has melted, remove it from the heat and add 25g/1oz (1 tablespoon) of plain flour. This mixture is now called a 'roux'. Put the roux back over a very low heat and cook for 2 minutes. This removes the starchy flavour often found in a sauce. After 2 minutes remove the roux from the heat and allow it to cool.

8 mins Measure out 600ml (1 pint) of milk. Using a balloon whisk or wooden spoon slowly stir the milk into the roux, making sure no lumps form. This is done off the heat. Stop once you have added three-quarters of the milk. Put the sauce back over a very low heat and allow it to thicken gradually. Stir all the time. The sauce should thicken and then come to the boil. If the sauce is very thick add the remaining milk to thin it down. Allow the sauce to boil and then simmer for a least 2–3 minutes before turning the heat off.

If at any point the sauce starts to become lumpy stop adding the liquid. Take a balloon whisk or wooden spoon and beat the sauce well until you can't see any lumps remaining. Then you can continue to add the milk. Make sure you stir the sauce all the time.

2 mins The white sauce is now complete except for the seasoning. Season with salt, pepper and a pinch of mustard powder. Use the sauce immediately or leave it to stand

If the sauce is lumpy you should sieve it. Discard the lumps and serve the sauce.

with a lid on. Don't forget to reheat it well before using it.

0 mins Wash up and clear away.

Variations

If you are making a cheese sauce. Grate 100g (4oz) of Cheddar cheese and add it to the sauce after it has boiled and simmered. Do not cook the cheese, otherwise it will go stringy. Season well and serve with cauliflower or a vegetable of your choice.

Hollandaise sauce

Serves: 4

Equipment

1 tablespoon
1 small saucepan
1 double saucepan OR
   1 medium-sized saucepan and
   1 heatproof mixing bowl
   which will fit inside the saucepan
1 balloon whisk
1 sharp knife
1 teaspoon

Ingredients

3 tablespoons of white wine vinegar
2 large egg yolks
125g (5oz) butter
salt and white pepper
2 teaspoons of lemon juice

Check store cupboard

Countdown method

Preparation time: 15 minutes
Cooking time: 15 minutes

This classic, rich French sauce is always served warm. It usually accompanies young or steamed vegetables such as new potatoes or asparagus and it is also delicious with hot salmon or shellfish. Assemble all the ingredients and equipment you need for the sauce. Remember, you must be very well organized and quick to prevent the sauce from separating or curdling. Set your timer for 15 minutes.

15 mins Put 3 tablespoons of white wine vinegar in a small saucepan over a low heat to boil, and reduce to approximately 2 tablespoons.

12 mins Take a medium-sized saucepan or double

Make sure the vinegar reduces well before using it.

saucepan and fill it half full with cold water. Slowly bring the water to the boil over a low heat.

8 mins Take 2 large eggs and separate them. You will not use the egg whites so cover them and place them in the fridge. Place the egg yolks into the top of the double saucepan or in a bowl away from the heat. Whisk up the egg yolks well with a balloon whisk. Slowly whisk the reduced vinegar into the egg yolks, a little at a time.

See Handy Tip 8, pxix for an easy way to separate eggs.

5 mins Take 125g (5oz) of butter and cut it up into small pieces. Place the egg yolks and vinegar over the hot water in the saucepan, allow the water to simmer not boil. Whisking constantly, add half the butter and allow it to melt. When the mixture becomes smooth and forms a thick cream slowly add the remaining butter. If at any time the sauce starts to get too hot, remove the bowl or saucepan from the heat and allow it to cool down before continuing.

Never allow the mixture to get too hot, if you are in doubt, remove from the heat and boiling water.

If the sauce does start to separate or curdle have an ice cube ready, place it in the sauce and stir. If you are lucky this might bring the sauce back together.

0 mins Season well with salt and pepper and stir in 2 teaspoons of lemon juice. Serve lukewarm. Wash up and clear away.

Homemade French dressing

Serves: 10–12

Equipment

1 measuring jug
1 large deep mixing bowl or 1 large jug
1 balloon whisk or 1 tablespoon
1 garlic crusher (or see Handy Tip 4,
   pxviii)
1 teaspoon
1 bottle or jar with a tight fitting lid to keep
   the French dressing in once it is made

Ingredients

*600ml (1 pint) olive oil
*200ml (7floz) white wine vinegar
*2 large cloves of garlic (optional)
*1 teaspoon of white or brown sugar
*1 teaspoon of lemon juice
*2 teaspoons of French mustard
*a pinch of dried mustard powder
*1 tablespoon of salt
*ground black pepper

*Check store cupboard

Countdown method

Preparation time: 10 minutes
Cooking time: None

Remember, this is a basic French dressing recipe and will need some testing and adapting before you feel happy with the taste as everyone likes different strengths and flavours. The dressing is best made in advance as this gives all the ingredients time to combine and mature, especially if you are using garlic. It will keep for 6 weeks in a bottle with a tight fitting lid, at room temperature. Always shake very well before using. Assemble all the ingredients and equipment you need for the dressing. Set your timer for 15 minutes.

15 mins Measure out the oil and place it in a mixing bowl or jug. Measure out the vinegar and place it in the bowl with the oil. Mix well with either a balloon whisk or a tablespoon.

10 mins If you are going to use the garlic, peel and crush it into the bowl. Add 1 teaspoon of white or brown sugar, 1 teaspoon of lemon juice, 2 teaspoons of French mustard, a pinch of dried mustard powder, 1 tablespoon of salt and ground black pepper to taste. Mix all the ingredients together really well and taste the dressing. You should adjust the strength according to your own taste.

Oils differ and can be difficult to mix with the vinegar so always mix them really well.

Experiment with this dressing, you will find your own ingredients make the dressing you like.

See Handy Tip 4, pxviii for an easy way to crush garlic without a garlic crusher.

Season the dressing very well before putting it away or serving it.

Variations

Here are some variations to the standard recipe that you can try.

Add 2 tablespoons of natural yogurt to 150ml (¼ pint) of French dressing.

Add 2 tablespoons of sour cream to 150ml (¼ pint) of French dressing

Fresh herbs such as chopped chives or parsley can also add colour and flavour to French dressing.

Vegetable chart

See Handy Tip 3, pxvii for a general rule on how to cook all vegetables.

Artichoke, Globe
Allow 1 whole artichoke per person.
Available all year.
Serve hot or cold.

Trim off the long stalk in line with the body and soak the artichokes in cold salty water for 1 hour. Remove the artichokes from the cold water and strip away the tough outer leaves. Bring a large saucepan of salt water to the boil and plunge the artichokes into water and cook for 35–40 minutes, or until the leaves pull away easily. Drain the artichokes upside down to remove any excess water. Serve hot and whole on a starter plate with some finger bowls. Allow your guests to pull off the leaves and dip them in either a Hollandaise sauce (see p195 for a recipe), melted butter or a cold vinaigrette. When you reach the heart, remove the choke or hair and eat the heart with a knife and fork.

Asparagus
450g (1lb) serves 3–4 people.
Serve hot or cold.

Wash the asparagus thoroughly under cold running water. Take care not to damage the delicate tips. Trim off the bases, cutting all the stalks to roughly the same length. Place the asparagus in a saucepan large enough to lie them flat. Pour on enough boiling water to cover them. Add a pinch of salt and simmer for 15 minutes or until tender. The cooking time will depend on the size of the stalks. Drain the asparagus and serve with a Hollandaise sauce, melted butter or vinaigrette.

Aubergines (egg plant)
Allow 175–225g (6–8oz) per person.
Available all year.
Serve hot or cold.

Wash the aubergines well under cold running water and cut them into 1cm (½ inch) slices. Lay them on a plate or board and sprinkle liberally with salt. (This is called *degorging* and it draws out the bitter taste that is sometimes found in aubergines.) Allow the aubergines to soak in the salt for 20 minutes before turning them over and repeating the process on the other side. Wash all the salt off before cooking. Aubergines can either be fried in margarine and oil, deep fried, or cooked in the oven. Serve as a vegetable, in a ratatouille, cut in half and stuffed or as a starter dip.

Beans, French
Allow 100–225g (4–8oz) per person.
Available all year.
Serve hot or cold.

Top and tail the beans and keep them whole if they are not too large. Place the prepared beans in a saucepan, add a pinch of salt and pour on just enough boiling water to cover them. Cook for 10–15 minutes. This will vary depending on how large and thick the beans are. Serve them hot with a small amount of butter or cold in a salad with a vinaigrette.

Top and tail the beans and remove the string down one side. Slice into diagonal 2.5cm (1 inch) strips. Place in a saucepan, add a pinch of salt and pour just enough boiling water over the beans to cover them. Cook for 12–15 minutes. The cooking time will vary depending on how large the beans are. Drain and serve hot with a small amount of butter or cold in a salad with a vinaigrette.

Beans, Runner
Allow 100–225g (4–8oz) per person.
Available July to October.
Serve hot or cold.

Twist off and discard all the leaves. Wash thoroughly and place in a saucepan. Fill the saucepan with cold water and add a pinch of salt. Allow to come to the boil and then simmer for approximately 2 hours. The cooking time will vary depending on the size of the beetroot. When they are soft all the way through, drain the water and peel and slice them into thin pieces. Serve hot with a white sauce or cold, diced or sliced with a salad dressing.

Beetroot
Allow 100–150g (4–6oz) per person.
Available all year.
Serve hot or cold.

Remove the beans from their shells and place them in a saucepan. Add a pinch of salt and pour over just enough boiling water to cover them. Cook for 20–30 minutes until the beans are soft. Serve hot with some butter, a parsley sauce or cold in a salad with a dressing.

Broad beans
Allow 225g (8oz) per person.
Available April to August.

Discard the coarse outer leaves and cut the stems off about 15cm (2 inches) from the head. If the heads are very large cut them in half. Wash the broccoli well and place it in a saucepan. Add a pinch of salt and pour just enough boiling water over the broccoli to cover it. Cook for 8–10 minutes. This time will depend on how large the pieces of broccoli are. Drain well and serve either with hot butter and toasted almonds or a Hollandaise sauce. Broccoli can also be served cold in a salad.

Broccoli
Allow 175–225g (6–8oz) per person.
Available all year.
Serve hot or cold.

Remove any damaged outer leaves and discard. Trim a small amount off the stalk and make a cross in the base of each stalk. Wash the sprouts and place them in a saucepan. Add a pinch of salt and pour over just enough boiling water to cover them. Cook for 10–12 minutes or until the sprouts are soft but still holding their shape. Drain and serve hot with a small amount of butter or, at Christmas, with some chestnuts.

Brussels sprouts
Allow 100–150g (4–6oz) per person.
Available September to April, best when cold and frosty.
Serve hot.

Discard any damaged, coarse outer leaves. Cut the cabbage into quarters. Remove the centre stalk and shred the cabbage. Use raw, as it is, for a salad. To cook, place the shredded cabbage in a saucepan and pour just enough boiling water over it to cover. Add a pinch of salt and cook briskly for 8–10 minutes until soft but still crunchy. When cooking red cabbage add 1 tablespoon of wine vinegar to the water. Drain the cabbage and serve hot with a small amount of butter and a little grated nutmeg, if you like.

Cabbage, white or red
Allow 100g (4oz) per person: 1 large cabbage will feed 4 easily.
Available all year.
Serve hot or cold.

New carrots: remove the feathery leaves at the top. If the carrots are very young, it might not be necessary to peel them at all. Cut them into even-sized pieces and cook them for approximately 10 minutes.
Old carrots: peel and top and tail them. Cut them into even-sized pieces either slices or diced. Place them in a saucepan with just enough cold water to cover them. Add a pinch of salt and cook for 10–15 minutes. The cooking time will depend on the size and age of the carrots. Drain and serve hot with a little butter or parsley to add colour. Carrots can also be served cold in a salad, either diced or grated. They must be peeled first.

Carrots
Allow 100–150g (4–6oz) per person.
Available all year.
Serve hot or raw.

Cut the cauliflower into sprigs or florets. If there are any large sprigs, cut them in half so that all the pieces are roughly the same size. Wash the sprigs in cold water, place them in a saucepan, and add a pinch of salt. Pour boiling water over them to just cover. Cook for 8–10 minutes. The cooking time will vary greatly depending on the size of the sprigs. Serve hot on its own, or with a white or cheese sauce poured all over it.

Cauliflower
Allow 1 medium-sized cauliflower to serve 4.
Available all year, best from June to October.
Serve hot or raw with dips.

Cut a small amount off the top and bottom of the celery bundle to separate the stalks. Wash each stalk well under cold running water. Depending what you are going to use the celery for, either cut it into even-sized lengths to use raw for dips or leave it in long lengths to serve in a jug of water on the table with cheese. To cook, pour boiling water over the celery, add a pinch of salt and cook for approx 20–30 minutes. The cooking time will vary depending on how large the celery pieces are. Alternatively par-boil the celery before putting it into the oven to bake for 1–1½ hours at 180°C/350°F/Gas mark 4. Serve with a hot white or herb sauce.

Celery
Allow 2–3 sticks per person.
Available all year.
Serve hot or raw.

Trim off any damaged leaves and using a sharp knife, cut the chicory into thin slices. Wash well and drain. Use in a salad or as a base for a starter. Chicory can also be cooked in boiling water with a little lemon juice for 12–15 minutes. Serve hot, tossed in butter or with a white or cheese sauce.

Chicory
Allow 1–2 heads per person.
Available September to June.
Serve hot or raw.

Wash the courgettes well under cold running water. Top and tail and cut them either in half down the centre or into thin slices. Sprinkle liberally with salt and leave them to stand for 10 minutes. (This is called *degorging* and removes the bitter taste often found in these vegetables.) Make sure you wash all the salt off before cooking. Cook halved or stuffed courgettes in an ovenproof dish in the oven at 180°C/350°F/Gas mark 4, for 30–40 minutes. Alternatively add a knob of cooking margarine to a saucepan or frying pan and cook sliced courgettes briskly on the hob for 5–8 minutes, until they become soft but still can hold their shape. Courgettes can also be served raw, thinly sliced in a salad, but they must be young to taste sweet.

Courgettes (Zucchini)
Allow 100g (4oz) person.
Available all year.
Serve hot or raw.

Wash the cucumber well if you are going to use the skin or peel the cucumber and trim the top and bottom. Slice the cucumber very thinly or dice it for a salad. Grate the cucumber if you are going to use it for a sauce. Cucumber can also be cooked. Add 25g/1oz (1 tablespoon) of cooking margarine to a saucepan or frying pan and cook briskly for 15–20 minutes. Season well before serving.

Cucumber
Allow 100g (4oz) per person.
Available all year.
Serve hot or raw.

Cut off the base stalk and separate the leaves, discarding any old coarse brown ones. Wash well and drain. Shred into small pieces. Place in a saucepan, add a pinch of salt and pour just enough boiling water over the leaves to cover. Cook for 8–10 minutes, depending on the the age of the greens. Serve tossed in butter with a little nutmeg.

Greens (Spring)
Allow 150–225g (6–8oz) per person.
Available February–June.
Serve hot.

Trim off the root, discard any damaged outside leaves and as much green top as necessary. Slice the leek in half and then into semi-circles. Wash extremely well to get rid of grit and sand. Place in a saucepan with a pinch of salt and pour just enough boiling water over them to cover. Cook for 8–10 minutes until soft but still squeaky. Leeks can also be cooked in the oven in an ovenproof dish with a small amount of cooking margarine at 180°C/350°F/Gas mark 4 for approximately 1 hour. Serve hot with a white or cheese sauce or cold with a vinaigrette.

Leeks
Allow 225g (8oz) person.
Available August–May.
Serve hot or cold.

Remove and discard any coarse outer leaves. Wash the lettuce well under cold running water and leave to drain well. Lettuce is usually used raw in salads and starters and served with a dressing. It can be cooked to make a lettuce soup; the lettuce is added to a saucepan with a small amount of cooking margarine and cooked briskly until it reduces. It is often puréed with the rest of the soup.

Lettuce
Allow 1 round soft lettuce for 2 people, Iceberg will go further.

Top and tail the mange-tout, wash them well, and place them in a saucepan with a pinch of salt. Pour just enough boiling water over them to cover. Cook for 5–8 minutes; but no longer as they are best served crunchy. Serve hot, tossed in butter and seasoned well with ground black pepper. They can also be served cold in a salad or as part of a vegetable dish.

Mange-tout
Allow 200–225g (6–8oz) per person.
Available all year but at a price.
Serve hot or cold.

Peel the marrow well, making sure you get through the thick skin. Cut it in half down the centre and remove the core and pips. These should come out quite easily using either a knife or spoon. Either stuff the marrow or cut it into 2.5cm (1 inch) strips. Cook stuffed marrow in the oven at 200°C/400°F/Gas mark 6 for approximately 60 minutes. Sliced marrow should be cooked in a saucepan with a small amount of cooking margarine; this is a mixture of frying and steaming. Marrow is often served in a ratatouille or in a casserole with tomatoes. It can be served hot or cold.

Marrow
Allow 175g (6oz) per person.
Available July–October.
Serve hot or cold.

Wash mushrooms well to remove any soil and trim the stalks. There is no need to peel cultivated mushrooms. Slice or cut into quarters depending how you are going to use them. Mushrooms can either be fried in a small amount of margarine, baked in the oven, grilled or deep-fried. They only take a few minutes to cook. Once dark juice starts to run out of them, they are cooked. (Add lemon juice and nutmeg to mushrooms for extra flavour.) They can also be stuffed and cooked in the oven, or served raw in salads.

Mushrooms
Allow 50–75g (2–3oz) per person.
Available all year.
Serve hot, cold or raw.

Peel off and discard the outer skin. Slice or chop, depending on how the onion is going to be used. Fry onions in a small amount of cooking margarine for approximately 5–8 minutes or roast in the oven with meat for approximately 1–1½ hours. Onion rings can be deep fried for 3–4 minutes or grilled. Onions can be served hot, cold or raw in salads.

Onions
Allow 175g (6oz) per person.
Available all year.
Serve hot, cold or raw.

Trim off the root. Discard any dirty, damaged outer leaves. Chop spring onions into fine slices and either serve them raw in a salad or cook them rapidly in a Chinese wok.

Peel the parsnips and trim them at the top and bottom. Cut into chunks or thin strips, depending on how you are going cook and serve them. Parsnips can be placed in a saucepan of cold water with a pinch of salt, slowly brought up to the boil and allowed to simmer for 20–30 minutes, depending on their size. They are delicious mashed with potatoes to make a purée or roasted alongside a joint of meat in the oven.

Most peas are cooked straight from the freezer. Cook frozen peas in boiling water with a pinch of salt and sugar for approximately 4–5 minutes, until they go wrinkly and soft. If you do come across fresh peas in pods, shell them and wash them well. Pour boiling water all over them and cook them with a little salt for 5–10 minutes. The cooking time will vary depending on the size and age of the peas. They are served hot with a knob of butter or cold in salads and rice dishes.

Old potatoes Peel the potatoes and place them in a saucepan of cold water with a pinch of salt. Allow the water to come to the boil and then simmer for 20–30 minutes, depending on the size of the potatoes. Alternatively: par-boil the potatoes and then roast them in the oven alongside a joint of meat; cut into sticks and deep fry them to make chips; or slice them thinly and sauté (fry) them in a frying pan with a small amount of cooking margarine. To cook baked potatoes, scrub the skins well and place the unpeeled potatoes in the oven for around 1–1½ hours at 200°C/400°F/Gas mark 6. Boiled old potatoes can also be used to make into potato salad.

New potatoes Wash the potatoes well, but do not peel them. Put them in a saucepan of cold water with a pinch of salt and (if you like the flavour and it is available) a sprig of fresh mint. Bring the water slowly to the boil and simmer for approximately 15–20 minutes, depending on the size of the potatoes. Serve them (skins on) with butter or a sauce. New potatoes are delicious eaten cold, either as they are or in a salad with a dressing.

Onions (spring)
Allow 1 bunch for 4 people.
Available in summer.
Serve hot or raw.

Parsnips
Allow 175g (6oz) per person.
Available September–May.
Serve hot.

Peas
Allow 225g (8oz) per person.
Available frozen all year. Fresh from March–December.
Serve hot or cold.

Potatoes (old)
Allow 2 potatoes per person, on average.
Available all year.
Serve hot or cold.

Potatoes (new)
Allow 3 to 4 potatoes per person.
Available spring to summer.
Serve hot or cold.

Remove and discard coarse stems and any discoloured leaves. Wash the spinach very well under cold running water and allow it to drain well. Place the spinach in a saucepan with a pinch of salt. Pour boiling water over the spinach. Cook for 5–8 minutes, until the spinach is soft. Drain well, as spinach tends to hold water. Serve as it is or tossed in garlic, ginger and butter or sour cream. Spinach can also be served raw in salads, but make sure it is well washed and young, otherwise it might be tough.

Spinach
Allow 225g (8oz) per person.
Available all year. Also frozen.
Serve hot, cold or raw.

Peel the swede and cut into even-sized chunks. Discard any root or top. Place the pieces of swede in a saucepan of cold water with a pinch of salt. Allow the water to come to the boil then simmer for 20–25 minutes until the swedes are soft. Drain well, serve with butter and nutmeg or mash well to a smooth purée and mix with butter and nutmeg.

Swedes
Allow 100–150g (4–6oz) per person.
Available September–June.
Serve hot.

Cut the peppers in half and remove the seeds, core and stalk. Wash the peppers well under cold running water. This will also help to wash out any stubborn seeds. If you are going to stuff a pepper you should only remove the core, stalk and seeds so that it remains whole. (Large peppers can be cut in half and then stuffed.) Slice the peppers as required. Peppers can either be sautéed, blanched or baked in the oven. They can also be served raw in a salad.

Sweet peppers
Allow 100g (4oz) per person.
Available all year.
Serve hot, cold or raw.

Remove the outside leaves from the cob so that all the yellow corn is visible. Take a saucepan large enough to hold the cobs and fill it with water. Add a pinch of salt and bring the water to the boil. Plunge the cobs into the water and cook for 20–25 minutes. This cooking time will vary greatly depending on the size of the cobs and their age. Test that the corn is soft with a sharp knife. Always serve hot with melted butter.

Corn-on-the-cob
Allow 1 cob per person.
Available February–May and June–November.
Serve hot.

This is bought either frozen or canned. It can be served hot or cold. Follow the cooking instructions on the packaging.

Sweetcorn

Wash the tomatoes well, unless you are going to remove the skins. Tomatoes can be cooked in a variety of ways: grilled, fried, baked, stuffed or raw in salads. Make sure you remove the core if you are cutting the tomatoes up. Serve hot or cold.

Tomatoes
Allow 1–2 per person.
Available all year.

Peel and discard any top leaves or roots and cut the turnip into even-sized chunks. Place these in a saucepan of cold water with a pinch of salt and slowly bring to the boil. Allow to simmer for 25–30 minutes. The cooking time will vary depending on the size of the turnips. Serve with butter and nutmeg or mash to a smooth purée, season well and add a small amount of butter and nutmeg.

Turnips
Allow 100–150g (4–6oz) per person.
Available all year.
Serve hot.

Glossary of cookery terms

I try to use as few complicated cookery terms as possible. I have stuck to words which you are probably familiar with and if not, they will be listed below.

Bain-marie This is a container of water which is put into the oven to cook delicate dishes which must not get too hot, such as egg custard. The water surrounding the dish stops it from overheating. I use a roasting tin as it is big enough to hold a dish and plenty of water. A Bain-marie should really be a double saucepan which is put into the oven instead of being used on top of the hob.

Baste To spoon hot fat or liquid over meat or vegetables to prevent them from drying out.

Beat To stir hard with either a wooden spoon, a balloon whisk or an electric mixer.

Blanch To plunge fruit or vegetables into boiling water for 1–2 minutes in order to start the cooking process. Vegetables are often blanched before being frozen.

Blend To mix either liquid or solid ingredients together.

Boil To allow the food to bubble rapidly on a medium to high heat.

Bring to the boil To allow the food to come up to a high temperature and to bubble.

Casserole A saucepan or dish with a tight fitting lid used to cook meat or vegetables slowly in a sauce in the oven.

Coat To cover food with flour, egg, milk or breadcrumbs in order to protect it, or add flavour.

Consistency The texture and thickness of a sauce or gravy.

Cook down To allow the ingredients to cook and shrink in size.

Cool To take the food away from the heat and leave it to stand for at least 5 minutes to cool down.

Cream To mix ingredients together (often fat and sugar) to make a light creamy constituency.

Curdle When ingredients separate and will not come back together.

Decorate To make a sweet dish look appetizing, pretty and colourful. (This does not have to be edible, but must be easy to remove if not edible.)

Degorge To sprinkle vegetables (such as courgettes and aubergines) liberally with salt to remove the bitter flavour often found in them.

Drain or strain To pass through a colander or sieve to remove water, or to separate solid food from a liquid. Sometimes the liquid is kept for a sauce or gravy, so it is strained into a bowl or measuring jug.

Flake To break up into small pieces.

Fold To mix gently and carefully, lifting the mixture all the time, trying to incorporate as much air as possible.

Fry To cook food fast in a small amount of fat in a frying pan on the top of the hob.

Garnish This is the same as decorating but is used when referring to savoury foods. Garnishes should always be edible, as they are often put into the food, i.e. parsley in a soup or watercress around a plate of meat or fish.

Glaze To give a dish a shiny finish, using beaten egg or milk. This is usually done to pastry.

Grill To cook meat or fish very quickly under a fierce heat or to brown the top of a dish to make it look appetizing (always use a heatproof dish).

Hold its shape A mixture that will

stand up in peaks in the mixing bowl and stay there for several minutes (e.g. egg whites when whisked).

Leave a trail When you have whisked a mixture for some time, take a spoon, lift some of the mixture up and mark the top of the mixture left in the bowl with a spoon. If the mark remains for a few seconds then the mixture has left a trail and is ready to be used.

Marinade A seasoned liquid (usually made the day before cooking) which is used to soak meat, fish or vegetables to add flavour to a dish.

Par-boil To place meat or vegetables into cold water, bring them slowly to the boil and partially cook them for 2–3 minutes.

Pith This is the white part of a citrus fruit that lies directly underneath the skin. It is there to protect the fruit but it is bitter in taste and should be avoided when grating the rind of the fruit as it can spoil the taste of a dish.

Plunge to immerse meat or vegetables quickly into a boiling liquid.

Poach To cook meat, fish or vegetables very slowly in a liquid, either in the oven or on top of the hob. The liquid is often used to make a sauce to accompany the dish afterwards.

Purée To sieve or liquidize a fruit or vegetable to create a smooth thick mixture.

Reduce To boil a liquid rapidly to evaporate some of the water, which increases its strength, especially for a special gravy or sauce.

Roast To cook meat or vegetables in a hot oven in a roasting tin with fat or dripping.

Roux This is a mixture of cooking margarine and plain flour which makes the base for all sauces. It should always be cooked for a few minutes to remove the starchy flavour, then allowed to cool before the liquid is added to form a sauce or gravy.

Sauté This is another method of frying food quickly over a high heat with as little fat as possible.

Season To add salt and pepper to a dish, to suit your taste. Sometimes you will need to add extra ingredients such as nutmeg, herbs and mustard powder. The recipe will give you details.

Sieve To remove lumps from food to give it a smooth consistency (e.g. to sieve flour to remove any lumps and to incorporate extra air for a sponge cake).

Simmer To allow the food to bubble very slowly on the lowest heat possible.

Slice To cut meat or vegetables lengthways into pieces or strips.

Soaking To leave meat, vegetables or fruit in a liquid for some minutes or hours, depending on the recipe.

Stew To cook meat, vegetables or fruit in a liquid either on the hob or in a moderate oven to tenderize them.

Stock A flavoured liquid. Stock can be homemade, bought fresh from a supermarket or made by adding water to the appropriate flavoured stock cube. Stock is used in casseroles, stews, sauces and gravy.

Tart This means that a fruit is rather bitter or sour and will probably need sweetening with extra sugar.

Whip To beat well with a balloon whisk or electric mixer. If you over-whip cream it will curdle, so do be very careful.

Zest This is the coloured outer rind of citrus fruits such as oranges and lemons. Zest is often used in dishes to add colour, texture and flavouring. It is usually grated on a fine grater, straight into the dish.

Index